WELL, THIS IS GROWING UP

Megan Street

Reviews:

"A self-help book that will actually work. Jam packed with inspirational thoughts and real life stories that you can relate to; Encouraging, thoughtful and easy to read. Guaranteed to inspire you regardless of any situation you might be in."
— Alison Lewis, Author of *Seasons of Life* and *Missing*.

"*Well, This is Growing Up* is the book I wish I had been given when I was in high school. Megan's advice is exactly what young women need to read – real and practical with a sprinkle of humour. Megan is the perfect role model to inspire young women to pursue their dreams no matter what obstacles they face."
— Amanda Coneyworth, Director of Gorgeous Presence.

"This book contains relatable stories for girls and guys going through their adolescence and encapsulates what everyone realises after they have finished school, how much fun it actually was and what they would have done differently. Everyone learns from their experiences and so this book can give you a head start on how to deal with adversity and different challenges growing up."
— Daniel Menzel Geelong Cats AFL football player and founder of MTMF (Mental Toughness Mental Fortitude).

"A must read for all young women in a modern world"
— George Owen, Editor in Chief *GC Magazine*

At last a book about growing up from a young girl who has been there and is still going it. Full of advice, optimism and scary stuff, this book discusses everything from being one of those 'nasty popular girls' we call knew at school to drugs, parents, teachers, virginity and suicide. I deeply admire this young womans courage and determination to help others.

Thanks Megan for reminding us what a tough but funny old world we live in. This book is an amazing discovery of how young people react to so many things that we don't even imagine enters their heads. It's scary stuff but Megan has the courage and talent to write this wonderfully put together book full of optimism, hope, humour and LIFE."
— John Morrow's *Pick of the Week.*

"Megan really breaks down why situations happen in your teens and how to look at it in a different perspective, as well as learn the progress from it. *Well This is Growing Up* will only benefit you and your relationship with yourself"
— Jessey Telford, Nutritionist and Social Influencer.

Published in Australia by Sid Harta Publishers Pty Ltd,
ABN: 46 119 415 842
23 Stirling Crescent, Glen Waverley, Victoria 3150 Australia
Telephone: +61 3 9560 9920, Facsimile: +61 3 9545 1742
E-mail: author@sidharta.com.au

First published in Australia 2016
This edition published 2017

Street, Megan
Well, This is Growing Up
ISBN: 978-1-921030-60-4
pp378

Acknowledgements

Thank you to my strong courageous and precious mum, Heidi Street, who made a miracle recovery. I cherish every minute I get to spend with you and appreciate your wisdom, support and, most of all, love.

Thank you to my awesome, super funny, softie dad, Ray Street. You are actually the best.

Thank you to my brothers, Leif and Jason, for putting up with my crap and always supporting me.

A massive thanks to my grandparents, especially Granny, words cannot describe how amazing you are, Gran. To my great grandma (Poppy), Aunty Paula, Aunty Marie and Uncle Paul.

To Rhonda Jamicson, you are incredible. Thank you.

My thanks go to my closest friends, especially Tori Quinn, who has been the most AMAZING best friend I could ever ask for! Without you none of this would have been possible. I love you.

And to Nickiee Stewart, Georgia Davis, Oaklee-Jade Hanley, Leah Cumming, Kristen Theodoropoulos, Emily Hutchins, Julia Robertson, Rachael Hunt and Sarsha Pruessner.

Thank you to everyone at Syndal Baptist (especially the girls).

Huge thank you to the boys who have helped me in many different ways: Cameron Worsfield, Ricky Maher, Michael Nadalin (Nadz), James Tee, Luke Betheras and JMack.

To all of my friends/ past friends: I love you guys so much and cannot thank you all enough for every second I have had the chance to spend with you!

Special thanks to my grade 6 teacher, Mrs Alkemade (Barbara).

To the man who knows who he is: I can't thank you enough. Thank you, thank you, thank you from the bottom of my heart for your guidance and everything. RIP.

I am so grateful for the teachings of Rick Warren of the Saddleback Church in California.

Thank you to God for giving me strength, courage and guidance to get through anything life throws at me. Philippians 4:13.

And, to anyone and everyone who has been mean/hurt me up until this day... Thank you, because what you put me through was the biggest blessing in disguise — without you *Well This Is Growing Up* would not exist.

Dedication

This book is dedicated to every single person who has lost their lives to suicide.
To everyone who struggles with the loss of loved ones to such a tragic death.
To everyone who struggles with depression and anxiety, day in day out, you are not alone.
Don't ever let it get the best of you.

Well, This Is Growing Up...

I was inspired to write this book after looking back on the last ten years of my life. I realised that some of the experiences that I have gone through while growing up may be able to help young women today go through some of the tough stuff that life sometimes throws at us.

Megan Street

Contents

To turn one's obstacle into one's advantage is a great step towards victory
– French Proverb

Introduction

Life can suck. Especially in this day and age with boys, social media, negative body image, eating disorders, everyone's eyes glued to their screens, people hurting you, friends being bitches, people disappointing you, you disappointing your parents, heartbreak, lies, nobody understanding you, depression and even suicide.

Even when you have good moments you may sometimes feel as though they won't last, that you don't even think you deserve to feel happy and it's just a matter of time before your good turns to bad again and your smile turns into a frown.

So if life can suck SO much, why do we live it day in, day out?

BECAUSE LIFE CAN BE AMAZING

It can be Awesome
Fun
Exciting
Thrilling,

Think about it, girl, when you're in pain, You can't have a rainbow without any rain.
–Unknown

And overall the best experience well...of your life.

Happiness is not the absence of problems;
it's the ability to deal with them.
– Steve Maraboli,
Life, the Truth and Being Free

Everything will be okay in the end.
If it's not okay, it's not the end.
– John Lennon

Just think about whatever it is you have already gone through, whatever it is you may have failed at, whatever hard, difficult draining and emotionally ruining situation you may have already been through... remember thinking 'How on earth am I going to get through this?' Look at you now. You got through it. And most of all you've come out stronger and an all-round better person because of it.

Take a moment right now to appreciate how strong you have already been throughout your life over the years... You are stronger than you think. And if you can get through all the crap that you've already gone through, of course you can get through anything life may throw at you in the future.

As I said earlier, life can *suck* sometimes but without the sucky times we have been through and will go through in the future there is nothing to which the good times can be compared.

The bad days make you realise
what a good day is.
– Aly Raisman

All the adversity I've had in my life, all my troubles and obstacles have strengthened me. You may not realise it when it happens, but a kick in the teeth may be the best thing to happen to you.
– Walt Disney

Not a literal kick in the teeth. Just wanted to clear that up… I don't want anyone to read that and literally go get someone to kick them in the teeth. Haha.

Where there is no struggle
there is no strength.
– Oprah Winfrey

So many times in my life I heard people say: 'I hate life', 'I hate people', 'I hate this', 'I hate that', 'Everyone sucks', 'All men are jerks', 'Why does she get everything and I don't?', 'When will life get better', 'I don't deserve this', and 'When is it all going to ennnnnnndddddd?'

And that's when I'm going to say to you - harden up: 'Build a bridge and get over it.' No, I'm totally kidding. But seriously, what I am going to tell you is:

Life isn't fair.

And

That happiness is not about having good things: situations, latest iPhones, clothes, make-up, money or getting the hottest boyfriend.

It's about playing the cards you are dealt and making the most of YOUR situation, not wishing that you had someone else's. And ultimately being the best version of YOU possible.

Happy people don't have the best of everything, but they make the best of everything.
– Unknown

This includes not just having bad times and hard experiences, but living through, learning how to deal with and having the ability to put a positive spin on what you may have originally considered a negative. The reality is that bad things are going to happen, that's just life, no one lives through life with no negative...it's impossible, so the sooner we can learn how to see the good in the hard times, the better and happier each of us will be as a person.

Life is 10% what happens to you
and 90% how you react to it.
– Charles R Swindoll

Remember: An arrow can only be shot by pulling it backwards; so when you feel like life is dragging you down with difficulties, it simply means that it's going to launch you to something great. So just focus and keep aiming.
– Unknown

What I will show you in this book using my own personal stories and experiences is that every negative situation or experience has a positive. You will begin to understand that some of the crap you may be dealing with is actually fuel for your fire and in the end will make you a better stronger and even happier person. You will walk away from reading this with your glass half full and with practice it will stay that way. You will know how to see things differently and turn your bad into good.

You will see how you can easily look at negative situations and experiences in a positive light, so believe it or not you might even be thankful for them.

Life really can be the best, best, best thing ever, especially if we can simply have the ability to see the good in every situation and train our minds to think outside the box and twist our thoughts so that we can look at things differently.

An example of this is:

Two different people get up on a cold winter's Monday morning, and have to be at school for the early class – what we used to call period 0, which had an 8.00am start.

One person may say: 'Oh yay! A new day when I get to go and study while making the most of the cool morning breeze in my hair... Today I will be working in a group and therefore will get to know my classmates more and hopefully make closer relationships.'

While the other may say: 'Ew, I have to go to the early class. Don't they know Monday morning is no one's best time? Even though I like school I only chose to do it because my parents wouldn't let me drop out. I'm just plodding through so that I can achieve a high school pass. It's so cold! Stupid winter! I just want to stay in bed all day. And the worst part about today's class is that I have to sit with a group of idiots and attempt to work with them... I would like never choose to be friends with these people even if the world depended on it. Life sucks. Today sucks.'

See what I mean – same situation but **DIFFERENT MINDSETS.**

I honestly believe that learning to see the good in almost any situation is one of the most important tools to have in the toolkit of life.

The earlier in life that you can see the world with positivity goggles on the better.

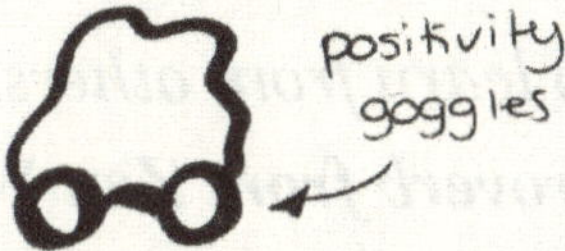

From a young age I realised that there are always two sides to the coin, two sides to every story and two sides to life.

We can either choose to focus on the upside or the downside. Over the years, I experienced many situations, hung out with many people, read a crap-load of self-help books and also looked up a LOT of inspirational quotes from books, Instagram and the internet. I have always had a morning and night ritual of closing my eyes and randomly picking a quote to read. If I am feeling especially inspirational-quote greedy, I'll read the one that's on the opposite page too. Naughty, I know. I would even get to school back in the day and people would ask me for 'today's quote'. I was known as the female Dalai Lama.

I know by writing this book that I will give you the opportunity to laugh at me, make fun of me and think to yourself how much of an idiot I have been in some of my stories and experiences. But more importantly, I will also give you the opportunity to learn from things I should have, could have, but didn't, do differently. This can hopefully prevent you from making these same or similar mistakes. By having the ability to learn from others' mistakes and experiences we can learn a whole lot more than if we were to learn from only our own.

It takes a wise man (woman) to learn from his mistakes, but an ever wiser man (woman) to learn from others.
– Zen proverb from Zen Wisdom by Mark Zocchi

I also hope that this book puts into perspective what is really important in life. When you (I'm guilty of this too) may think that having tongue hockey with the guy you like is the most important thing in the world, trust me, it's not. There's more to your life than getting the boy you like, or being the most popular girl in school, and looking pretty.

I don't want to see a whole generation wasting their precious brain space on things that seem important at the time but may not be as important or even important at all down the track.

People often ask what inspired me to write this self-help book for young adults. I usually reply with something along the lines of 'Oh, you know I think a lot of gals can learn from my mistakes' or 'I guess I just want to try and change the world.' but these generic responses are just the tip of the iceberg. There were two occasions that really stood out to me which inspired me to write this book and I'll share them with you.

The first one was when I was out watching my 16-year-old cousin attend her debutante ball (what most people know as 'deb'). I went to watch it with my family. As I sat there, I looked at the absolutely stunning 16-year-old girls, who had probably spent the last 24 hours freaking out because their hair, makeup and spray tans needed to be perfect, ready for the deb. And as I looked at them in awe I was aware they had definitely achieved perfection.

As they stood there in their beautiful white dresses, some wearing princess crowns to top off their already stunning look, part of me even felt a bit jealous as I sure as anything wasn't feeling like a princess sitting there in my LBD I'd already worn like 5000 times before, along with rushed hair and make-up. I thought, 'Man, these girls are young and beautiful and have their whole lives ahead of them to achieve whatever they want.' As each one of them walked down the steps and aisle, I listened to their hobbies, interests and goals that the MC was reading over the microphone. I kind of zoned out while a few of the girls went by but my ears pricked up when I heard one of their goals, which was to marry a rich man. That's all. I thought to myself, 'Oh girl, you are being silly. There is so much more you

can do in your life than to just marry a rich guy.' It just passed me by and I thought, 'Oh well there is always a silly person at school.' Then the next girl walked out, her hobbies and interests were read out, then her life goals and, to my disbelief again, her goal was 'to marry a rich man'. I thought, 'Ah well, whatevz. Those two are probably best friends'. But I was amazed as, after her, girl after girl came out and the same goal was read out for each! About 75% of the beautiful stunning girls with the world at their feet had one lousy goal, which was to marry a rich man. I sat there shocked, unaware that my jaw had dropped. My mum told me to close my mouth. I was just too shocked though. I couldn't believe that so many of them (including my cousin, mind you!) had that one goal. In that moment I felt hugely inspired to show these girls that they were capable of so much more than just marrying someone rich. I wanted to shake some sense into them. But talking to them (or shaking them) wouldn't have worked and the last thing I wanted to do was act like a teacher, or worse, their mum. The other thing I thought about was that if about 75% of girls at this school only have that one dream, imagine how many girls in all of Melbourne, let alone Australia, or even the world, also had it. I felt a strong need to show girls that with self-belief, high goals can be set, aspired to and achieved. I needed big scale exposure. Talking to the small group of girls that were doing that deb wouldn't have been good enough. I needed to get through to as many girls as I could.

The second occasion was actually when I was just chilling at home and randomly got out my high school year book...Okay fine, I lie – I'd recently hooked up with a guy I went to school with and wanted to kiss his year-12 photo goodnight. #talkaboutobsessedalready #imweirdIknow #stage5clinger. After I kissed him goodnight I started to reminisce about the good old days of high school or should I say the 'pretty sucky I used to cry all the time' days of high school. I thought about the friends and everything that went with 'growing up':

Bullying
Bitching
Heartbreak
Meanness
Being popular
Being unpopular
Being shy
Overcoming shyness
Boobs (or in my case lack of)
Failing, failing and failing
SUCCESS
But then more failing
Drugs – saying no when everyone else was doing them
Getting WAY too distracted by boys.

WHAT ON EARTH DID I WANT TO DO WHEN I GREW UP? (Career wise)

The breakdowns.

The tears (thanks Mum for dealing with those).

Beginning to think that I was a boy it took me so long to get my period.

Telling mum I needed to go to emergency when I got my period (I thought I was dying).

Teachers hating me.

Students hating me.
In fact feeling like *everybody* hated me.
Being a virgin for like forever.
Part-time jobs.
Realising who was really a true friend, and who was not.
THE LIST GOES ON.

I thought to myself that I'd gone through so much over the years (both good and 'bad') and realised, three or four years after high school finished, everything that I'd gone through had actually made me who I was today. I was stronger, better, way more resilient and loving life and, without sounding arrogant, loving the person I'd become. I also had a heap of stories to share, all of which had ultimately turned out for the good.

Although everything is awesome now, I'll never ever be able to forget the nights when I would come home from school and cry and cry and cry to anyone who would listen – my mum, my best friend, my grandma, and even the Kids' Help Line (free counselling hotline for kids and young adults). It was important that not only did they listen but they made me realise that life doesn't suck forever, school/growing up can be hard and that it will and DOES get better.

Everything changes once you leave school, I promise you.

Three years down the track everything was and still is great. Everything that was crap about school I had turned around and used the pain to make me fight harder for what I really wanted in life... Happiness...and it worked.

It was then that I thought that if I, one of the biggest idiots in school, who was known for being 'dumb', can turn negative experiences around and use them positively and become a better person, anyone can. And, I realised, this needed to be shared...☺

I thought that I cannot just keep my experiences that started out badly and ended up well to myself. I needed to use them (as embarrassing as some of them are) to inspire other young women who live in this crazy crazy world that 1: It's not easy but you'll get through it, and 2: There IS good in every situation/ experience, even if it feels as though there is not.

I hope the experiences I share with you guys make you realise that you are not the only person in the world going through bad or difficult times. YOU ARE NOT ALONE. Also, that the inspirational and motivational quotes can be ones to be remembered for the rest of your lives to help you to achieve your full potential and achieve true happiness. Feel free to highlight the book too, so that you can open anytime to any place and see your fave quotes/stories!

YOUR NOT ALONE!

Through my stories and experiences I show that everything works itself out in the end and that whatever it is you may be going through/will go through helps you to become a better person if you can just open your eyes and see the blessing hidden in disguise. ☺

– Megan Street

So no matter who you are, what you have already been through, what negative thoughts you may have previously had about yourself, know that with the right mindset and attitude you will develop after reading this book you can and will live the happiest life ever.

SO WHAT ARE WE WAITING FOR? LET'S BEGIN! Before we go any further, here is something to remember every time you look at a $20 note. (Random I know, but bear with me.)

If I offered you $20, would you take it?

How about if I crumpled it up?

Stepped on it?

You would probably take it even if it was crumpled up and stepped on... Do you know why?

Because it is still $20; its worth has not changed.

The same goes for you.

If you have a bad day, bad week, bad month or even a bad year or if something bad happens to you, you are not worthless.
– Unknown

If anyone or any situation crumbles you up or makes you feel as though you are being stepped on, your worth does not change. You are still as valuable as you were before.

To...

the girls who overhear their 'best friends' bitching about them,

the girls who didn't have / don't have a date to their formal,

the girls who no one wants to sit next to on the bus,

the girls who are told they are 'too dumb' to get anywhere in life,

the girls who can't stand looking in the mirror,

the girls who get bullied by the guy they have the biggest crush on,

the girls who are in love with a boy who doesn't even know their name,

to the girls who have been hated on, kicked when they're already down, pushed until breaking point,

and
to all the girls who have ever been called weird / 'weirdo' / loser / loner/ freak or any names similar.

This book is for you.

And

S
T
A
Y

W
E
I
R
D

(:

Friends (Bitches)

A good friend is like a bra... Hard to find

Supportive
Comfortable
Always lifts you up
Makes you look better
And is always close to your heart
– Unknown

Something I found that I was VERY worried about when I first started high school was friends. I was sent to a high school where I did not know anyone at all and the only thing I really cared about at the start of high school was making friends. I was not interested in the school work, the environment or the teachers; all I was focused on was if I would make friends and not be a 'loner', someone that nobody wanted to talk to or hang around with. I was scared that girls would become my friends as a joke and then suddenly stop being my friends so I had no one.

- Choosing the right friends is VERY important
- The right friends may or may not be popular kids

Remember that some children in disadvantaged countries don't have the luxury of going to school. They have to work hard with little or no education.

Yes, school is a social battlefield but school is also a place for study and work. **At the end of the day we go to school to learn** – yes, to make friends and create connections with others, but the main reason we go to school is to learn.

It may feel like a place where you *have* to go and where you see and make friends, but the bottom line is we go to school for an education. Don't forget that.

Remember that next time you complain about going to school. Try your hardest to make school a place you enjoy. The majority of adults will say although school was hard and they complained about it every day, they believe that their school years were the BEST years of their lives. So lap it up, make the most of it.

TRY to associate school with fun and make it a place you WANT to be.

Try to put positive spins on things. E.g., if you have to work by yourself because the class Science/Foodtech has an odd number of people in it and you are supposed to be working in pairs, don't fake a sickie and go to the sickbay because you are embarrassed that no one wants to be your partner. Try not to be angry at your friends because no one would be your partner. (Who would want to be partners with an angry friend in the future?) Make the most of the situation and think, yes, I'm going to prove to myself and the teacher that I am strong and independent and can work well on my own AND when I'm in a pair. In life you are going to be on your own a lot so you may as well adapt to it as best you can now. Try not to get upset, as, at the end of the day, you have made a great achievement 1. By not getting upset because you have no partner and 2. Because you have proved to yourself how well you work alone.

The most important single ingredient in the formula of success is knowing how to get along with people. ***–Theodore Roosevelt***

Having a good support system is important...and remember that being nice to everyone will always get you further in life than being negative and mean. Having the ability to get along well with ANYONE even if you don't like them is a great personality trait to have throughout school and in life and work (when you get a part time/full time job).

How you get along
with other people
will change your life

Here is an example of a positive spin on a negative situation that happened to me when I was in my first year of high school at 12 years old.

I was one of the popular kids (I don't know how I fell into this group) for about four/five months. These girls were HEAPS of fun to hang out with, but we were kind of rebellious. We would be silly in classes and the most popular girl, Tiffany, was my best friend at the time. When we were in one of our first maths classes, the teacher wrote 'Algebra' on the whiteboard and when he wasn't looking she went up to the board, grabbed the whiteboard marker and circled the work 'bra'. The whole class found this hilarious. We would also hang out with and flirt with a lot of the guys in our year level. Our group of girls was made up of Tiffany, Sophie, and me. We were all really bitchy behind each other's back and basically downright mean. They were very 'out there' people and I was quite reserved, so I was often left out.

A
L
G
E
B
R
A

I was that person who was too scared to put up my hand and answer questions in class.

They were also more developed than me…they had boobs and their period and I had no period and a chest as flat as a surfboard. I still haven't got boobs ten years later; just hoping they'll come one day!

I felt like they were fun friends but I never really connected with them on a deeper friendship level. We would always talk about going to the Bluelight Disco, boys and who was dating who and they even forced me to go out with this guy I literally had NO interest in just so that I had a boyfriend. It was cool to talk about this sort of stuff but not all the time.

My mum for some reason never really liked Tiff or Soph and I never really knew why. Now girls, remember, as much as you deny it, your mum usually does know best. But at the time I was popular and these girls were the only friends I had.

The plus sides were that it was great as I'd been a dork/loser for my entire time in primary school and to come to high school and be popular and talking and even flirting with boys and stuff was **awesome**.

I remember at our camp in first year of high school about one month into high school Tiff threatened to shave this girl's eyebrows off. And we would also have fights with the boys, throwing each other's underwear at them – mine even ended up being shown to the entire year level when they were going through all of the lost property at the end of camp. I obviously didn't claim them – and we would even be seen as 'cool' for sleeping on the top bunk of our cabin.

THEN ONE DAY…

It was after dancing. I used to do dancing with the main popular girl (Tiffany), who literally told me in these words: 'Megan, you're just not "radicool" enough to hang out with us anymore'. I was shattered. My first friends at high school were ditching me – just what I thought would happen! It was terrible! I went home and cried all night to my mum.

**R
A
D
I
C
O
O
L**

Luckily I have always been someone who likes to get to know people and when I was hanging out with Tiff and Soph I made sure that I talked to almost everyone in the year. It was like a little goal I'd had when I was in primary school to NOT be shy in high school. So luckily, although it sucked that my friends ditched me, it was kind of all right as I had made friends and been friendly to everyone in the year by now and had other people that I could hang out with. (This is a message to treat other people with respect throughout your years of school. If I had been mean and nasty to these people when I was popular I would literally have had no friends.) Being nice to people will ALWAYS turn out to be a good thing. Never forget that.

I remember reading a book that my mum bought to read herself when I was in first year of high school. It was *The Friendship Factor* by Kenneth H. Rubin with Andrea Thompson. It had a chapter about popularity and I remember reading it. It said that there are different types of popular kids. Two of these types are:

Two Types of Popular Kids

- The popular bullies who get their popular status from being mean and treating others as lower than them, and basically everyone is scared of them

  And

- Popular kids who are generally well liked as they are friendly and approachable and people enjoy hanging out with them.

I remember thinking to myself if I am going to be popular I am going to be the right kind of popular – well-liked and nice.

If you are popular, try to be the nice, friendly, 'everyone wants to be around you' popular, not the 'I'm better than you, be scared of me' popular.

As bad as it sounds, I also figured that being popular was a great way to get to know everyone as people have respect for you when you are popular. Basically I knew that when I talked to people they wouldn't shut me down…so try and use being popular for the good if you happen to be a part of the popular group.

When I was with Tiff and Soph I would always talk to other people to not only make friends but to make sure that people weren't intimidated by me… I wanted to give off a friendly persona to everyone.

- You want people in your year to like you and feel like they can approach you as a friend, not just as a popular kid who will intimidate them.
- Also you don't want people to think you are stuck up and, if you ever feel yourself looking down on someone, remember that you want to be friendly, nice, approachable, 'fun to be around' popular, not 'stuck-up, intimidating people to be scared of you' popular.

Making friends with people in other classes is also a good idea. You want to be able to walk into your locker bay and say 'Hey' to a lot of your friends.

People who are loved always have a glow to them
– Megan Street

***Being genuinely interested in other people... their lives and hobbies and what makes them who they are**... will get you far, not only in the school ground – it is something to remember for the rest of your life.*

If you happen to be in the popular group, use it as a good thing and improve yourself because of it, for instance, make yourself more confident. Being confident made me realise that I can go and talk to someone and not be shy-a BIG thing for me when I was 12. (If you are shy or an over-thinker, then you'll understand.)

Remember girls, confidence is the key. One of the most attractive traits for both guys and girls is confidence... If you don't feel it, fake it till you do.

Anyway, I went home and told my mum about the whole not being radicool enough to hang out with the popular girls anymore. My mum knew how important it was for me to have friends and a good support system so she got out the school photo from my first year at high school and literally pointed out a few of the girls in it (I know this is realllllyyyyyy embarrassing), and said, 'Why don't you make friends with them?' (Mind you, my mum was probably having a party in her head now that I wasn't hanging out with Tiff and Soph anymore, as she never really liked either of them from the start.)

The next day I literally went up to one of the girls Mum had pointed out and said, 'Let's get to know each other.' Seeing I was popular I had this new-found confidence to do this sort of thing (even though I look back and think, hahahaha, I was such a dork). We sat and talked all lunch. That's when I realised **I enjoyed hanging out with this girl more** than Tiff and Soph! Now in the past, I'm not going to lie, I thought she was a little bit of what people would call a 'loser'. BUT once I got to know her I realised how AMAZING she was and that just shows, you really shouldn't judge people until you get to know them properly.

In fact, don't judge them at all, as everyone is different and that is what makes the world and other people exciting.

So now I had become a bit of a floater (someone who floats around friendship groups), hanging out with different people throughout the day. I would usually just hang out with Tiffany out of school at dancing and we all had our own different friendship groups now. Kind of like in Mean Girls, when 'The Plastics' broke up. Later that year Tiffany told me that she was moving schools. I was sad because she was my first friend at high school but I was happy that I'd made other friends, not only because I wanted to but in case this sort of thing happened.

Being nice to people will always be the best way to live.

Tiffany and Sophie both left the school and I found a friendship group that I fitted into properly and, even though we weren't popular, I enjoyed the company of these girls a lot and felt like they would be a great support system to have throughout school. It just shows that it is more important to enjoy who you're hanging out with more than just hanging out with people to be popular.

We were not popular and we were not complete losers (and that doesn't matter even if you are in that group, if you fit in with whoever you are hanging out with great – if you don't, find some new people.) I'm sure you'll be able to connect with at least one girl/boy in your year level, and, if not, someone in another year level at school. ☺

My group was just average, more on the loser side actually. But I didn't care. They were great to be around and our topics of conversation ranged further than the Bluelight, boys and boobs.

Some of these girls were in my class and some were not.

I always placed high value on getting to know people; so although these girls were my immediate group I would actively hang out with other groups as I enjoyed many people's company, not just one group. It's important to remember that **people are so very interesting and each and every person is so exciting to get to know.** No two snowflakes are exactly alike; no two people are exactly alike... and yes, even twins may look the same but anyone who knows twins knows full well that they have different personalities.

Back to the story...I'll NEVER forget my 13th birthday party – one of the girls I had made good friends with held a surprise birthday party for me. I remember driving to her house and all my friends jumping out of the bushes and yelling SURPRISE... At this point in time I almost cried I was soo happy

SURPRISE!

that I'd found such an amazing group of friends. Even though we weren't 'popular' I was soo much happier #loser4lyffff

To this day, over ten years later, I am still close friends with most of these girls; they have definitely been an amazing support system and helped me to achieve my best throughout the years.

WE MUST REMEMBER THAT PAST EXPERIENCES SHAPE OUR LIVES...so try to put a positive spin on your situation and be grateful for the experiences you have been through, as every experience makes you a stronger, happier, more motivated person.

Tiffany and I used to be regulars in detention and got a bad rep; she escaped from this by moving school whereas I stayed at the school. As much as it sucks, reputations can be formed easily and can be hard to break free of...often people are stubborn and will believe what they want to believe (even teachers), so try your best to keep a good rep at school... I know I sound like a mum but stay out of detention if you can.

A few other ways a good support system can help you (and helped me) over the years:

- So many fun times and laughs with your friends even if it is over something really silly.
- They helped to motivate me to get into university.
- They set the bar high-what they were doing I wanted to do (make sure that your friends have goals and aspirations).
- Often people follow what our friends do, for example, studying, wagging, smoking, drugs,

so staying with the right crowd can hugely benefit you.

- My friends helped me to get through exams and tests while also motivating me, even tutoring me and telling me that I could do it.
- Without these great people I probably wouldn't be where I am now.

When you are younger, friends can have a HUGE impact on your life and how you turn out to be as a person. Some people will get involved with the wrong crowd, start taking drugs, get addicted and for the next ten or even twenty years, be addicted to drugs. Please remember that the people you hang out with can positively and negatively impact your life. Choose your friends wisely.

Try to choose nice friends: don't just try and get into the 'popular' group as, although it might seem great to be popular at the time, choosing friends that you connect with and will push you further in your life is waaaayyyyy more important.

And focus on being 'friendly popular', which is being nice and friendly to EVERYONE despite what 'group' they are in or 'label' they have.

If you don't find anyone to connect with at school, try to find a good support group somewhere else. E.g., I met some great friends at tennis, dancing, and even hanging out with my friends from primary school who went to different high schools.

Church is also a great place to meet some awesome, nice people who are almost always accepting and friendly. Even if you don't follow religion or believe in God, it doesn't matter – it's just a great place to meet cool people and make new friends. A range of exciting activities is held that I guarantee you'll have so much fun on/at – examples being camps, lasertag and rollerblading. I know a lot of kids who come to youth functions held by the church who don't believe in God at all. These kids just enjoy coming and meeting new people and having a great time.

Even if your good friends are not in school it may be a blessing in disguise, as maybe you are being shown that you should be studying at school and focusing on your education. And outside of school you can then hang out with your friends. I know some of my friends have had this approach to school and even university. Some people like to keep friendships and study separate. It's your choice. I personally prefer to have friends wherever I go, but it's a personal choice if you choose to work at school and play outside of school. It's totally up to you.

- Although remember that working with other people on schoolwork is extremely beneficial to your learning…I learned about it at uni last year…as Peter Jarvis states: *Learning always started with experience and experience is always social.*

Even if you have to study in the library at lunchtime, who cares? I know it may be hard but at the end of the day you have awesome friends outside of school and it a really smart and mature thing to study in the library at lunchtime. So you go, girrllll...

Another thing I highly recommend in school is to GET INVOLVED. Yeah it may be loserish or geeky but I guarantee it will be worth it. I remember the group of girls I was friends with in school began a 'book club' in about year nine/ten. They would all meet in the library at lunch once a month and discuss a book they were all going to read over the next month. I honestly thought it was dorky and embarrassing at the time but now I look back and realise that if you are interested in something, GO FOR IT. If you enjoy it, do it! Don't worry about what others think. If you take anything from this book please take this: DON'T CARE WHAT OTHERS THINK, DO WHAT MAKES YOU HAPPY... It was great that these girls all swallowed their pride and strived for what they enjoyed, despite my and other people's opinions in the year level. And if the club or society thing doesn't exist, MAKE IT! Schools love when students have amazing ideas and I'm sure the teachers will be keen to help organise the activity you want. There are also many other activities that can be done and are probably already organised, e.g., swimming, tennis, badminton, cross country, or any sort of activity that basically gets you out of your comfort zone and enjoying life is great. Not only are you practising the skill, you are also learning valuable life lessons such as handling defeat in a sport/competitive activity, learning more social skills and how to get along with others, and punctuality. Learning more social skills is an important one, as the majority of activities

you do in life requires getting along with others. I've met great friends at extra-curricular activities. E.g., I met my best friend at aerobics training for school. I've met many friends playing tennis over the years and down at the tennis club, also at dancing, school footy and soccer. Basically at any extracurricular activity, you are bound to meet some cool people that you enjoy hanging out with, so you'll be learning a new skill and making new friends at the same time. WIN WIN SITUATION.

If you are shy and scared to begin a new activity, remember that you can do ANYTHING if you put your mind to it. Start small, such as pushing yourself to join a group or activity and as life and school goes on, you will push yourself further. You may even end up being the school captain in five years (if you want to be that is).

You can do ANYTHING if you put your mind to it

BELIEVE IN YOURSELF

This also comes in with living outside your comfort zone. Often it is quite scary to begin something new, especially if you are doing it by yourself. I know even the most confident people still get nervous in some situations!

A quick and easy guide on how to make friends anywhere!

Obviously there are many ways to make friends, but if you are a little bit shy and get nervous around people, especially new ones you have never met, I suggest using a few or all of these tactics.

The main thing to remember when making friends is to **genuinely be interested in the other person and their life.** 'Curiosity is the key.'

Often I will make a conversation as soon as I sit down next to someone saying pretty much anything to break the ice!

Icebreakers

'Man, I'm so happy that you are early too, being the first to class is so awkward!'

Or give someone a genuine compliment. This is a fail proof way to start a conversation.

Ones that I have used are: 'Hey that's an awesome jumper. Those big pockets are massively in fashion at the moment! ' Or 'I like your watch. Where's it from?' (Only do this if you really mean the compliment. Don't be fake.)

It's always great to make others feel good. Not only that but they will feel more comfortable around you now and feel as though you are a nice person and they will NOT be intimidated by you. Try not to be intimidated by attractive people either; at the end of the day, people are people and we all want to be loved. Often models don't get many people talking to them as many are intimidated by their beauty.

Remember, just because someone is beautiful it does not mean they are stuck-up. Give them a chance. I'm sure they'll be happy to talk to you and would be really happy that you actually got to know them before judging them.

Once you have broken the ice, you can ask them a few more questions to get the conversation rolling, like the ones I like to ask people (because I am genuinely interested. You can ask ones that YOU are interested in, or just use mine, which are below). But be genuine; don't be fake. People can see through fake and will not be interested in talking to you.

Remember that people are your teachers, every person you meet you can learn from if you look hard enough.

These are all open-ended questions that can't just be answered with a yes or no response:

Say we are in a first class for the year, start with a few ice breakers; then, ask questions like:

So where are you from?

How long does it take for you to get to school/uni?

What bus do you catch? If the same as you, GREAT common ground.

If you know someone else who lives in their suburb, ask if they know them. (Don't speak badly/negatively about this person, kindness is your aim.) If they do, bang, you have some COMMON GROUND.

The bottom line is you want to get common ground with people. This could be a similar interest e.g., music, sport, reading or anything that can establish a better friendship. It could even be that you both have Jack Russell dogs who are always full of energy!

Most people will often ask you the same questions back, such as, 'Where are you from?', 'How long does it take for you to get here?' or 'What type of dog do you have?'

BUT if they don't, don't get disheartened. Just think they are probably enjoying the conversation so much that they forget to ask you these things back.

People Love Talking About Themselves

Once someone is talking about a subject they like, they can go on for hours.

And personally I love, love, lo-o-ove listening to someone talk about something they are passionate about, even if I am not interested in the subject. I just love hearing people discuss and express their passions in life. E.g., once I was listening to a guy talk about video games so passionately I was enjoying the conversation even though I have almost no interest in video games at all. It's beautiful to listen others express their passion because everyone is different. Next time the conversation drifts to something you may not be interested in, still listen, as watching people discuss what they are passionate about is an awesome thing to watch. Listen, listen, listen (and ask questions if you have any).

We have two ears and one mouth so that we can listen twice as much as we speak.
– Epictetus, Greek philosopher.

Don't just think about what you are going to say next...try not to get caught up in your own head. Genuinely listen to their words and respond accordingly. The conversation flows better if you listen and fully comprehend what the other person is saying.

I've found that being interested in others and their lives and stories and hardships has been one of the greatest things I have ever done in my life.

If you are just talking about yourself all the time, when are you going to learn from what the others are saying?

If you cannot find common ground with a person, be interested in what they are doing

BE CURIOUS AND ASK QUESTIONS.

E.g., if you are talking to a vegan and are not even slightly considering becoming one yourself, you don't have common ground.

I personally would ask:

So what made you decide to become a vegan?

How long ago did you start becoming a vegan?

Do you feel healthier?

Is it difficult to go out for dinner?

Do you take supplements for iron?

Opportunity is often missed because we are broadcasting when we should be tuning in.
– Unknown

Try not to make your conversation sound like an interview. Rather than having question after question, try this:

YOU'RE COOL!

Ask follow-up questions to develop the conversation.

You: So what made you become a vegan?

Them: Oh, I've always loved animals and have been extremely against animal cruelty.

Y: Yeah, it's terrible, hey. I wish I could help to stop it too but I just don't think I'd want to give up meat. Do you know any other ways I could help?

T: YEAH. There is this seminar in the city about stopping animal cruelty tomorrow night. You can come with me if you want.

AND BANG, NEW FRIEND!

It's really that easy. Once you understand and are interested in people it's EASY peasy to make new friends.

By being interested and curious about someone else's life/activity and choices you can almost always make a new friend.

Basically the bottom line is to find other people interesting.

Once I sat down in the MCG at the footy in Melbourne; mind you, it was the Anzac Day match (a big match for AFL). There were 92,000 people attending and I thought to myself, 'Hey I wish I could get to know all these people, their stories, their hardships and heartbreaks and whatever makes them who they are. Why he did he choose to do his hair in a mohawk? What inspired the footy players to work so hard get so far in their careers? I know that it would probably be physically impossible to really get to know ALL these people in my lifetime, but hey, I can defs try!

I love to ask people questions like what makes them push themselves harder and not give up? What gives them the motivation to succeed in whatever they may be successful in?

E.g., one of my close friends runs 100km marathons. Often she trains so hard every day to be able to achieve this high level of fitness. She is absolutely INCREDIBLE and the reason that she has the motivation to do this is because she says it helps her to connect with her dad who passed away when she was younger. She says that she feels really alive when running and that her dad is looking down on her and is proud of her.

Now, from discussing and knowing this about her, I have LEARNT that to achieve at such a high level of success as she does, a HUGE motivation must be there, a motivation that is bigger than the pain of the activity. Your thoughts and feelings can help you to overcome anything and will help you to achieve your full potential.

I got to know my marathon runner friend by asking her about her passion (running). I asked a lot of open-ended questions about motivation and I have now LEARNT that to be as successful as she is there needs to be a HUGE motivation to do it. Therefore I have learnt from this conversation and am bettering myself.

EVERYONE IS OUR TEACHER.

If I had been busy talking about myself in this conversation (broadcasting when I should have been tuning in) instead of listening and asking questions about my friend, I would have never learnt what her motivation was to succeed and may have never realised its importance.

My motivation to write this book is to HELP PEOPLE. I've even saved it onto my computer as 'Help people' rather than 'Book'. This is so that I can trigger my brain to 'see' writing this book and appeal to my 'wanting to help people' (my huge motivation). If I was to name it 'Book', I may make an association that it is a chore to write and that I HAVE to do it (like homework) and put off doing it. Finding a way to make yourself enjoy what you are doing is a great tool in your toolkit for life.

Sure there have been days when I'm lazy and can't be bothered writing BUT my motivation to help you guys is way stronger and no small setback is going to stop me. At the end of the day, if I can help just one person with my advice, all of these hours of writing, typing and editing will be worth it.

Persistence is the key.

One of the best-selling books in the world, Jack Canfield and Mark Victor Hansen's *Chicken Soup for the Soul,* was rejected by over 140 publishers before it became a success.

Even the stunning Miranda Kerr was rejected for modelling jobs before she was recruited as a Victoria's Secret Model.

Henry Ford went bankrupt five times before the success of Ford Motor Company.

These are just a few people who persisted and didn't lose hope from one (or many) rejections or setbacks.

PERSISTENCE IS SO IMPORTANT.

Anyway I'm getting off topic. Sometimes when you try to make friends with people, you may not be successful. Some people have reasons why they may not be as friendly and open as you'd like them to be. Some people are just not interested in friendship. For example, a placement student teacher at my high school said to me that she was not interested in making friends at university, as she liked to keep friends and uni separate to ensure that she concentrated at uni and hung out with her friends outside of uni. Some people may have this mentality wherever you may be trying to make friends. Even friends of friends may not be interested in getting to know you. 'I have enough friends, I don't need anymore' may be their mindset. (I suggest to you to not have this mindset because you can learn from each and every new friend you make/person you meet.) BUT it's up to you how to live your life and if you feel like you have enough friends, by all means don't make more, but you never know how well you'll click with someone until you give them a chance. A point to remember: If the people who have the 'I have enough friends' mindset, shut down your friendliness, don't let it get to you/make you sad. As my dad says, 'Treat it as "water off a duck's back".'

Remember, it's their loss if they don't want to get to know the awesome person you are. You know within yourself that anyone is lucky to get to know you and don't ever let one person who doesn't want to be your friend get you down. They'll probably soon realise how cool you are and want to talk to you anyway. Don't be rude if they try to be friends after they blew you off the first time. Give them a chance. People always deserve second chances.

True friends want nothing from you except the joy of your presence. No matter what you do, they will always be your friend.
– Paramahansa Yogananda

Associate yourself with people of good quality if you esteem your own reputation; for 'tis better to be alone than in bad company.
– George Washington

So who do you choose to be with you? ☺

Bullying

Don't you worry about those who make you cry...people try to bring down those who fly high.

From when I was a kid, going to school it felt like you were in a meat grinder. It chews you up and pours out this mess that can't function.
– Gerard Way

Bullying, bullying, bullying. Where do I start? It really does impact on people strongly. It's crazy to think that if you speak to most adults they can remember clearly who bullied them in school and exactly what those who bullied them said and did. The bottom line is **it hurts** and we remember the physical and/or emotional pain we were put through. Almost everyone has been bullied in one way or another, whether it be physical, psychological or cyber, and bullying can occur in many different places – school, workplace, bus stop and even on the street; in fact, anywhere. When I was getting bullied in school, I assumed that as people and I got older they would get more mature and wouldn't feel the need to bully others. And yes, in my three years out of school, bullying (especially at uni) has been virtually nonexistent. Although we must remember that there will ALWAYS be people who don't like you.

You can be the ripest, juiciest peach in the world, and there's still going to be somebody who hates peaches

– Dita Von Teese

Sometimes there is no logical reason as to why someone doesn't like you... Some will like you, others won't; it's just how life is...and if you go around trying to please everyone, let me tell you now, you can't. You can try...but tell me how that goes for you because I promise you not everyone is going to like you in life and it's better we realise this sooner rather than later.

From my experience, high school was most definitely the place where bullying was at its worst. I'll never forget when I was catching the bus home from school and people (including the boy I liked) threw their old lunches at me, and when I got off the bus, hurled names at me.

BUT you can take one of two mindsets when it comes to bullying – either that of the victim or the hero. If you take the VICTIM mindset you will only feel sorry for yourself, and think, 'Why me? What did

I do to them?' (More often than not you have done NOTHING wrong to them!) You will also be hard on yourself and down on yourself. In actual fact it's the bullies' insecurities that drive them to bully you and you actually make THEM feel insecure. People have weird ways of showing their feelings especially when they are teenagers and young adults.

Bullies just want to feel more powerful than you and by making you feel worse about yourself, it makes them feel better about themselves. Humans can be very strange.

OR you can take the HERO mindset. Remember that what someone says/does to you mainly shows how insecure and unhappy with themselves and their lives they are. My grandma (who is one of the most amazing inspiring ladies on earth) once said to me, 'Megan, when people are mean to you, don't be mean back. Just feel sorry for them that they feel they want to treat someone like that.'

People who are happy and confident within themselves don't feel the need to bully and bring others down; they are the people that want to bring others up.

- Try to be someone YOU would want to meet.
- Treat others how you would like to be treated.

What Suzie says of Sally says
more of Suzie than of Sally...
REMEMBER THAT.
– Instagram, Unknown

- Belittling others makes bullies feel powerful and they get a kick out of being mean to you.
- I know it's hard but DON'T LET IT GET TO YOU.

Little people belittle people.
– Rick Warren

Try not to retaliate and bring yourself down to their level... You know you are better than that.

My suggestions

- If in class, walk out.
- If on bus, put music in and ignore.
- If at lunch/recess, walk away.
- If on computer, deactivate/block person.

All these suggestions are a lot easier said than done.

But it is important to remember to try and remove yourself from the situation (if you can). You are better than the people who are trying to bring you down, and by walking away/taking yourself out of the situation, you are showing a great deal of maturity by not acting on impulse (most likely anger) and probably saying/doing something you might regret.

You can even move to a new school if bullying gets really bad. I know a girl from my high school (one of my close friends now) who was bullied A LOT and she moved to a new all-girls school and the bullying completely went away. Sometimes completely removing yourself from the situation can be the best action to take.

Another useful tactic that I wish I'd known in school when I was being bullied is this:

Often if you knew only just one more thing about that person's life, you would completely understand why they are treating you how they are.

For example, if someone is calling you too skinny and telling you to 'Eat a burger, babe' or 'You are definitely anorexic', they may be struggling with their weight themselves and wish they were your size. By making you feel bad about yourself they are making themselves feel better.

You never know if the kid who is being mean to you is getting abused at home physically.

They might even be dealing with their parents getting a divorce at that point in time.

They might feel really sick and need to let out their feelings on someone…and that someone could be you.

They may be really annoyed at themselves because they didn't get into the footy team they wanted to play for.

Or even something as small as they have to walk home and can't be bothered.

Although it is not acceptable to let out your frustrations on someone else, everyone does it.

Next time you get annoyed, actively take note of who you are letting your inner frustrations out on. Often it is those closest to you, e.g., Mum, Dad, brothers or sisters, but it could be anyone.

Have you ever had a bad day and, in a really bad mood, walk into a clothing shop where the shop assistant is happy and chirpy, ready to help you – and you completely blow her/him off or are rude to or even ignore her/him because of YOUR circumstances? Did the shop assistant do anything wrong? No. YOU are the one putting your negative frustrations onto a completely innocent person. This is an example of how people 'work' and how people act when facing negative circumstances, and a great example of why and how people bully others. We are all guilty of this in one way or another.

Discussing bullying, another story comes to my head. It's the story of a troubled girl I used to know. Ever since my first year of high school, she was always with the boys. She was girly but was just one of those girls that preferred boys' company rather than being with girls. She was the girl that always had a boyfriend (usually a hot one, mind you). Now hanging out with boys is fine. A lot of girls I know choose to be around boys more than girls as boys can be 'less drama'. But this girl was different. While hanging out with the boys she would also be really mean and hurtful towards almost every girl in our school and everyone (including me) was super-intimidated by her. I always got the feeling that she enjoyed that; almost like she loved the power of everyone being scared of her.

I was never a huge target for this girl's bullying. But there were a few incidents where she had a few stabs at me. E.g., once I was walking past her in her locker bay and I had sprayed myself with perfume and she said, 'Ew, that stinks.' (It SO didn't; it smelt awesome.) Then she and all the boys laughed at me. She also didn't like the fact that I was dating her ex-boyfriend a few years after they had broken up (we only lasted like a month anyway).

But as I grew older and more mature, she acted almost strangely in her ways with boys (part of me was most likely a little bit jealous as I didn't have any close guy friends except the gay guy in my class). But anyway, she was always flirting with boys and getting their attention. She had quite large boobs for her slim figure and would definitely knew how to make the most of them! (.) (.) She was also a massive flirt and knew how to get any guy she wanted and I'm not going to lie; she did a great job of it!

The one time that stands out more than others was when my friend was in health class with her when she was openly talking and flirting with the teacher (male) discussing her vagina. He was a married man with a wife and children. Apparently, as everyone walked out of the class they were all talking about how this girl was way too full-on with details (even though it was health class, there is a certain line you don't cross).

We thought that it was a bit strange but soon got over it as anyone would when you are a teenage girl (your brain being filled with so many other things). Time passed and no one was impressed by this girl, and she didn't really have many, if any, friends. The friends she did have were what people called her 'sheep'. They would do anything she told them to, they were intimidated by her while at the same time loved her. But friends are friends in high school. Whether they are 'sheep' friends or real friends they are friends, and it usually feels better to have 'any' friends than hanging out alone. If you are wondering how I know all of this about this girl...she was so popular with boys that practically everyone at school and in the area was super jealous (yes, me included).

But anyway as I matured, I actually got to know her as she sometimes caught my train. I really started to like the girl despite all the mean things she had said to and about both me (behind my back when I was dating her ex) and my friends. I was past all that and gave her an actual chance and really started to enjoy her company.

She was awesome. We were never close friends but we were friends. Somehow I understood at a young age that behind her meanness and ways she'd treated others, I knew that there was a reason as to why she is who she is and why she acted how she did. I was also not near as intimidated by the girl as I used to be because, most of the hot guys were not around coz they had dropped out of school to pursue trades. I didn't care if she embarrassed me in front of the girls and the guys who didn't tickle my fancy. Also because I was more happy and sure of myself, and because popularity tends to fade out as you grow up, both in and out of school (popularity and cliques seem to fade as you get older and more mature. A lot of people also drop out of school to pursue their careers. And basically everyone forms closer bonds with everyone, e.g., 'Nerds' talk to 'jocks', 'popular girls' are friends with 'nerds' or this is how it happened at my school but every school is different). By this stage a lot of people didn't have the time/respect for this girl due to how she used to be and how she used to treat them and she was always waiting by herself for the train. Often I would go and sit with this girl because I knew that she did enjoy other people's company.

Anyway, one day this girl and I were catching the train home together and she (almost out of the blue) completely started to open up to me. She started to tell me about her mum and how she left her dad and her when she was young and had actually spent time in jail, and how she used to try to kidnap her from primary school at lunchtime. Now for a primary school student I imagine this would have been pretty scary as school is a place where children, especially primary school-aged children, are meant to feel safe. She explained that every recess and lunchtime she was scared to even leave the classroom.

She told me other stories about her life, such as growing up with a sibling who had leukemia. It was at this point that I realised that this girl had really gone through so much crap throughout her life. I could not even begin to imagine this sort of stuff happening to me, especially at such a young age with no brothers or sisters around at the time. My biggest worry in primary school was whose sleepover party I was going to that weekend. This girl had to think about things such as her mum, who had been to jail, kidnapping her at lunchtime.

It all seemed so unfair to me that people at our school had lost respect for this girl without really properly getting to know her, understanding her story and what she had been through. And yes, I know it's not okay to be mean to others to express your own feelings but this girl learned this as a coping mechanism when she was young and may have thought it worked well and therefore stuck with it. I admit we all 'think' we are doing the right thing at the time and again high school is a social battlefield. **The majority of people will do anything to fit in/not stand out and /or get bullied.**

As my friends would bitch about this girl (hardly even knowing her, mind you.), I would always fight back and say, 'You guys should really think deeper into why she is how she is. I know that girl has gone through a lot in her life that all of us wouldn't even begin to understand, so I think it's a good idea to stop talking negatively about her, until we have walked two yards in her shoes.' (This will probably never happen, and even if the same things were to happen to us, we would interpret the situation very differently to the way she did as we are now adults, while she was a child then). I'll say it again and again: childhood shapes our current reality whether we are aware of it or not.

Being negative and bitching about other people and laughing at people's problems while sitting in a group of 'friends' is not at all positive energy. It's rude and cheap with negative outcomes from YOUR own negative emotions.
– Benjamin 'Casper' Eade

As people kept discussing this girl negatively there was one person who had the same mindset as me and that was my best friend's mum. My best friend's mum would say to my best friend, 'Stop being mean to this girl as she has gone through so many things that couldn't be understood by someone who hasn't experienced them for themselves.' I gained so much respect for her when she said that and it also made me realise that I was not the only person who thought and understood that this girl was troubled and not just the 'Bitch' that everyone knew, and labelled her with.

The reason I told this story is because whether you realise it or not, often the people who are the meanest and nastiest towards other people have many issues, both great and/or small, going on for them, which you may have NO idea about. Don't stoop to their level and be just as mean and nasty back. Just remember that next time someone, either someone who is young or even an adult, is mean/nasty towards you, there may be MANY things that you don't know about them and/or about their lives that make them feel and act negatively towards you. FEEL SORRY FOR PEOPLE WHO ARE MEAN TO YOU...DON'T FEEL SORRY FOR YOURSELF AND MOST OF ALL **DON'T BLAME YOURSELF.**

Sticks and stones may hurt my bones, but mean names sting like anything! ***– Unknown***

Sympathy is the key...you could even say something like 'I hope you feel better one day; I wish you all the best' because you must remember that truly happy people are NOT mean to others. And if people have ever been mean to you, DON'T be mean back... I know it's hard to be the bigger person but just think... you don't want to hurt the already hurt person back. Once mean words are said, someone may never ever forget them.

MY ADVICE ON WHAT TO DO WHEN OTHERS ARE MEAN TO YOU:

People hurt you to fix their own hurt and pain.

- Feel sorry for them...happy people are not mean to others

SMALL PART ON JEALOUSY

You probably have something that they want, whether they realise this consciously or not, e.g., caring friends, good boyfriend, hot body, nice eyes, fun personality or even something deeper for example. The girl whose story I just shared had an insanely unfair childhood. (Remember that the person who is teasing you may have problems bigger than you could ever imagine.)

I know what you are thinking... BUT NO I don't have any of these qualities...no boyfriend, caring friends, hot body, nice eyes, fun personality... OR SO YOU THINK. Often people see the beauty in you that you don't even see yourself.

E.g., I know a girl who went through all of her years of primary school and high school wishing she wasn't so skinny. She hated it and just wanted to be heavier. She used to look at the girls in her classes who were healthy and carried more weight than her and WISHED that she could look like that.... People were always mean to her about her weight throughout all of her years at school. When, after high school, her best friend told her that she thought that people were jealous of her weight, she could not believe it as she was jealous of theirs! It was insane. My point is that there is often something about yourself you don't find beautiful that other people do. Jealousy can cause people to do horrible, horrible things, especially to girls. I heard on the news the other day that one girl poured gas and set alight another girl because this girl was 'attractive' and she thought her boyfriend liked this girl more.

Honestly, jealousy is a terrible feeling and can cause people to do unimaginable things.

My advice is, if you are jealous of someone, use it to improve yourself. If you are jealous of a girl who does yoga to keep fit and you admire her flexibility, start yoga yourself. Hating her is not going to make you a better person...but getting inspiration from her and using this girl as motivation to get fit and flexible is a great way to turn jealousy into success for you.

You are amazing.

- Don't ever, ever, EVER forget the good qualities about yourself. If you feel you don't have any, ask a trusted person – Mum, Dad, a friend, or even a counsellor, to point out a few positive qualities they think about you...you may be surprised at how much people love things about you that you are unaware you even possess.

I am on placement at a primary school right now (during university) and there is a girl who gets really upset because she thinks that she's 'bad at maths' and wishes she was fast at maths like the other kids. But then I saw her drawing skills and, no joke, she is like a mini-Picasso. She's amazing! I made a point to explain to her that even though she feels crap when she does maths, to remember that she is super-talented and skilled in other areas such as drawing.

It's SO important to point out other people's strengths not weaknesses.

- Remember that I'm 22 (nearly) and four years after high school, and a lot of the bullies are addicted to drugs, doing illegal work (such as selling drugs) and are living off the dole. While YOU will be living the life of your dreams: studying what you want to be studying, and/ or working at an amazing job that you love and enjoy, while getting yourself to the top of the career you want, or even travelling overseas and making the most of your life. At the same time, your bullies may be just trying to get their next drug hit or selling drugs at clubs every weekend.

I LOVE, LOVE, lo-o-ove the saying: 'Be nice to Nerds. You may end up working for them'.
– Charles J Sykes

- Remember that these bullies may be standing on top of you now and they may hurt you temporarily BUT what they don't realise is that what they are actually doing is giving YOU more motivation to succeed in the future. The more people bring you down the more you need to store all of that 'nastiness' then convert it into motivation to succeed at whatever you want in the future, not only to prove them wrong but to lead a happy life that YOU enjoy.

- There is nothing worse than seeing the person you hate being happy. E.g., how angry does it make you if someone you hate smiles at you? When you see them happy it hurts you more than seeing them upset. *Happiness is the best revenge.*

- I will never ever forget when people used to call me the nastiest names while I was sitting down on the bus minding my own business. I just used to sit and think and try so hard not to cry. I was like 'Don't cry', 'Don't cry', 'Don't cry', the entire bus trip home. But I used this nastiness and bullying as motivation and since then we have all grown up. These boys have matured and now we are friends. Not close friends, but friends. I choose to believe that because I went out and lived my life to the full and followed my dreams (I know it sounds super cliché) and didn't let the bullying affect me (tried not to at least), these boys have learnt to respect me for who I am. Remember to use these bullies as

> motivation to succeed and prove them wrong. You know you are higher than what they say about/to you… You know yourself what you are capable of achieving (whatever you want). GO OUT AND DO IT! Don't let other people's opinions of you get into your head and ruin your self-confidence. And when you do succeed don't say it to everyone just use your actions to show it… According to https://www.psychologytoday.com/blog/fulfillment-any-age/201511/4-signs-someone-is-probably-insecure bragging can actually be a hidden form of insecurity. Karma will come around to them (those bullies), trust me. What goes around really does come around.

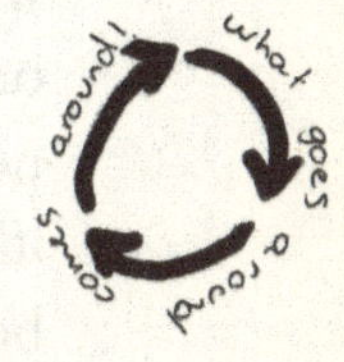

I have seen it happen many times to everyone, both to people who have taken stabs at me and also to myself when I have been mean and rude towards others. And even watching my friends be mean to others – it bites them back in the ass, either quite soon after they said it or a little while later. Even if you don't ever find out about your bully in terms of karma, just remember and have the mindset that it will come around and get them… Often you don't realise a lot of bad things that have happened in someone's life. You never know the pain someone may be going through until they tell you. So don't think, 'Oh, it looks like my bully has the perfect life,' because I can almost bet 100% that they don't have it all together. A lot of people put up fronts against the world and are a lot different to who you may think they really are. You don't really know or even see who they truly are behind closed doors. Even if you are not someone who believes in 'karma', the mindset of knowing that everything evens itself out in the end or that somehow the person being mean to you will pay, makes bullying a lot easier to deal with. I know you should never wish mean upon others but if you have to think that mindset to get through your high school days while being bullied, do it, because you KNOW it will help you make it through those years alive. Remember to be the bigger person you know you are. Don't fight back by pointing out karma to people who have been mean to you...this will feel good but only make them not like you even more. Watch the negativity happen to them and think in your head that it's karma.... And even if you don't see their karma, still believe that karma will reach them one day or that it is reaching them now but you are unaware of it.

I was told by my year 12 English teacher and my careers teacher that I wouldn't be able to achieve the marks to get into university. And from that point on why I wasn't listening to them anymore... when someone tells me I can't do something I remember that it's their opinion and NOT the truth.

People will try and put limitations on you but the only person who can truly limit you is YOU.

Your value and worth is not based on what any other individuals think of you whether it be your teachers, mum, dad, best friend or school mates.

Even people you trust and have a lot of respect for may try to put limitations on you because THEY believe it is not achievable. As hard as it can be, try not to put your value in other people's hands...keep your self-esteem at a high and healthy level because deep down you know what you want...and you know you CAN achieve it. My aunty has always said to me from a young age, '*The world is your oyster – it's up to you to find the pearls* – Chris Gardner'. Obviously there will be setbacks on your way and there will be struggles. But keep your head up and, girls, **keep wearing your invisible crown**...despite what you have gone through in the past, from this day forward you are going to not let other people's opinions of you get you down. You are going to keep a healthy self-esteem and know that, despite what others say (especially bullies) of you, you KNOW what you can achieve.

I actually did get the marks to get into my course (only just scraped through) but I did get them. Now that I look back on the situation, the lesson I learned from this experience was actually probably just as, if not MORE important, than the grades. I learned that just because somebody doubts you, you can push past the limitations they put on you. Even if you have an immense amount of respect for the person or the person is a higher authority such as a teacher, if you believe in who you are, believe in yourself, know that you are amazing and capable of achieving what you want, **you can do it**. How amazing the look on their faces will be when you have done exactly what they said you couldn't. No words can describe the awesome feeling of doing what others claim you cannot do.

Do just once what others say you cannot do and you will never pay attention to their limitations again.
– Captain James Cook

As for those teachers who made those comments about me never being able to get the grades to get into university, I now look back and truly should THANK them for their words, which stung and hurt SO much at the time but honestly made me so much better of a person today. And surprisingly if you look at what I'm doing four years out of school: I am writing a book (when my average mark in English was a D+) and my marks at university somehow average at a High Distinction level, it's funny how only four years ago I was told I was not smart enough to even get into uni. Please don't take this story as bragging. I honestly am just trying to show you that if ANYONE says something bad about you, DON'T believe it for one second (**that's their reality, not yours**), because once you believe it, you live it and begin to think it's true… even if it's not. You don't need that person's negativity in your life. Remember, even if people are being mean and doubting you still give them respect. You don't have to like them or be their best friend but do pay them respect, even if they don't deserve it.

Holding negative thoughts about someone is like holding hot coals and intending to throw them at someone...but in the end you're the only one getting burnt.
– Buddha

Being mean to others won't get you any further in life. Love and appreciation for everyone and everything will bring you a lot more happiness. I know it's hard when people are treating you badly and putting limitations on you but be the bigger person and go about your life being nice and prove them wrong, not for the revenge but for yourself. My favourite saying in school was, 'Don't doubt me'.

For a person who cherishes compassion and love the practice of tolerance is essential, and for that, an enemy is indispensable. So we should be grateful for our enemies, for it is they who can best help us develop a tranquil mind.
– The Dalai Lama

Compassion also means loving friends as well as loving enemies which isn't easy.
– The Dalai Lama

Remember the gem cannot be polished without friction, nor the man perfected without trials.
– Chinese Proverb

Although I am throwing all these quotes at you, it is honestly easier said than done. Just because you know these quotes, it's a completely different thing to have the ability to LIVE by these quotes.

If you are going through hell
– keep going.
– Sir Winston Churchill

When I was ditched by my friends (story in Friends (Bitches) chapter), I decided that I was going to purely focus on bettering myself, gaining new confidence and making new friends. I took up tennis and dancing, singing and school production were looking up. Four years later the 'popular' girls had left my school. I bumped into the old 'queen bee' when I was working at my part-time job. I will never forget the day she asked me if I worked at the shop (as I was standing behind the register, haha), and acted so surprised that I worked at a 'cool' clothing shop. A few weeks later she came into my work again and asked me if I'd go clubbing (underage) with her and her friends. I was so happy because it felt as though she was asking for my friendship back after being so cruel to me four years earlier (maybe I got radicool). I said yes, and I hung out with her for a little bit and she kept wanting me to go clubbing with her every week after that. But by this stage in my life, I was busy with other things and other people and wasn't really interested. But looking back on that experience, it's crazy how in four years the person who was really mean to you wants to so badly hang out with you again.

But girls, there are a few messages in this story:

Your Consent
Keep bettering yourself despite what anyone says or does to you. Try to have unshakable confidence.

- In a matter of a few years the tables can turn and the people who treated you poorly can be begging for you to give them another chance... Let them – people deserve chances.
- What someone thinks of you is NOT true unless YOU believe it. If someone calls you dumb, ugly, idiot, slut, the only way these words can affect you is if you believe the names they are giving you yourself.

No one can make you feel inferior without your consent.
– Eleanor Roosevelt

Looking back in school I was called a 'slut', 'slappa', 'whore', 'skank', many, many, many times BUT I never let it get to me because I knew myself I was never any of these. I was getting called a slut when I hadn't even had sex/done anything sexually yet. What matters is what you know within yourself...what anyone else says of you is their opinion NOT your reality. Even if thousands of people call you mean names you know that there is only one person's opinion of you that matters and that's your own. Keep your head high.

One quote that I live by now is:

What he thinks of me in no way controls what I think of him. And I have the utmost respect for him.

– Rick Warren Saddleback Church CA

I love this because it is about loving others, even people who are mean to you.

Treat others how you wish to be treated

– Lou Holtz

NOT

Treat others how they treat you.

– Unknown

At the end of the day I know for a fact that being nice will get you further than being mean. Negativity brings on negativity.

My brother was also a target for bullies at school. Initially he reacted, which fuelled the bullies, making them worse, until he realised that putting his iPod in (on the bus) and ignoring worked a lot better. These bullies used to physically hurt my brother, who was quite tall although rather skinny. Two years down the track my bro saw his bullies at the local gym; he'd been working out for the past three years and now was definitely not what you'd call skinny. He was about three times the size of his ex-bullies! He didn't even say anything...he just looked at the bullies and smiled. Within a few years there is so much that can change and the people who bullied you and who you were so scared of will not frighten or intimidate you at all. My brother would have loved to rematch his bullies, but he realised he was happy with how he is now. Beating the bullies now was not going to make him feel any better about the past, so he took the mature approach and just smiled and moved on with his life.

Contacting Kids Help Line/Beyondblue or Lifeline is always a great plan of action to take when you are feeling down about bullying or anything in general. It's a free telephone counselling service (in Australia) on which you can talk to someone about what's upsetting you. I have called them many times throughout my life when I was feeling misunderstood and not listened to or bullied by others. I can't recommend them more. They are amazing and next time you are feeling down, shoot them a call. I can almost guarantee that they can help you feel a lot better. Kids Help Line –1800 55 1800; Lifeline –13 11 14; Beyondblue 1300 22 4636. If you have a serious emergency or are suicidal, ring 000 (Australia) or your own country's emergency number.

Everything is going to be all right. ☺
And don't let anyone ever bring you down.
Stay true to you. It's all you have to do.
– *Megan Street*

Failing

You don't learn to walk by following rules; you learn by doing and falling over
– Richard Branson

You know what 'FAILING' stands for?
It stands for:

- *Finding*
- *An*
- *Important*
- *Lesson*
- *Inviting*
- *Needed*
- *Growth*

– Gary Busey

Success is how high you bounce when you have hit bottom.
– George S Patten

I haven't failed, I've found 1000 ways that don't work.
– Thomas Edison

It takes 20 years to become an overnight success.
– Eddie Cantor

Failing happens
Even Walt Disney was fired because he apparently *lacked imagination*!

I failed in some subjects in exam; my friend passed all. Now he is an engineer in Microsoft and I am the owner of Microsoft.
– Bill Gates owner of Microsoft

Many, many, MANY times I have 'failed' and things have not gone to plan. I've failed tests at school, exams, driving tests, university exams, failed at achieving many of my goals, becoming school captain, house captain, even failing at having my crushes like me back! Job seeking, when I was 15 years old and first able to work, I applied for, no joke, about 100 casual jobs. The aim of the game is not to get disheartened when you get rejected by anyone – an employer, your crush, your friends, your parents – ANYONE.

- A close friend's boyfriend still struggles with applying for jobs due to being afraid of rejection or failure. He (like many people) gets one rejection, gets disheartened and gives up trying to find a job.

My contrasting opinion is that you should use failure to drive you HARDER to achieve your goal. I learned in primary school that

persistence

confidence

being organised

and

getting along well with other people

are four traits that can greatly help you to achieve any kind of success you wish.

– From 'You Can Do It' Emotional Resilience Program

Eventually I got a job after many days of handing out résumés, applying online and calling employers. AT MACCAS! And even though it was at Maccas I was ecstatic that I had landed my first real job after so much persistence and patience. And yes, I know what you are thinking – it's just Maccas, but it was so much more to me than just a job at McDonald's...it was a huge goal reached. It didn't matter where the job was; it mattered that the goal was completed (ticked box). I knew that I wasn't going to stay there forever and that it was a great stepping stone to other future part-time jobs. You need to remember that you must take small steps towards your goal. No one is an overnight success. They have usually spent a long time working their way up to the success that they have.

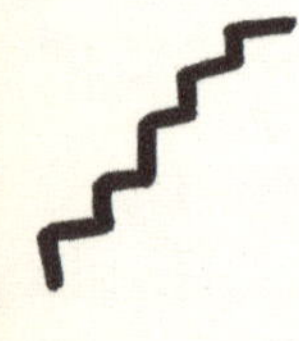

After a year or so at Maccas (I quit because I was over cleaning up vomit from all of the 'burger eating comps' customers would have.) I tried for a few more part-time jobs; then landed my dream part-time job at my fave clothing store! Wooo!

The manager of the clothing store said to me, 'It's impressive that you have worked at Maccas as they have great training.' Later, on one of my shifts, the manager of the clothing store told me half the reason she hired me was because I'd worked at Maccas. If I had turned down my first part-time job at Maccas because, let's be honest, it's not some prestige job... it's McDonalds, I would have never made the first step to getting a job at my fave clothing store. Not to mention the awesome friends I made and fun experiences I had while working at McDonalds – spraying each other with cleaner, water fights, hiding in the freezer, attempting to make a burger, even getting my first boyfriend to lick the chocolate sauce off my hands.

My point is that it doesn't matter where you start. It matters that **you make the most of the experience**, learn from it and get better from it. My advice is to give it a shot. You may love working at Maccas (or that place that you would NEVER work at and keep turning your nose up at). Stop with the 'Ew, I couldn't work there', or the 'They wouldn't hire me, there is no point in even applying!'.

GIVE IT A SHOT.

YOU NEVER KNOW UNTIL YOU TRY.

Even if you do hate it, try, try and try again, until you like one of your jobs. If you go into a new workplace or any situation for that matter with the right mindset there is almost no doubt that you'll enjoy yourself there whatever you may be doing. Remember it can be a stepping stone to greater things.

Each and every opportunity you are given, take it, as you gain experience from everything you do in your life.

Another time that persistence paid off for me was after year 12 (final year of school). I knew that I wanted to be a teacher...although I didn't know if I was able to achieve the grades high enough to get into university.

CRITICISM = MOTIVATION

My results throughout the year were average, until I decided to fully put my head down and study like there was no tomorrow. I said to myself that I wouldn't let ANYTHING get in the way of me and my career goal of becoming a teacher. I had a goal of 'ACE-ING' my exams and NOTHING was going to stop me.

As you know I had teachers telling me I wouldn't be able to achieve any higher grades; teachers telling me that I would never be able to become a teacher; one teacher even told me not to try because I wouldn't be able to reach a certain study score. The people in my year called me 'dumb' and one boy even said, 'Why do you bother studying? It's not like you'll ever get into university.' (I will speak more about this in the Boys/ Heartbreak chapter.) And as you know to this day I thank them all for their criticism and harsh words as that was my motivation to study, I knew I had the ability to prove them all wrong and I did. ☺ I aced my exams and got As, B+s and a C+. As my mum always said, ***'The best revenge is massive success'***, a Frank Sinatra quote.

Even though I got those grades, they were still not high enough to get into teaching… BUT I did get into another course and then university to study creative arts, which I was extremely interested in. I studied this course for a year and then transferred to my double degree of teaching (primary and secondary) and was credited with the entire year of creative arts. I had finally, after years of hard work, got into teaching at university. And to this day I am more than halfway through my Bachelor of Education Prep to year 12.

SUCCESS IS TRULY THE BEST REVENGE.

My point to this story is not to give up on your goal. People are most likely going to try and bring you down with their harsh words and criticism. DON'T let them. Use criticism as motivation. People bringing you down are only trying to fix insecurities they have in themselves. They may be jealous of you or may just genuinely get a kick out of saying hurtful things to others.

Brick walls are there for a reason.
The brick walls are not there to keep us out.
The brick walls are there to give us a chance
to show how badly we want something.
– Randy Pausch, The Last Lecture (book)

Most of the important things in the world have been accomplished by people who have kept on trying when there seemed to be no hope at all.
– Dale Carnegie

Don't give up... You may be two seconds away from your treasure (goal).

Genius is 1% inspiration and 99% perspiration.
– Thomas Edison

Obstacles are those frightful things you see when you take your eyes off your goal.
– Henry Ford

Our greatest glory is not in never failing, but in rising up every time we fail.
– Ralph Waldo Emerson

When you reach the end of your rope, tie a knot in it and hang on.
– Franklin D. Roosevelt

Defeat may serve as well as victory, to shake the soul and let the glory out.
– Edwin Markham

Mistakes are the portals of discovery.
– James Joyce

It's closer than you know; but you've gotta keep going for it to show.
– Megan Street

Ugh, Parents

Don't bite the hand that feeds you.
– English Proverb

Do not cut down the tree that gives you shade.
– Arabian Proverb

Your parents are doing the best job that they can do.

A crazy thing that my parents did when I was younger was give both me and my brother (who was about four years old at the time) a go at smoking one of my dad's cigarettes. I know what you're thinking. What crazy insane parents would let their 6-year-old daughter and four-year-old son try a cigarette? It was such an out-of-character thing for both my mum and dad to do; so why did they do it? Now that we are older, mum and dad have explained why they did this to us – it was to completely turn us off smoking. So when my brother was four and I was six we both coughed and coughed and almost threw up BUT to this day Jason (20) and I (22) don't smoke. A lot of our friends do but we don't and do not feel like we want or need to; we are just not interested. This is

an example of how parents are trying to show you the right path, but are doing it in a different way to what you would expect and/or think is right.

Another thing my parents have always been big on was 'finding our own way around'. Often, when I was growing up, I would have to find my own way home from places I went to by either public transport, lifts from friends and even taxi rides, rather than getting picked up by my parents. At the time it absolutely **sucked**, as a lot of my friends got picked up and taken everywhere and I was always that girl on the bus or the train. At one stage I felt like they didn't even care about me. BUT as I grew up and matured, I realised that what they were doing was actually a blessing in disguise. I now look back on it as a great way to bring up us children, as we learned independence and how to do things on our own with little or no help from others. This has been a huge lesson/part of my life as now I try as hard as I can to do things and not rely on others unless I really have to. Independence is a great quality that I learned from something that I hated at the time. But now I respect my parents for doing that back then. Just because you don't understand your parents' actions, it doesn't mean you should hate it/them.

I firmly believe that no matter how far-fetched, crazy, cruel, mean and annoying they are being at the time, your parents really are trying to do what is best for you either in the short term or long term. **Cut them some slack**...because I can almost guarantee you'll be thanking them one day. Just remember – where would you be without your parents? Show them your love and appreciation.

CHANGE YOUR MINDSET – I grew to love the train and bus rides, chilling out, listening to music, talking to people, making friends. Sometimes I used to even take the longer bus route home so that I could talk to people for longer on the bus. There is no escape on the bus. Whether the person wanted to talk to me or not, they kind of had to because they were stuck on the bus – hehehe. If you hate the train/bus/tram change your mindset. Think about all the good reasons for catching the bus/train/tram, e.g., time alone, listening to new music, playing scenarios in your head about you and your crush, relaxing, thinking about your goals, what you want to do in the future or enjoying the scenery. A bit of quiet time by yourself without your phone/ social media can be great, so just sit back enjoy the view and practise your 'bus patience' even when the bus is stopping at almost every stop and you are already running an hour late. Remember this chapter and your 'bus patience'. *Patience is a virtue* – Proverb-and a very good place to practise such an important life skill is on the bus.

I guarantee if you can master 'bus/train patience' you can master patience in any situation.

Parents ARE trying to help you. They may think and say things differently to what you would say/do to help. A lot of people in your life are trying to help you; try not to push them away. Two quotes that I also need to be reminded of constantly are: *Don't bite the hand that feeds you* – English Proverb *and Do not cut down the tree that gives you shade – Arabian Proverb.* Think of everything that your parents do for you and honestly, where would you be without them? Oh wait, that's right – YOU WOULDN'T EVEN EXIST. They cook, clean, love, drive you around, enrol you in school, buy you food, give you clean water or help you with homework. Whatever they might do for you, just remember to be grateful for it, because at the end of the day, although it sometimes may seem otherwise, they do love you and want what's best for you. Even though you feel like you want to let your feelings of anger and frustration out on those closest to you, take a step back, take a breath, cool down and remember...

Be grateful for what your parents/family do for you.

If you are younger, your parents are most likely trying to teach you, NOT work against you and hate you (which it may often feel like). Trust me, from someone who's been and gone through it, **you will thank them when you are older.**

One story that pops into my mind on this subject was when I was about four years old (yeah, I know, crazy that I even remember that far back), but the reason I remember it is because it caused me pain at the time. I now look back on it and realise it was a huge blessing in disguise. One day my mum, brother and I were all coming home from a trip to the local swimming pool and as we all know you always crave super delicious foods after you go swimming. When I was a kid we weren't allowed to eat a lot of the things the other kids ate as my mum can be a bit of a health freak. The nicest thing we were allowed was fruit finger sticks. (Honestly they had almost no fruit in them and were absolutely jam packed with sugar. I think mum thought they were semi-healthy because they were sold at the fruit shop.) But anyway as we were leaving the swimming pool we had to walk straight past the canteen where all our friends were buying yummy treats that we were not allowed (I would have killed for just one jelly snake). My brother and I used to get so jealous and beg Mum for some treats after swimming. She would just give us one lousy fruit finger while saying, 'You'll thank me when you're older.' We were so annoyed at the time and definitely could not see how in ANY way we would be thanking Mum when we were older for not giving us scrumptious treats from the swimming pool canteen. Even though it took me a good 14 years or so to realise this, my mum was doing what was best for our health. And to this day I'll never know what may have happened to our health if she had fed a lot of junk food to both my brother and me when we were younger. So this is a lesson in itself. Although it may take you a long time to realise the reasons behind their actions, almost always, they are for your benefit in the long run. At the end of the day you can't have everything you want always and that is half the beauty of life. Patience and understanding about why your parents act/acted as they did will help you to live

no jelly snakes for you!

with and respect the choices that they have made or are still making for you.

We often remember our pains and just see them as pain. Whereas if we look at our pains and what GOOD the pain has/will bring in the future or has already brought us, I promise you are one step closer to happiness.

Choices – Drugs

Hugs not Drugs

Try not to be influenced by others –
be true to yourself and YOUR beliefs
– Megan Street

Not being influenced by others will probably be one of the most challenging things that you will have to do in school and life as a young adult.
– Megan Street

Know who you are and don't
give in to peer pressure
– Megan Street

If you don't want to do drugs and they are offered to you by someone who is pressuring you to do them, just politely say thanks but no thanks. And if you feel uncomfortable with everyone doing them around you, try to leave the situation/environment if you can.

It can be really hard because people might and probably will call you names such as weak, loser, dork, scared but when you walk away and look back on the situation, the feeling you get from the ability to stand up for yourself and say no is huge. You gain more respect for yourself and walk away, knowing who you are as a person and what you will and will not stand for. And most of all you will feel proud that you didn't give in to peer pressure.

A memory of drugs I will never forget was when I was on Schoolies after year 12, my final year at school. I was 18 and I was at the house of a friend's friend and was sitting in a small room full of about 12 people, all passing around marijuana in a bong. I did not try the bong although my best friend did (mind you people were pressuring us). Even though all of these people my age were pressuring us to do it, I knew myself really well and knew that my health was more important than the small high I might get from trying marijuana (weed). I was not interested and politely said no; then left the room and went to the toilet and just sat on that toilet feeling dizzy and out of it. It was a weird but scary feeling. After I left the toilet I went and hung out with some people downstairs who were not doing any kind of drugs.

Another time a similar thing happened was when I was at the home of a friend who was having a gathering.

Probably about 15 people were there. I had gone with three other girls. They were all offered some weed and they used it. Within a few hours, all three of them were vomiting and really sick. After seeing this, I was really happy that I hadn't tried it as I probably would have been sick with them.

THE CHOICES YOU MAKE ARE WHAT MAKE UP WHO YOU ARE.

Let's not forget that 'Drug misuse increases the risk of developing schizophrenia or a similar illness' that a person may have never had otherwise. http://www.nhs.uk/Conditions/Schizophrenia/Pages/Causes.aspx. It's honestly not worth the risk from any amount of fun you get from it (in my opinion). And, I know, you may be thinking, 'Oh yeah, but that won't happen to me.' Well, trust me. I know a few people that I used to be really close with and have THE BEST fun at parties with. Ever since they started doing drugs they have developed mental illnesses.

A piece of me:

A lot of people ask me, 'Why haven't you just tried drugs?'; 'You know you'll have a good time'; 'I know you won't get addicted'; 'C'mon it won't hurt anyone'; 'Just try it once'. Now I stand very firm with my choice not to do drugs because:

- When I was younger my aunty told me that mental illness runs in our family and I'd have to be so silly to play with fire and even just try drugs (maybe it was her tactic to not get me to go near drugs…but it definitely worked). When you already have the genes that are predisposed and could easily turn into mental illness, you really must think twice and even three times before you take any sort of drugs (even just marijuana which people have told me is a 'safer' drug), as everyone is different. It may affect your friend for the Saturday night he/she did it – but it may affect you for life. Ask your parents if anyone in your family has had mental illness, because often you may think people who haven't had any mental health problems actually have. I've noticed that people who have had mental health problems can hide it very well. The other thing that I have noticed is that some of the happiest of people have had depression or some kind of mental illness which they have overcome, and now 'life now' in contrast to 'how life used to be' is absolutely amazing. They are the LAST people you would have expected to have had mental illness or depression. Looks and outward exterior can be deceiving. So ask around…sus it out and look after yourself first.

- I have always been prone to little things such as OCD and anxiety my entire life...even when I was really young...so again taking drugs would be playing with fire.
- I have a really addictive personality... I get addicted to things (or should I say the feeling things give me) really easily whether it be gambling, coffee or even just cola... When I want something it's hard for me to say no to myself. This all comes from knowing yourself and knowing your own personality. The best way I can try to explain it is that it's like the feeling that you want something, you know you SHOULDN'T have it but you cannot help but have it. I can sit there for hours thinking I'm not going to have a cola (drink) and coffee but then I eventually give in to it. This is because the good feeling of having the cola or coffee outweighs any feelings that I shouldn't have it. Addiction is hard to explain.

Another thing which has made me know even when I was younger that I have an addictive personality is that I used to always want to have a go on those claw machine games...over and over again with the chance that I'd win. I'd almost never win and just spent all my pocket money on these claw gaming things. My brother would save his money to spend on what he wanted but I was addicted to the high I got of the 'chance' that I might win big on the claw machine. Evaluate your personality...work out if you have an addictive personality because I know all too well addiction can be SUPER hard to beat especially if your brain is just wired that way.

I've seen many people fall into drugs, people you would never ever expect to have a drug problem. It often starts small but then they believe that they can't have fun without drugs and only enjoy being around others who do drugs or even think they are 'cooler' than everyone else coz they do drugs. Or they may adopt the 'I can stop anytime I want' motto, which is also common with smokers who insist they are not addicted or are only 'social smokers'. Before you know, they can't go a few hours without a cigarette. Or the 'I only do it once every never' motto and start doing drugs once every never, which turns into once every month, which turns into once every weekend, which turns into many times a day and the person can't survive without drugs.

My best friend was heavily into marijuana (weed) when she was 19/20 years old. She was smoking literally about four bongs an hour, she couldn't eat, sleep, function without it. She had no job and lived off the dole (Centrelink) and didn't have any plans to change her ways. I have a few friends who have been heavily addicted to drugs but I have chosen to interview Rose as she has made the biggest turn-around and is such an inspiration to anyone who may be struggling with drug addiction. She has now been clean of drugs (other than alcohol and tobacco) for over three years now. She is working, studying, saving, has healthy relationships and apart from the ups and downs everyone has, her life is pretty much on track now. For someone to go from such an extreme addiction to completely turning around her life and habits is absolutely amazing. She is a massive inspiration to anyone hooked on any type of drugs, has a friend who is addicted and anyone wanting to kick addiction...because if she can do it anyone can. I asked if I could interview her and she swallowed her pride agreed to be totally honest when I asked her the below questions, I hope that her truthful answers can help you or someone you know out of drug addiction.

How did you get into drugs?
Well, I was 18 and I was at friend's house having drinks. His brother was there smoking weed and he looked like he was having an awesome time; that was when he offered me a drag. I was drunk and thought why not, so the drag turned into a whole cigarette/joint; then the joint turned into many.

When did you hit rock bottom and realise you needed help?
So I was at home doing my typical routine before bed to get me to sleep and a moth flew into my room and I was like whatever. Then I went to lie down to sleep and I could hear the moth and started to get really anxious. I started thinking that the moth would fly into my ear while I was asleep and go into my brain, then sit on my brain and kill me. At the time my heart started to go funny and I had heart palpitations and it felt like it was coming out of my chest. I freaked out, had a panic attack and ran into my dad's room. I couldn't sleep and that's when I realised something was wrong and I needed help.

What was it that kept you so addicted?

The feeling, the cloudy feeling, relaxed, deep thought, fun, helped me forget about my problems and escape life as I didn't have a job and felt like I was going nowhere in life; but the weed made me feel like a completely different person.

Did you ever think in school and before you hit 18 that you would become a drug addict?

I was 110% against drugs, especially because my mum has schizophrenia, which was caused by her doing drugs at a young age/teenage years. I was always quite studious, kind of a nerd, goody too-shoes, and almost never got in trouble; but all it took was one night to change that.

If you are going to try drugs (illegal) make sure you are in a positive mind frame beforehand.

What is your advice for people/kids experimenting with drugs?

Don't give into the temptation/peer pressure. Definitely don't do it on a spur of the moment decision, or when you're sad or upset. If you ever are going to try it, which I believe you definitely shouldn't, think about it, research it, research if any mental illness is in your family and realise it's not all it's cracked up to be. It's not as good as you think it might be – weed. As for other drugs, don't ever do them. You never know exactly what you're taking.

What advice would you give to occasional users?

- Make sure you don't have an addictive personality.

- You don't realise you're hooked until it is usually too late.
- Realise who and what bad influences are.
- Happens so fast going from occasional use to frequent use.
- You know you are becoming a frequent user when you are doing it alone and not social.
- Your relationships can be hugely affected.
- You may move away from the right people/ real friends
- Shut off to real friends.
- Watch out for Personality changes.
- You see yourself becoming different, more rough and scummy (as much as I hate to say it now).

(Rose was using the 'C' word in like every sentence. Three years down the track she is disgusted at the foul language she used to use.)

Once I got off the drugs I lost most of my 'drug friends'.

I then realised I had pushed away my true friends, but was lucky to get some of them back. You might not be so lucky.

How did you beat addiction?

I knew that I never wanted to experience those bad experiences again: anxiety, panic attacks, not being able to sleep, smoking to have to get to sleep, psychiatrists, and all it took was one bad experience, and I'm lucky that it wasn't a worse experience.

How was it for the first few months?

IT WAS REALLY HARD.

- Couldn't sleep properly for the first three months. I tried drinking, medication (sleeping pills) but nothing would work
- I felt like I had forgotten how to fall asleep, severe anxiety every day
- I slept in Dad's room for 6 months on a mattress

Why did you do that?

- Because I was anxious and afraid I would not wake up if I finally got to sleep
- I had severe panic attacks, heart palpitations, passing out, sweats, shivering
- Valium helped a lot for the first three months

If you had a friend who is a drug addict, how would you approach the situation?

Rose: Tell them I would stop being friends with them, if they don't stop doing it. Try to understand and help the situation first. If you see little to no improvement, give them an ultimatum. (Rose's opinion)

Me (author): First tell them that they should stop; it makes people 'not themselves'; creates worst version of self. If it got to the point where it was toxic on my life, e.g., they were getting into trouble with the law and dragging me into it, and having a negative impact on my life and I had to deal with their problems, I would most likely let the friendship go.

What is your advice to people who think 'it won't happen to me'?

Don't think you're invincible because YOU ARE NOT. It is best to stop a drug addiction before it's too late – cold turkey; or slowly wean yourself off. Maybe find a new hobby that will distract you.

- Seek professional help. You have to be willing to stop for yourself, not anyone else. You must want to stop.

SAY NO!

Do you ever want to go back?

Yes, especially when other people are doing it around me or when I'm worried and feeling down – needing to relax. Triggers are everywhere, for example, plants, leaves, even looking at a water bottle (used to make a bong out of a water bottle).

How do you deal with it when people do it around you?

Think about how much I don't want the anxiety, bad experiences and panic attacks to come back, and remember how far I have come and how much I have accomplished since quitting.

What does it feel like to be clean for over three years now?

Clear, amazing, proud and going somewhere in life. It feels like you can conquer/achieve so much if you can get through something as hard as drug addiction. You feel truly yourself again.

Have you had any problems that last, which were caused by your addiction?

- Anxiety
- Panic attacks
- Hypochondriac
- Depression
- Sick easily
- Bad overall health, which has improved now
- Stomach issues
- Headaches

Anything else you want to share?

Yes, this is a poem that I did not make up but read on Facebook. Read it through, take in every word and if you ever think of touching anything, just read this over again... Coming from a prior drug addict, everything this poem says is entirely true.

HELLO, MY NAME IS DRUGS

Hello my name is drugs – I destroy homes, tear families apart, take your children and that's just the start.

I'm more costly than diamonds, more costly than gold; the sorrow I bring is a sight to behold.

And if you need me, remember I'm easily found; I live all around you in schools and in town, I live with the rich, I live with the poor, I live down the street and maybe next door.

My power is awesome; try me you'll see, but if you do, you may never break free. Just try me once and I might let you go, but try me twice and I'll own your soul.

When I possess you you'll steal and you'll lie; you do what you have to just to get high.

The crimes you'll commit for my narcotic charms will be worth the pleasure you'll feel in your arms.

You'll lie to your mother, you'll steal from your dad; when you see their tears you should feel sad.

But you'll forget your morals and how you were raised; I'll be your conscience I'll teach you my ways.

I take kids from parents and parents from kids. I turn people from God and separate friends, and no, that's not even the beginning to where it ends.

I'll take everything from you, your looks and your pride; I'll be with you always right by your side.

You'll give up everything – your family, your home, your friends, your money; then you'll be alone.

I'll take and take till you have nothing more to give. When I'm finished with you...you'll be lucky to live.

If you try me be warned, this is no game. If given the chance I'll drive you insane.

I'll ravish your body, I'll control your mind; I'll own you completely...your soul will be mine.

The nightmares I'll give you while lying in bed; the voices you'll hear from inside your head.

The sweats, the shakes, the visions you'll see; I want you to know these are all gifts from me.

But then it's too late and you'll know in your heart that you are mine and we shall not part.

You'll regret that you tried me...they always do, but you came to me, not I to you.

You knew this would happen the many times you were told, but you challenged my power and chose to be bold.

You could have said no and just walked away; if you could live that day over now what would you say, my slave? I'll even go with you when you go to your grave,

Now that you have met me what will you do? ***Will you try me or not... it's all up to you.***

I can bring you more misery than words can tell...come, take my hand, I'll take you to hell.

– Unknown

Now Rose has been completely clear of drugs for just over three years and she is very happy with her job and has found an amazing loving boyfriend and is ultimately 'loving liiioffff'. Whereas if you had looked at her three years ago you would have assumed this girl's future was not looking too sunny to say the least.

Rose's situation is a very lucky one as the marijuana has not affected her long term mentally. I know a few people who have gone to rehab for drug addictions and honestly you miss the person that they used to be. Drugs change people's personalities and who they are.

I also know of a friend's friend who was heavily hooked on ice and accidently OD'd on it and died.

A few years ago I used to even date a boy who would party for two/three days straight on the weekend on drugs and it's very hard as a girl to give the guy you like the same emotional high that he gets on drugs. Eventually I stopped dating him, as every weekend he would pick drugs over me (maybe he didn't actually like me that much, I don't know). But what I do know was that he was hooked. I watched him go from the 'once every never' type to the 'every weekend has to be

done with drugs' type. I don't even know what he's like now because we don't talk but I hope he has got off the drugs and is leading a happy life.

- DON'T LET THIS HAPPEN TO YOU OR ANYONE YOU KNOW.
- Another similar problem is smoking. I went to school with a really kind, sweet nice girl who said she would never ever, ever smoke in her life. What do you know – a few years later this girl is smoking round the back of the school between almost every class. She was the last person you would have expected to smoke. Another example was a very studious girl who, as mean as it is, was called a 'nerd' for all of her schooling, left school and started smoking. People can change. People have different ways of dealing with things. Smoking helps anxiety and helps people to relax and calm down. Often I think everyone sometimes needs to relax more too, but I think that there are safer healthier ways to relax such as yoga, breathing techniques, thinking about a calm place and even exercise (which really helps). There are always better and safer ways to relax. ;)

It was so hard for me to watch my best friend Rose go down this path. I never knew what to do at the time. It was really hard. She would panic all the time and once she interrogated me with questions, having a go at me because I was apparently 'not sitting close enough to her' and then she had a panic attack. It freaked me out as she was acting so strangely. She would panic and freak out all the time over normal things. As I said earlier, she has been completely clean of drugs (except tobacco and alcohol) for three years now. Unfortunately there is one downside to her story, as she has become a hypochondriac, freaking out over small things she thinks are wrong with her. E.g., if she gets a mild pain in leg she will honestly freak out, have a panic attack and literally think that she needs to go to hospital. She walked away from heavy drug use with only this small mental illness. She is lucky because some others develop serious illnesses such as schizophrenia, which was exactly what had happened to her mum, who therefore was unfit to bring her daughter up.

I heard another story about drugs when I was 16 that has stuck in my mind ever since. I was working at my fave clothing shop (one of my first jobs ever) and I was speaking to my 19-year-old manager. She told me a true story about a friend of hers who smoked some weed and lost all control of her bladder and bowel. She had diarrhea everywhere and almost everyone at the party was laughing at her…except for the few friends who helped her. Could you imagine being at a party, shitting everywhere? Imagine how embarrassing school would be on Monday morning, let alone your life, because the word gets around. Is it really worth your dignity?

I went to the MCG (giant sporting ground in Melbourne) recently on an excursion with the school where I was doing my university placement. A tour guide showed us the backrooms and then let us stand on the oval. He was telling us all about football, cricket and the history of the MCG. He went on to footy players doing drugs. He naturally had a really soft voice but when he shared this point he practically yelled it... What he said was that if you take one thing from this whole day make sure that it is this: 'Don't do drugs; it'll screw up your life!'.

Parents should be told if their child is doing drugs.

It's most definitely not 'COOL'; don't ever think it's cool. How cool is ruining your future, friends, career and especially, your HEALTH. A longitudinal study published in Child Development showed that if the child is 'cool' in school that when they get in their 20's they have a higher chance that they will abuse drugs and alcohol, have interpersonal issues and even engage in more serious criminal behavior. Try not to forget that– 'Let It Go' issue of *Psychology Today* Magazine 2014, *The Attractiveness of Personality Traits* article. Remember, '**Being a tool is not cool**'. Situations most likely will occur where you are offered drugs but you know that within yourself you have the confidence to say, 'Thanks but no thanks'.

If people are pressuring you too much it may be best to find a new group of friends to hang out with or just to distance yourself for a while.

Bad company corrupts good character.
– 1 Corinthians 15:33

BE STRONG. YOU ARE YOU AND DON'T EVER LET OTHERS CHANGE THAT.

If I have one standout piece of advice for this book, this would have to be one of my fave ones.

The feeling of saying no to drugs and being strong and different beats any feeling you could ever get from letting yourself down and giving into drugs.

Drugs can honestly ruin lives and cause serious health and mental health problems... At the end of the day it's up to you but do you really want to end up in a mental institution? It can so easily happen. Think twice, three, even four or five times, before you look at or even think of taking drugs, because people you know love you for who you are. They don't want your brain and entire personality to change.

Is one pill really worth the thrill?

Choices – General

Your world is in your hands.

decisions, decisions...

Short skirts, lots of make-up, wagging, detentions... all of these are our choices. I believe some people take risks more than others but even if you are a risk taker, you need to remember sometimes that choices that may seem good at the time may have negative consequences later on in life/down the track.

There are so many choices we make in a day. At school, they place a lot of importance on certain choices, such as your career. You may think that you want to do one thing at 16 and then two years later, when you realise you hate what you left school for, you also realise that you don't have as many choices as you would have had career-wise if you had stayed at school. People change their minds. I know a few mums who have completely switched careers, such as my best friend's mum, who went from being a primary school teacher to being a nurse. Even MY mum went from being a scientist to going back to uni at 48 to study social work... People do change their minds and change their career paths. Once you pick something it's never set in stone.

Although I say it is important to keep your options open, it is also important to remember that there is almost always a way into what you want to be/do career wise even if it comes to university. Now I know they place SO much value on your final year scores these days, and yes, I do agree your final score is important. BUT IT'S NOT YOU. Your score does not define how smart you are. I promise, promise, promise you! I know many people who achieved hugely high final year of school scores but don't have the mindset and discipline to finish their courses. They drop out; they burn out from too much study and not enough inner drive and mental persistence. However, with some courses such as Medicine, Law and most sciences, the score is super important because frankly if you don't get the mark, you don't get into the course. There are usually pathways in – like studying an arts degree then transferring across to your other course. I firmly believe that with majority of careers...

score DOES NOT = intelligence

When there is a will, there IS a way.
– Proverb

DUMB

Now I will tell you this story even though I have only shared my final score with very few people (probably about five) because I was SO ashamed of myself at the time. As I've mentioned in previous chapters I was always considered 'dumb'. 'Oh Megan she's so dumb.' You know that sort of thing. This hit a nerve because I never felt smart. I failed a lot of tests and subjects and exams throughout both primary school and high school. These comments truly did hurt me...at the time. I was always enjoying the more creative subjects such as art, drama, creative writing, food tech (the more hands on subjects), which some people, as much as it sucks, considered the 'dumb' subjects. Yes, I was no 'brainiac' but I decided to choose subjects that I enjoyed so that I would work hard doing what I loved. Now for about half a year of my final year at school I partied a lot, didn't study heaps or take it very seriously, until one night my best friend borrowed my fake ID and had it taken from her by a nightclub bouncer, because it wasn't actually hers. I was soooo angry because that meant no more underage clubbing for me. BUT to my disbelief this was actually a huge blessing in disguise. The night she told me it was gone I thought, 'How can I make the most out of this situation? What can I do to turn this bad news into good?' So I said to myself that for the next five months or so till exams I am going to STUDY MY BUTT OFF. AND SMASH MY EXAMS... So I did. And what do you know I smashed them. I got an A, B+, B+, and a C+, AND AN A for my art assignment! I didn't believe I was dumb anymore after this. I just knew that I had to work harder to achieve these results.

Whether you think you can or you can't...
You're right.
– Henry Ford

Most successes are because of a mindset about application and trying your best. Successful people often seem to have achieved easily because of their natural abilities, but if you really looked into it, you would find that they have worked very hard to pursue and achieve their goals. They most probably pushed and pushed and never gave up.

One of my fave quotes is:

Success is going from failure to
failure without any loss of enthusiasm.
– Winston Churchill

Now to keep going with the story: Bottom line is I got a final high school year score that was below average. I was shattered because all I wanted to do was get at least 50 (half) to get into a university course...and I didn't. I'm not even joking with you. I called up almost every Bachelor course in the careers guide in not only Melbourne but also regional Victoria to ask and beg course coordinators to let me in, so that I would study in that course for 6 months; then transfer to teaching... But no one would accept me. They all said that if you get 50 we could squeeze you in but we can't do anything with anything lower than 50. Mine was lower than 50.

I went to TAFE (hands on education) for 6 months and hated it. I didn't want to be there I didn't want to be studying Child Care; I wanted to be a teacher. (I also probably hated it due to the fact that I went into it with a negative mindset.). What kept me sane and at TAFE during this time was the fact that I did the course with one of my best friends.

While I was at TAFE I kept applying for any Bachelor Degree course that I could and finally I got an acceptance letter. It was for the Bachelor of Creative Arts. I was so excited especially coz I love art and when the coordinator asked me to send her my final high school results she was impressed by my art mark. She also liked the fact that I had acted in a TV show that had aired all over the world (performance studies) and let me in. After all that time, perseverance and persistence I got into university! :D

Now take this story as a lesson...if you want something, **keep going**. Don't let people who tell you 'no' get in your way. You know where you are going and you know what you are capable of achieving. Don't let ANYONE, even your parents, dull your sparkle. 'No' can turn into 'maybe' and 'maybe' can turn into 'YES'. Don't believe someone's 'no' as a definite 'no'. Even guys who you say no to will try and try again, despite your first answer being no, because they believe that they can sway you. I guess we can learn something from sex-hungry men – persistence.

No=
MAYBE=
YES

I eventually grew to love this course (Bachelor of

Creative Arts Industries) because I wanted to be there. It is so important to choose what YOU want to do, not what your parents want you to do or what pays good money or what your friends are doing.

It's your life; own it.

I love the saying, *Choose a job you love and you'll never have to work a day in your life* – Confucius. Aim for your happiness and go towards what will make you happy. I am also doing this new thing where I don't call work 'work'.... because it's way too much fun to be called 'work'. I love doing this and it keeps me happy and excited to do what I do...try it. Instead of saying, 'Hey, I'm going to work', say, 'Hey, 'I'm going into the shop'. Or if you are like me and work with kids, say, 'I'm going to see my little friends today'. Or if you work with clothes, say, 'I'm going to sell some clothes at the shopping centre'. It really works and takes you out of the 'Oh, booo, I have to work today' mindset.

You're lucky that you have the health to even attend work... Some people don't.

Another of my stories that I want to share is about careers. When I was 16 I thought to myself 'YES I want to be a hairdresser!' I was looking into leaving school and pursuing a career in hairdressing. I went to all the Open Days, saw the careers teacher and got brochures and letters sent to me about the course. I was dead set on the idea of leaving school to become a hairdresser. One night I went to my grandma's for dinner and I told my aunty that I wanted to leave school and become a hairdresser. She yelled at me and said, 'No, that's a bad idea. If you want to do hairdressing, at least finish school and go into it after school, or study it while you are doing VCE as a subject. That way, in case you don't like it, you have your VCE behind you and can fall back into another job or course'. I was really annoyed with her at the time. I thought, 'No way. I'll do what I want, thank you!' (being the little brat of a 16 year old that I was). BUT later that night I went home and actually gave it a bit more thought, and I came to the conclusion that I didn't know how much my mind and passions would change in the future. So I decided that I would finish school. And what do you know? One year later, I decided that no way did I want to do hairdressing-I love art, kids and people. That's when I decided teaching was for me. (I haven't changed my mind since, although I may in the near future want to study a different course or go into a different field of work/study. But even if I was to, I am so happy to have a year 12 pass under my belt). Sometimes it takes an adult who has been on this earth a lot longer, and someone who is a lot more experienced in life, to tell you a harsh bit of truth, because at the end of the day, a trusted adult's opinion is very valuable to your future. Adults have gone through more than us and often know what is truly best. So cut your parents or trusted adults some slack and try your best to take in some of the knowledge that they have, as they have probably learnt the hard way and are trying to give you some advice that THEY wish they'd known at your age.

At such a young age, it is almost unfair to ask

people what they want to do with their lives. It is such a big decision to make when all your mind can really think about is boys, clothes, sex, parties, boys, boys, sex, fitting in and more boys. Although your mind is swamped with other things, such as your crush's smile and how you swear he was flirting with you when he asked you if he could borrow your rubber today, you need, need, neeeeeeed to try to focus on your career and future. Giving things a go is a great way to do this. If you feel that you would like a certain field of work, give it a shot on work experience. If you maybe want to pursue a career that one of your parents has, go along to work with them one day. Get a feel for some types of jobs which you may wish to pursue in the future.

Give it a shot!

So don't stress and worry too much about finding what you want to do and the choices you may have to make and how things turns out, as it may be how it is meant to be. It could turn out like my hairdressing – it wasn't meant to be. Also if failure occurs or a certain company doesn't offer you a place for work experience, don't stress. Just re-read the 'failing' chapter. (It may FEEL like failure at the time, but in the future, this thing you call failure will and can easily push you to better things and twist itself into success.)

Another key choice that you should make sure of with almost everything you do whether it be study, relationships, friendships, sports and even learning to drive is choosing to put in effort and time and truly focus on it. Not many great things were achieved without a lot of time, effort and focus.

Michelangelo said:
If you knew how much work went into it, you wouldn't call it genius.

Also, do you think it took Thomas Edison ten minutes to create the light globe? No way. It took heaps of long tiresome hours and a huge amount of focus and effort to create it.

Remember:
Patience is a virtue
– Proverb

When I was in school I used to always be drawn to and really enjoyed art classes. I went to them, did my work but I never gave it my all. I even remember for some strange reason actually NOT expressing myself through my artwork as I was afraid it would be too 'weird'. BIG MISTAKE! When I got to final year of high school, I decided that I was going to put 110% effort into my art project. I did it every art class, most lunchtimes and after school, and actually came in on weekends. I even remember staying back till 6.00 after school when all the teachers had left. I just loved doing my art project-it was really relaxing and so much fun. It was then that I realised that I was passionate about ART! It was my passion and my way of expressing my emotions through a creative outlet. And now I am currently studying at uni to become an art teacher. But most of all I found my passion by giving something 'my all'. I got awesome marks for this art project and folio – A and B+ – which is a huge achievement for me (who is used to 'failing' a lot of things). So remember, please take my advice and really put your mind to whatever you do. Don't just get through; put your mind to it; really give it all of your effort. A good quote I read somewhere by Richard Nixon was: '*Remember, always give your best. Never get Discouraged.* Really make the CHOICE to dedicate yourself to it, and don't just choose what your friends are doing. Be YOU!

Believe you can and you're halfway there.
– Theodore Roosevelt

Something Anyone Can Do To Instantly Be Better

There was a man,
They called him mad…
The more he gave
The more he had
– John Bunyan

Kindness

Now I'm going to start this chapter off in a little bit of a different way, so try to bear with me and listen up… I actually want you guys to begin with a little bit of an exercise, right now in your head. Think about someone who you have been rude/mean to in the past and whether you said this thing to their faces or behind their backs. (I'm talking about comments/bitching that you have either verbalised to another person, about someone else or to the person themselves.) It may have been your mum, aunty, cousin, friend, ex-boyfriend or even an acquaintance...anyone.

Now if it was behind the person's back, imagine that they found had out that you said whatever it was about them. And if it was to their face, then just think about when it was said.

So now I hope everyone is sitting here thinking about a time when they were mean/rude to another person... everyone has done this; we are not perfect people.

Now think about something someone has said or done to YOU in your life which has cut you deep and hurt you very much whether it was a situation or words. Do you remember how upset it made you and how much pain you felt when this was said or happened to you? You will probably never forget what was said or that situation for the rest of your life – that's how much it hurt you. The pain was real and if you are anything like me, even years after it was said or the situation happened, it still hurts.

So the next step is to think about the amount of pain you felt after hearing those words or going through that situation and then think about the first part of the exercise which was the thing that YOU said that was mean to someone else... Now imagine if the pain you felt when someone hurt you was felt by another person BECAUSE of you and what you said to hurt another.

What if you made that other person feel the exact or worse pain you felt when someone was nasty to you, hurting you. Basically I want you to imagine yourself in their shoes.

How would you feel if you are walking around living a happy life doing your day-to-day things and you found out that even though it was years ago, what YOU had said to someone had hurt them so much they still remember it clearly and are hurt by it to this day?

With us watching our tongues and being nice to each other, we can work together to help each other through this crazy, strange, sometimes harsh world.

So let's be nice to each other.

No good deed goes unpunished.
– Oscar Wilde

It's absolutely ridiculous how rude to others some people can be in this day and age. A recent example of this was literally two days ago when my cousin was driving and a wheel actually fell off her car. She crashed her car and the entire side of it was smashed. She was super blessed/lucky to walk away not having hurt herself or any others in the crash. But anyway the point of the story is that when she had the accident (mind you she was freshly 18 and had only had her licence for four months), she was crying and freaking out after the accident WHILE OTHER DRIVERS WERE HONKING, YELLING, SWEARING and even shaking their fists and putting their middle fingers up to her.

She had just been in a car crash, lucky to not be injured and let alone alive and all these people cared about was that she may have caused a slight inconvenience to them by holding them up.

The only word I can use to describe the attitude that was shown towards my cousin on that day is disgusting. Does anyone care for anyone anymore?

When I was getting told this story, I couldn't believe it. Are people really in that much of a rush that they can't stop to help an innocent 18-year-old girl whose tyre just fell off and who had just survived a car crash?

I'm hoping that this situation is just a once off and will never happen again but for some reason I think that this sort of treatment happens often. It's seems to be almost a normal way to treat others in society.

SOMETHING NEEDS TO CHANGE.

What happened to ***'Do to others as you would have them do to you?** – Luke 6:31* Does anyone even know what kindness is anymore? Or are we too busy staring at our phones waiting for the next ego boost when someone 'likes' our photo? Are we too busy, too stressed, to get out of our own heads and stop thinking about our own needs to help another person?

GIVE

Happiness comes from giving...yes, receiving is great too. But giving wins, according to *The Secret to Happiness? Giving.* Article published on www.newssciencemag.org

Giving will make you feel truly feel alive.

Another little story I actually read in *How to Persuade in a Minute* by Tony Wrighton – great little book. There was a section of the book I read that was about interviews of successful people by the author.

And after interviewing these people and asking them what the secret was to their success? Interestingly, he actually found a trend...and it was that all of these people interviewed mentioned that relationships are the key to success. A few of the quotes the interviewees said were 'being really good friends with people and getting to know people I work with is key', 'not only build those relationships and network but keep in contact with people' and 'I believe deeply in relationships. Knowing people is 50 per cent of this business'. *It's not what you know; it's WHO you know* –Origin unclear, but a widely used quote. It's not just knowing people but actually having a real lasting connection with them. They said that if they had a secret that would be their secret to success.

I speak the same way whether he is the garbage man or the president of the university.
– Albert Einstein

Be kind, for everyone you meet is fighting a battle you know nothing about.
– Wendy Mass

Kindness is the language which the deaf can hear and the blind can see.
– Mark Twain

Kind words can be short and easy to speak, but their echoes are truly endless.
– Mother Teresa

People who are intimidated by you talk bad about you in hopes that others won't find you so appealing.
– Unknown

Let no one ever come to you without leaving better and happier. Be the living expression of God's kindness: kindness in your face, kindness in your eyes, kindness in your smile.
– Mother Teresa

Three things in the human life are important. The first is to be kind, the second is to be kind, and the third is to be kind.
– Henry James

Here is the simple but powerful rule...Always give people more than they expect to get.
– Nelson Boswell

A kindness tip that is important to remember is that when people are rude/mean to you, try your best to be kind back to them. Remember that we don't always succeed but we should at least TRY to undo meanness with kindness, or simply walk away.

Now I do understand and know all too well how easy it is and how good it feels to bite back and hate someone who is mean to you, is rude to you and/or has hit a nerve with you and hurt your feelings. BUT hating them back is almost being as bad as them...you are just stooping to their level, and literally just bringing yourself down. The person that has been mean to you wants you to get angry, frustrated and upset. Don't give them that satisfaction. Walk away and be the bigger person.

– Megan Street

A great example of this was on a controversial episode of X Factor when two of the judges were ripping into one of the contestants and even got fired in the end for doing it. Take a watch of it in this video (link below) and 1. Watch how rude and mean they were to this guy on international TV and 2. Most of all watch how he handled the situation and shut down the negative situation... Amazing.

https://www.youtube.com/watch?v=LuZ1TvBZNB8

If you can't be bothered watching the whole thing through, the part to watch from is about 5:10 through to about 7:01 and it's at 5:06 where the magic happens. It's small and right to the point and was a great response to someone treating/bullying him.

He handles literally a horrible nightmare of a situation really well, without biting back or even responding negatively, with a simple, 'Thank you, you're beautiful.' I can't even begin to imagine how hard it would have been to reply with something like that to someone who had literally shut him down COMPLETELY on international TV. I have a massive amount of respect for him and believe he has a taught us a great lesson on how to handle negative criticisms.

On the topic of this incident/kindness, somebody on my Facebook wrote a great status about this situation, which is too good for me not to copy and paste his best points below.

It's horrifying to think that these judges can sit there in their comfortable position (also a metaphor for their professional career) and completely shit on, and downgrade, and completely humiliate and abuse someone completely out of their comfort zone performing their talent to THE WORLD. To pick on someone who's trying to train and better himself and entertain other people at the same *time, all whilst fighting his own fears of public opinion and stage fright?* ***It's fu*king bullying.*** *I think he's doing a great job, he put on a good show and sounded great. Those judges should be fired (which they were), and/or worse...put in the same position and completely shunned for the world to see.*

– Benjamin 'Casper' Eade

After watching the video and reading parts of Casper's Facey(Facebook) status I hope we have all realised that it's so important (even though difficult) to sometimes not bite back... If he had bitten back he would have stooped to the judges' level, and we all would have seen him differently but because he had an awesome approach to their response, we all have a HUGE amount of respect for him now. I really, really hope we have all realised that being mean to people will get us nowhere... These judges lost their jobs, their media image is ruined and to put it in a nutshell, the majority of the viewers hate them (now that we have the lovely internet to share videos with the entire world). Now I know we are not in this situation but what we have learnt from this, we can all apply to our everyday lives.

1. Don't stoop as low as the person who's being mean to you
And
2. BE NICE and treat people how you wish to be treated.

TREAT OTHERS HOW YOU WANT TO BE TREATED

We reflect on paradox: water wears away rock; spirit overcomes force. The weak will undo the mighty. May we learn to see things backwards, inside-out and upside-down.
– Lao Tzu

Remember: ***Rudeness is a weak man's imitation of strength.***
– Eric Hoffer, The Passionate State of Mind: And Other Aphorisms

Throw kindness around like confetti.
– Unknown

People are often unreasonable and self-centred; forgive them anyway.
If you are kind, people may accuse you of ulterior motives.

(It is crazy to think that our society thinks that behind someone being nice is the fact that they want something; this needs to change as some people [most people] actually gain happiness by making someone else happy. How much do you looooovvvve doing nice things for the guy you like? Some people have no ulterior motives. They want nothing from it but to put a smile on someone else's face.)

BE KIND ANYWAY.
If you are honest, people may cheat you.
Be honest anyway.
If you find happiness, people may be jealous.
Be happy anyway.
The good you do today may be forgotten
tomorrow. Do good anyway.
Give the world the best you have,
and it may never be enough.
Give your best anyway.
– Mother Teresa

Before you speak, ask yourself if what you are going to say is true, is kind, is necessary, is helpful. If the answer is no, maybe what you are about to say should be left unsaid.
– Bernard Meltzer

It's best to never forget that what you say and do can affect people in ways you can never imagine.

Do you gossip?

Exclude and punish others for no reason?

Envy others?

Wish to cause harm or pain on someone? Either physical or psychologically.

We are all in his world together; let's work together to make it a better place!

Help each other.

Love and forgive.

BE THERE FOR OTHERS,
especially in times of need.
Your good karma will be off the charts.

It's absolutely insane how much our words can affect someone either positively or negatively.

I still remember certain things people said to me over ten years ago that STILL hurt when I think about them. It was when I was being bullied in school and they defs hit a nerve, and I have been self-conscious ever since. It's crazy how easily one slip of someone else's tongue can change our whole outlook on, not only ourselves, but the world in general.

How many times have you heard people say, 'Oh, screw everyone. I don't need anyone. I've only got myself', or make generalisations such as: 'All men are jerks' or 'I only associate with punks' or 'I hate the world'? Now if you are walking around saying these things (mind you I am SO guilty of this), you need to try to remember not to let one person, or a few people who have made you think this way, sway your view and mindset on life.

There are going to be people who aren't nice, who will bring you down and may even seem to hate you for no reason. Just because one person or a few people hate you, **it doesn't mean every person sucks.**

What ever happened to one of my favourite sayings: *Everyone is a friend until they prove otherwise?* ***– Unknown***

Yes, you may be a little bit 'unlucky' in love and have dated not one, but a fair few jerks, in your life but that by all means DOESN'T mean that ALL men are jerks. (Mind you, I'm not saying there aren't jerks out there because there defs are. Haha.)

The next guy who tries to pick you up at the bar may actually be your dream guy but because you are walking around with such a negative mindset like 'All guys are jerks' you don't give him a chance. Therefore you have just thrown away a great guy who, guess what, IS NOT A JERK. (He may have even been the love of your life, but I guess you'll never know.)

Another great example of this is when people decide to only associate with a 'certain type' of person (Remember, I'm generalising here by stereotyping people, but I'm doing it because it is easier to make my point like this.). It might be punks hanging out with only punks. Or hipsters only hanging out with hipsters ('hipsters' is a slang name for kind of hippy/indie people). Or, the one that annoys me most, 'attractive' people only associating with 'attractive' people. Grrrr.

A word on forgiveness: If somebody does wrong by you, how many times do you forgive them?

Two?

Five?

No, not seven times but
70 times 7 times!

– Matthew 18:21-22

Just because you may 'feel' like you fit in with a clique or a certain crowd of people, this does NOT mean that you shouldn't give anyone a chance that does not fit into your clique or style or with the way you are. Don't be so judgmental. And just because you choose to live your life the way you do, you shouldn't be looking down on people who are not like you/don't live like you.

One of my fave sayings is: *Don't judge someone because they sin differently than you.*
– Lauren Elise

I'm not going to lie to you guys. I know so many people who do this. I do it sometimes as well and it's downright mean and purely unfair. Why can't 'punks' date 'Barbie dolls'? Why can't 'hipsters be best mates with 'losers'? Why can't the 'chess club president' hang out with the 'jock boys'?

Why does the 'hottest girl' have to be with the 'hottest guy'?

Ever seen a really hot girl with a guy way below her, looks-wise? This is because she gave him a chance and his personality 'charmed' her.

LET'S JUST REMOVE ALL THE LABELS AND STEREOTYPES AND GIVE EACH OTHER A CHANCE.

Don't act stuck up and don't be judgmental. Open your mind; open your heart; and feel the love for each other. <3

A song that has been playing over and over in my head while I've been writing this entire chapter is *Where is the Love?* by The Black Eyed Peas

A little exercise I want you to do when you go out next is to talk to someone you have already judged negatively...we all do it. Next time you do, say you are in a clothing shop and you have judged the shop assistant as a slut/bitch because she is wearing slutty clothes and isn't smiling (she may be not smiling because she WANTS someone to talk to her!), go up and talk to her! Get to know her and you may realise that number one, she's a super nice person, not a bitch at all! And number two, (highly doubt she will tell you this right when you first started talking to her) she's actually a virgin who has never been with any guy sexually ever. MAN, WERE YOUR JUDGMENTS WRONG when you thought she was a 'slutty bitch'.

Watch these people that you judged prove you wrong... just give them a chance to let them show you that they are not who you think they are.

I have another very real example of this that actually

happened to me one night. I had decided that I wanted to play netball this season and I saw my local netball club were looking for people and had an info night to sign up for it… Now I went down there by myself not knowing anyone. (Yes, I was a bit scared it would be awkward, but an awkward situation is not the end of the world.) I sat down in a group of girls and I'm not going to lie, I felt super intimidated by all of them. They all looked like amazing netball players and here I was rocking up in my converses. (Real runners would have been a much smarter idea, espesh coz we were meant to be running around.) And some of them were girls I had heard got into physical fights with other girls in their high school years.

So anyway I sat there and tried to conceal the fact that I was super intimidated. When it came to the end of the talk/intro to netball part, we all got up and to my surprise a lot of the girls came and introduced themselves, saying, 'Hi', and they were ALL **so lovely**. And to think just five minutes before I had been super intimidated by these girls and had just wanted to go home. I genuinely thought that they would hate me because I didn't 'look' like a profesh netball player. Haha, one of the girls even suggested we run around the oval and do a few stretches to get our fitness levels up. I ran around and had good chats with a lot of the girls. By the time we were going home I had made some awesome friends who I was excited to start netball with. Whereas if I'd left because I was scared and intimidated, I would have never realised how nice and fun these girls really were and wouldn't have even thought about going back to play netball.

So the point of this story is to not look at people /a person and assume anything. You don't know them, you don't know about them, (**even if you have heard rumours and judgments, make up your own mind once you get to know them**), and you haven't even given them a chance. So what are you waiting for? Get yourself out there and get to know them. :D

One of my fave lines from the poem *IF* by Rudyard Kipling is: *If you can bear to hear the truth you've spoken twisted by knaves* (dishonest untrustworthy person) *to make a trap for fools.*

In a nutshell to me, that line of the poem means if you can listen to the truth you have said and someone twists it and changes what you said to make you look bad... the only people who will believe these lies and twists are fools. If they weren't fools they would be getting to know you themselves before ever even considering thinking anything negative of you.

Try not to judge a book by its cover. It's hard but it will be well worth it considering the friends you will make. ☺

I know some guys who literally 'look' so rough and, as my family put it when they saw a pic of a few of these guys, 'Oh, they look like criminals who would smash your face in', but when you get to know them, they are actually the sweetest kindest people who wouldn't hurt a fly. Kind of like gentle giants... their muscles are huuugggge but their hearts are also huge. <3

Now what I'm NOT saying is: 'Don't be part of a clique that you feel like you fit in with', as it's great to have people that you are similar to and connect with well. Just try not to 1, feel and act like you and your group are better than everyone else and 2, judge someone or a group of people just because you have assumed you know who they are and what they are like. The bottom line is YOU DON'T. Despite what you have heard about them/the group, try to remember that a smart person gets to know someone themselves, rather than believing what they have heard from others about the person.

And if you are one to sit around in your clique/ group laughing at others and bitching about how they choose to live their lives, just read this quote which I mentioned earlier it's so true and perfect!

> *Being negative, bitching about other people and laughing at people's issues/problems, while sitting in a group of 'friends' all bitching, is not at all positive energy. It is rude, cheap outcomes of your own negative emotions'.*
>
> ***– Benjamin 'Casper' Eade***

Let's just take a minute for that to sink in...

It hit home hard when I read it. I am without a doubt guilty of this and I'm sure almost everyone is. That's why we are going to change our behaviours.

If you do find yourself looking down on others because they 'aren't like you' or 'just don't get it' or choose to live their life differently to you, realise that you are doing this to increase your own ego and self-worth. In other words it's to make yourself feel better about who YOU are. It has little to do with them; the fact is, thinking you're more superior to someone, makes you feel better inside.

Many of us are guilty of this and aren't even aware that we are doing it. I've had times when it's crept in on me as well. I'll give you an example which is a common one for me...

So I am on a strict Paleo (mainly veggies, meats and nuts) diet (for health reasons) and am not allowed to eat many 'normal' foods. It sucks, but everyone has their problems. This is mine. Sometimes when I hang out with other people, they are ordering a massive stack of pancakes from the Pancake Parlour, a large cheeseburger meal at Maccas or a delicious battered chocolate bar mmmmm. When I can't even order anything on the menu (I lie, a garden salad if I take out half of the ingredients), but I think to myself, 'Haha, at least I'm healthier than you.' (It's mean, I know.) Then I try to stop myself in my tracks and remember that I'm only thinking this negative thought because I'm jealous that they can eat that super yum food and not feel sick. BUT by me thinking 'I'm healthier than you' it makes me FEEL BETTER ABOUT MYSELF, INCREASES MY EGO and ultimately helps me deal with my problems/downfalls.

Here is another example. Have you ever had a friend who brags and brags and brags about how much alllllllll the boys love her and that she has such a selection of guys to choose from? You almost think that she may be bragging about it so much to piss you off. Now I'm not saying 'definitely' and 'all the time' but according to the article 'Why We Feel Insecure, and How We Can Stop' on the Psychology Today website 'some people compensate for insecurities by trying to show that they are better than others. They may constantly brag about their achievements, remind others about their successes (even if others are well aware of these) or belittle their friends and family members'. Therefore, people sometimes cover up their insecurities by acting the opposite to who they really are. That girl who's bragging about how much/many guys love her might not be entirely truthful. She might just feel the need to brag about the guys she gets to convince herself that she is desirable, sexy, hot and wanted by many, which ultimately makes her feel better inside and increases her ego. The hottest most desired women I know almost never says a word about how many men are in love with them because they know it as truth and don't feel the need to explain it to anyone.

does she really get allllllll the guys?

Be humble. Try to remember one of my favorite quotes:

If we judge people, you have no time to love them.
– Mother Teresa

People don't consciously think this; they just act it out. For example, they don't think, 'Oh, I'm going to brag about alllllll of the boys that love me tonight when I hang out with my girlfriends because I am actually insecure about the fact that I don't FEEL like boys like me.' NO WAY. People do it without even realising.

CONFIDENCE IS SILENT…
INSECURITIES ARE LOUD.
– Unknown

At the school where I did my university placement we had a 69 (don't be immature lol)-year-old grandma come in who was the grandma of a few of the students at the school and actually a principal herself of a school over in California. She had also run a lot of summer camps with kids and has been hugely successful in the education industry over in America. She gave a really great talk to my placement class. She asked if anyone had any questions and I shot my hand up and asked, 'if you were to give one piece of advice/motivational words to the students and us teachers what would they be?'

*She replied, '**We can learn so much from others**, and we are all the same (no discriminating others).'*
– Mary Lou Johnson

A little pic I saw on Instagram might explain my point a little better. It applies a lot to some 'spiritual' people. Let's try not to get on our high horse because we believe that our way of living is better than anyone else's. A huge point of being 'spiritual' is loving each other, not looking down on others thinking that we are better than them. This can also apply to any belief system that makes you feel better than anyone else. The 'spiritual' one I have written about below is just the one I saw on Instagram...

Ego Traps

- If you think it's more 'spiritual' to ride a bike to work or use public transportation, but then find yourself judging anyone who drives a car, you're in an ego trap.
- If you think it's more 'spiritual' to stop watching television because it rots your brain, but then find yourself judging those who still watch TV, you are in an ego trap.
- If you think it's more 'spiritual' to avoid reading gossip, tabloid or news magazines, but then find yourself judging those who read those things, you are in an ego trap.
- If you think it's more 'spiritual' to listen to classical music or soothing nature sounds, but then find yourself judging those who listen to mainstream or pop music, you are in an ego trap.
- If you think it's more 'spiritual' to do yoga, become a vegan, buy organic, buy healing crystals, practise Reiki, meditate, wear hippy/thrift shop clothing, visit ashrams and read enlightened spiritual books but then you judge anyone who doesn't do these things, you are in an ego trap
- Always be aware of the feeling of superiority. Self-righteous superiority is your biggest clue that you are in an ego trap. The ego loves to sneak in the back door. It will take a noble idea like starting up yoga, and then twist it to serve its own ends by making

> you feel superior to others; you will start to look down on those who are not following your righteous 'spiritual' path. Superiority, judgment and condemnation...they are ego traps. – Unknown

Everyone has insecurities; it's just whether you let them rule your life or accept that you are not perfect and live your life how you want to, not feeding your ego at any chance you can. When you are with others, the best way, I would say, to do things would be to be in the present moment.

Do not dwell in the past; do not dream of the future; concentrate the mind on the present moment.

– Buddha

Also truly listen to what the other person has to say. Other people are so fascinating if we can stop thinking about what we are going to say next and truly give our attention to them. By doing this you can create real and lasting friendships easily, and learn so much about the other person/people you are talking to.

I'll give you a quick example:

Say you were talking to someone about learning techniques for exams; you could ask them how THEY study.

1. They will be flattered that you are asking them about themselves.
2. They will tell you about their study techniques. You may be wondering why you would be interested in THEIR study techniques; this has nothing to do with YOU but remember, not only are you showing interest in them, showing them you care and getting to know them, but you could learn something new that will be beneficial to you. You may find that their study technique makes you into a genius. BAM you just got to know this person while also learning a new way you can study. It's simple stuff but it's common for people to get caught up in their own heads and struggle when it comes to listening and learning from others.

And most of all if this study technique you learn from this person works well and practically makes you the next Einstein, DON'T FORGET TO THANK THEM! I'd even be giving them flowers every day for the rest of their lives if their technique made me as smart as Einstein. But seriously, don't forget to thank the person if they have helped you in any way. I know it can sound a little bit embarrassing especially if you aren't used to doing it but being kind shouldn't be embarrassing. It can be sometimes (especially if you aren't used to doing it), but the more you thank people and are kind the less embarrassing it gets.

- Another quick note on thank you and gratitude: an awesome thing to do which I only started

> doing a few months ago was a 'gratitude journal'. There is always something to be grateful for and in your gratitude journal you write a dot pointed list of things you are grateful for and when you are feeling blue, just open your gratitude journal, and you will remember everything you have jotted down in life that you are happy about. It really works Try it. ☺

A story on being kind: Once I was at the supermarket when I said to an older lady (not too old, like 50s – if I called a lady in her 50s old, my mum would kill me, coz she's 50) that her eyes were really pretty. As she said, 'Thank you,' I looked into her eyes again and they were actually welling up with tears. This lady was crying from happiness when all I did was shoot her a quick compliment.

Just remember it's really, really, really easy to make someone else's day. Set a goal for yourself to say three genuine nice things about someone every day.

Here is another example. Ask the next person you see what they do for fun. They may say an activity or pastime that you may never have considered before like rock climbing or dodgeball (yes, real competitive dodgeball teams exist. In Melbourne Australia. Hopefully it's the next new sport in the Olympics too). After you ask your friend or stranger on the street this (whoever floats ya boat), they may invite you to the 'Bring a friend' night at dodgeball training. You go, you LOVE IT. And what do you know? You have just found yourself a new, awesome, fun, exciting hobby (which, if you prove to be super good at, you may even represent

Australia internationally at the dodgeball tournament – yes, I'm not making this up. You really can represent Australia in dodgeball.) But just think about it. If you'd never asked what your friend or someone you know does for fun, you would have never known how much you love dodgeball. And that's really sad because no one could represent Australia in dodgeball better than YOU. ;) IF THIS HAPPENS, **DON'T FORGET TO THANK** THAT PERSON!

Now think about this – if in both these instances would you have become another Einstein or an Australian dodgeball team member if you had talked about yourself and not the other person?

{Let's imagine that you didn't speak to this person because you had pre-judged him/her as someone not worth talking to:}

3. By being judgmental you are simply projecting your negativity onto them as you 'think' that you are better than them or 'think' that for whatever reason you don't need to give this person a chance.
4. How are you supposed to make friends/and meet new people if you are going around judging people? I admit I used to do it too alllllll the time. But then I took a step back and learned from experience and realised that some of the people I wouldn't have even spoken to five years ago (because I judged them) I now know and they are the most awesome, amazing people, who I love spending time with!

Next time you go out anywhere, give it a shot and TRY not to judge anyone before you talk to them. For example, if the cashier at the supermarket has a 'resting bitch face', try not to automatically think that she's a bitch. Have a chat to her about how her day's been. Watch her eyes light up as she becomes so friendly and nice and happy. Notice how wrong you were.

Try to listen carefully to other people and limit the amount of time you sit there and talk about yourself. As you guys know, other people can teach us SO many things if we are open to it and just listen to them. Remember that **EVERYONE IS OUR TEACHER IN THE SCHOOL OF LIFE**, if we can simply swallow our ego and listen.

Some of the most important things you will learn will not be in a classroom. They will be from the experiences you have. I am a huge witness to this as when I am at uni I learn a lot about teaching, although when I'm in the teaching environment actually teaching at a school I learn 10,000 times more on the job. I believe the best way to learn is not only from your own experiences but by listening to other people's experiences and learning from theirs.

A quick example: I have learnt from not only my experience but my friends' experiences that (bear with me I am a 22-year-old girl who talks about boys and dating A LOT) when I have been super keen I have messaged the guy I like allllllllll the time coz I think about him alllllll the time. I have now I realised that by doing/experiencing this, it almost never worked. The guys would judge me as clingy, needy and obsessed with them (which I probs was) so I learned from my own experience not to act that desperately. And my friends tell me how they are going with the guy/s they're dating and they explain that sending him messages alllllll the time and acting realllllly keen isn't working very well for them either. If we had discussed this topic earlier and learnt from each other's experiences I'm sure we probably wouldn't have scared off so many guys with our excitement aka. Neediness.

Also, you can read so many books on a certain topic, such as 'Interacting with people' or 'How to Win at Creating Your Own Business' or 'How to Become the Best School Teacher'. But if you don't have the ability to apply what you have learnt from your book into real life, you have only gained a lot of book smarts (mind you it's great to have knowledge on things), but not practical smarts. For practical smarts you need to be in the environment and in real life. A lot of university students will graduate with a degree (congrats coz degrees aren't easy to get) but then they get a job and get into the workplace and don't have the practical knowledge to apply themselves and adapt to not only the new-found workplace but the people they are working with. Some studies even show that street/social smarts (Emotional Intelligence) may actually be more important than book smarts (it depends on the job in my opinion.) Some people have book smarts and know how to full well ace the exam and assignments buuuuutt when it comes to life they need a little bit more help. Research carried out by the Carnegie Institute of Technology shows that **85 percent of your financial success is due to skills in 'human engineering', your personality and ability to communicate, negotiate, and lead.**

Shockingly, only 15 percent is due to technical knowledge. Additionally, Nobel Prize winning Israeli-American psychologist, Daniel Kahneman, found that people would rather do business with a person they like and trust rather than someone they don't, even if the likeable person is offering a lower quality product or service at a higher price.

(Jensen, 2012)

In saying this, I know it isn't always the case, but I know many employers who have said to me that they will hire someone who's friendly, nice and takes initiative, over someone who is well qualified but frankly doesn't 'click' with their peers/workmates. But the bottom line is experience and other people are possibly the best teachers and we understand things so much better when done in real life.

It will teach you so much in a completely different way you can ever get from books. It's almost like comparing apples and oranges. They are both great but different. Learning in general is great but make sure that if you are learning in book smarts you are also learning in street and social smarts too; and be nice to your workmates – you never know how far it will get you.

Kids – What WE can learn from THEM

Now I know this is going to sound a little bit silly at the start but bear with me: for the last five years I've been working with children mainly from ages four-twelve and I'm not going to lie. I've learnt SO MUCH from working with kids at different schools, kinders, child cares, holiday programs and after-school cares. Now you may be thinking, 'Dude, is this girl serious? What on earth can we learn from kids? It's more like what do they learn from us! They are so innocent and don't know much about the world.' But I beg to differ. Kids actually have an awesome understanding of life. 'How?' you may ask. These are my observations:

- Kids are free spirited, they are open and look at the world with excitement.
- It's rare to see kids with anxiety and worry. The world is awesome; they don't need to worry.
- They do things with courage and aren't scared of failure.
- They do what they want and aren't affected by what other people think of them...to an extent.
- They don't worry about who's going to be their boyfriend or who's going to marry them.
- They don't really care about how they look and if people will find them physically attractive.
- They make friends with people for who they are, NOT what they look like or what this friend may bring to the table for them.
- They just go for it. Ever wanted to go and jump on that pile of sand you walk past everyday but know you'll look like an idiot if you do it, let alone get sand all over yourself? Well, you know what? Kids just go for it!
- They feel free to share their thoughts, even if it completely doesn't make sense. E.g., if two kids are outside playing in the sand pit while talking about making sandcastles, one of them randomly, without caring that it is

such a random question, asks, 'So what's your favourite animal?' They will keep on changing from one random topic to another and won't be at all concerned about sounding weird.

- They are honest: if you ever want an honest opinion, ask a kid. If a kid calls you pretty, take it as a big compliment because kids mean what they say.
- Ask a kid about their dreams and they will tell you huge ones that haven't been dampened by the world. Once a kid I know was asked what he wanted to be when he grew up. He replied with 'A rooocckkkkk sssttttaaarrrrrrr', while doing the air guitar. Now ask an adult what he wants to do, and even though he may want to be a rock star, I highly doubt he'd say it with enthusiasm and excitement like the kid doing the air guitar, and also because he may not think it's achievable and doesn't have huge dreams and goals, unlike the child.

Shoot for the moon. Even if you miss, you'll land among the stars
– Norman Vincent Peale

- Let's all try to let go, set our goals high, believe we can, like children!
- They question everything: 'Why this, Mummy?', 'Why that, Daddy?' They are curious about everything. When I was four, my mum wanted to tape my mouth shut

because all I would ask her was why, why, why. Haha! Keeping a childlike curiosity about the world helps us better ourselves and helps us to learn from every day.

The wisest keeps something of the vision of a child. Though he may understand a thousand things that a child could not understand, he is always a beginner close to the original meaning of life. **– *John Macy***

Keeping a bit of a kid in us is an awesome way to not take things too seriously. Children have a charm that's hard to resist and if you keep a little bit of a ten year old in you, trust me, 'charm' will be your middle name.

A story to back up my point happened to me last school holidays on the YMCA (great company to work for if you are looking for a job.) School Holiday Program. I was sitting at the back of the room. Disney's *Frozen* movie was playing and a little girl, who was about seven, came up to me and smiled at me. I said something along the lines of 'Hey, what's up?' or 'Hello (her name)' and she just stood there smiling at me. After a few more seconds she said to me, 'Megan, I love you.' (I really wanted to give her a massive hug but when working with kids we aren't supposed to hug them.) I just smiled back with the biggest grin on my face and said, 'Thank you (her name).' I gave her a pat on the back and went back to watching the movie. As the day went on, I thought about how sweet it was of her to come and say that to me and that people, especially older kids and adults, should be doing this sort of thing more often.

She wasn't scared

She wasn't nervous

She was happy and relaxed and genuinely just wanted to share the love. It was a really kind sweet thing for her to do.

Now think about how many friends we love and don't

say it to. Think about how many family members we enjoy spending time with and love being with but we don't tell them. How many workmates that make work so much better, you love spending time with them and the day goes SO much faster when they're around.

IF YOU HAVE SOMETHING NICE TO SAY, SAY IT.

IF YOU LOVE SOMEONE, TELL THEM.

In saying that, when I've told boys I like them, they have run for the hills, haha. I wouldn't recommend running up to the hot guy who works at the local surf shop and telling him that for the last two years you've had a secret crush on him and always go into the shop pretending you need 'help' finding a new bikini. Or tell him that you love him he will probs think it's very weird. I would avoid following your crush home and sneaking into his bed at night and then when he jumps into it, surprising him and then confessing how much you love him. You may think you're being cute and sharing the love but really **you are being a creep** and he'll most likely call the cops.

But seriously, we should let people know we enjoy their company, love having them around and love who each person is. So many nice things go unsaid these days, and just by letting someone know how much you love them or enjoy being with them will not only make the person/people you are saying it to feel good, but it will also make YOU feel good. As I said earlier in the book, one of the greatest forms of happiness is giving love to other people. Giving is just as good as, if not better than, receiving.

From now on let's be more childlike, letting go of being scared and letting people know how much we love them. Let's learn from kids as they have so much to teach us. If you are sitting next to your parents right now, turn to them and tell them you love them and thank them for being great. Tell your friends tomorrow you love them. Tell your workmates you love being at work with them. If you like someone's new hairstyle, tell them you love it.

Let's not forget other simple ways you can show someone you love them.

An interesting concept by Gary Chapman is the five Love Languages, which classes people into categories in ways which they prefer to have love shown to them.

The five categories/ways are:

- Physical touch
- Words of affirmation
- Acts of service
- Receiving gifts
- Quality time

Simply Google 'Five Love Languages Quiz' to do the quick quiz to work out your most preferred way to have love shown to you. (We are not just talking about romantic love only. We are talking about friendship love and the love that is shared with you and love in general, not just specifically romantic love.)

In my eyes, a hug can show so much love, but in someone else's eyes, an act of service may be preferable, or a gift. Remember that everyone is different. An example of this is: I have always and will always be a hugger (which appaz I'm awkward at), but there have been a few instances where some people have not hugely appreciated my hugs. By all means, they didn't reject them but they did get awkward about it. Not everyone shares your love language and it can be really beneficial to not only work out your love language but also the love language of other people close to you. This is so that you know the best way that you can make your loved one/ones happy! :D Remember the 'It's better to give than to receive' thing? I had my brother do the test so that I could work out his love language and it's so fascinating to see how other people view things and think completely differently to you. For instance one of the answers my brother gave during the test was that he would prefer a gift in comparison to a hug. I was shocked as in my head I'd choose the hug anyyyyyyday. If you ever meet me, hug me. :D

Look the test up and do it not only on yourself but on your loved ones and work out the best ways to share love and kindness, specifically tailoring it to the ones you care for and love. ☺

It's literally like a three-minute quiz, but what you learn from it you can remember forever.

So overall I know it's been a loooonnngggg chapter but I believe it's one of the, if not the most, important chapters in the entire book.

Although we have discussed lots of different ideas and things, they all stem back to and relate to the one thing that instantly makes you/anyone better... you guessed it. KINDNESS. <3

I hope this chapter (and this book in general) opens your eyes, challenges your way of thinking and inspires you to improve on the awesome person you are now. To finish up, I'm going to give you guys some of my fave quotes, which tie in well with the chapter. If I were you I'd read them over a few times to let them sink in; even highlight/underline any if they stick out at you heaps.

Then you can try your best to remember and live by them throughout your day-to-day life. ☺ Good luck. ☺ xx

- *Create a beautiful inside and you will look beautiful on the outside.*
  – Charles F Glassman, *Brain Drain, the breakthrough that will change your life*
- *The way you treat people who are in no position to help you, further you or benefit you, reveals the true state of your heart.*
  – Mandy Hale, *The Single Woman, Life, Love and Dash of Sass*
- *Be kind to unkind people. They need it the most.*
  – Ashleigh Brilliant (Pretty brilliant quote, hey?)
- *If only our eyes saw souls instead of bodies, how very different our ideals of beauty would be.*
  – Unknown

Be the person your dog thinks you are!
– JW Stephens

- *Be kind, hold doors for people, compliment them on their shirt, ask them how their day's been, offer them a taste of your snack, give them a hand, show them you care. Being kind doesn't have a cost.* ***All you need is a heart... and we all have one of those.***
  – Unknown
- *A person has two hands; one for helping himself and the other for helping others.*
  – Unknown

- *When a happy person enters the room, it is as if another candle is lighted.*
  – Unknown
- *You don't need a reason to help people.*
  – Zidane Tribel
- *See the light in others, and treat them as if that's all you see.*
  –Wayne Dyer
- *Make someone smile today.*
  – Megan Street
- *We rise by lifting others.*
  – Robert Ingersoll
- *I'm a true believer in karma. You get what you give, whether it's bad or good.*
  – Sandra Bullock
- *Be helpful...when you see a person without a smile give them one of yours.*
  – Zig Ziglar
- *Let your light shine so brightly that others can see their way out of the dark.*
  – Timber Hawkeye
- *The greatness of a man/woman is not how much wealth he/she acquires...but in their integrity and* ***ability to affect those around them positively.***
  – Bob Marley
- *So don't wait for other people to be kind, SHOW THEM HOW.* ☺ ☺ ☺
  – Boonaa Mohammed

Let's start sharing the love!
LOVE ya xx

Boys and VCE

Let me start with a story. When I was in VCE (final years of high school) and I was actually dedicated to study, believe it or not, I said to myself there is absolutely no way I am going to have a boyfriend – get distracted by a guy in this final year (probably the most important year of my education ever).

Now I said this due to the fact that I know myself well, and know that when I really like someone, no joke, like 90% of my thoughts wander to thinking about him, whether it be thinking about dates with him, kissing him, how I can 'run' into him, and even just about us going to the supermarket together. Maybe I'm a little bit of a psycho girl...but aren't we all when we like a guy?

So here is a little bit of a story that will make you realise that you are not the only 'crazy psycho he-better-fall-in-love-with-me' girl when you like a boy. It's all totally normal and part of growing up.

I remember an insane thing my friend and I used to do to 'run' into the guys we liked (as the boys were both best friends, and so were we). Oh yay, match-make made in heaven! I used to do it almost every day, but she and I only did it once, so basically, it's just a crazy ME story. I used to get up to catch the 7.00 train rather than the 8.30 bus, just so that I could SEE the guy I liked and his friends at the bus-stop train station terminal thing. There was only one time the guy I liked even came over to say hi. Every other time all he did was a wave from afar.

So to put it into perspective I got up a whole two hours before I usually got up (we also need to consider the amount of time I spent on hair, makeup and hitching my skirt up for him). I look back on it now and think, man, I was actually insane. It wasn't even love. It was just a huge crush, almost fair to say obsessive crush. Then I realised this whole waving at the bus terminal thing wasn't working out for me so I had a plan B. As I'd be too scared to do this on my own I had to bring along my best friend Candi as she was my friend who liked the best friend of the guy I liked. So Candi stayed at my house on a school night (I know, rebels) and we were planning on catching the 7.00 train to see the boys, but this time we were going to take a different approach...we were going to CATCH THEIR BUS WITH THEM! Argghhhh, whyyyyyy? (They would have known full well the only reason we were on their bus was to see them. The boys and my friend and I knew our school was in the completely opposite direction to theirs.) So anyway we missed the train (we had to catch a train to get to the bus terminal)...but did we take that as a no, we won't see those hot guys we liked? It's not meant to be or try another day?

NO WAYYY. This was just a small obstacle for a couple of 16-year-old high school girls who had universe-sized crushes. My mum wouldn't drive us any further than the local station and the next train didn't come for another half an hour and by that stage we would have missed the boys. SO there was only one thing to do... We called a cab at 7.00am on a school day and asked the cab driver to take us to the station (not to school, which would have cost the same amount) but to the station two stations down from my home train station). So he did and $20 later he dropped us off (oh man what idiots we would have looked, getting out of a cab at like 7.15 in our school dresses), AND WE MADE THE BOYS' BUS. They saw us. As we got on their bus there were no seats left so we had to stand right in front of them. The entire trip they kept yelling at us and trying to talk to us and yes, this was a perfect opportunity to get to know our crushes properly as we only really saw them at parties and the train station... but what did we do? WE DIDN'T SAY A WORD. We were both too scared to. Hahahahah (what a waste of time effort and money). But anyway, there is one positive to the story and that is that when we got off the bus, one of the boys yelled, 'See you at the deb after-party!' (That was on that coming weekend.) And we did see them and you know what we saw – both of them hooking up with heaps of other girls...heartbreak 101.

Candi + Megan = DESPERATE!

So clearly by this story you see why I HAD TO keep away from boy/s in my final year of school. All of my mental focus needed to go towards study. I have written and told this story not just to embarrass myself but so that YOU can see that

- You are not the only crazy girl when you like a guy.
- Hopefully make you feel LESS crazy in

comparison to me (and a little bit of my friend).

- So that you don't make silly mistakes wasting time and precious sleep on guys who treat you like crap and are never really into you.
- So that you don't waste money that could be saved on a taxi ride to see the hot guy/s.
- So that you don't get your heart broken by people who never really try with you or care about you.
- AND MOST OF ALL TO FOCUS ON SCHOOL NOT BOYS.

This is just MY story. I know many, many girls and guys who had great relationships throughout their final years of school but honestly I can only think of two couples that are still together now at 22. It kinda just depends on the person. Some people are really good at managing their priorities and are very organised as in they have a set amount of study time, set amount of boyfriend time, set amount of sports time. I greatly admire these people because, for me, when I like someone, I'm pretty much screwed. My emotions go nuts and I find it extremely difficult to do things that require a lot of mental work such as study. So by all means I'm not telling you not to have a boyfriend while in your final years of school because sometimes it's great to have someone who's there for you AND you may have even found 'The One' in school. BUT just remember to try not to do a 'Megan' and fall head over heels for someone who doesn't really like you and focus ALL of your mind and time on them...in other words, try not to go crazy when you like a guy in high school.

I know it can be really hard but you need to remember you are at school to learn, not to pick up guys. I mean great if you can do both but I sure know that I couldn't.

Balancing Life

Includes tips to scoring a part time job

Life is like riding a bicycle.
To keep balance you must keep moving.
– Albert Einstein

Now as I said earlier it's important to be healthy and balance your life. This would be my rough guide on things you should try to include, with or without a boy in the picture. The definition of health is 'A state of complete physical, mental and social well-being and not merely the absence of disease or infirmity' – World Health Organisation.

Good health is not just being free of an illness or disease. It runs a lot deeper than that. Good health is feeling happy or content, enjoying mental and social well-being as well as good physical health. Would you feel happy if you didn't have people around you? (Now I know some of you may answer yes to this although, at the end of the day, you need social interaction. You just have to find it with the right people.) Would you be happy if you had depression? Most likely not. On a side note we all need to stop hushing up about depression and work out how to help people who have it. Telling them to 'snap out of it' or to 'lighten their mood' is almost definitely not going to help. Being caring, considerate, non-judgmental and letting them know you are there for them can be a HUGE help. And last but not least is physical...if you have broken your arm and are in a lot of pain do you think you are going to feel happy? I doubt it.

So here is a healthy lifestyle plan you may like to follow or just take bits and pieces from for your years of growing up.

FRIENDS

You don't have to have them in school. You can always find friends out of school — join a team or an activity you enjoy...your best friends may even be your cousin/brother or sister; you never know where you might meet your new best friend. My mum met one of her best friends in the food court of the shopping centre because she offered my mum a table when it was really busy. It's crazy how nice people can be if you give them a chance.

SOCIAL/EMOTIONAL –
Friends can give a great amount of emotional support and you should truly thank them deep down if you have some great emotionally supportive friends.

FAMILY

Family time may not seem important at this point in your life as there are so many other exciting things happening, but sometimes you need to take a step back from your crazy life to spend a bit of time with your family. It may sometimes FEEL that they don't love you but at the end of the day they raised you and deep down have a HUGE amount of love for you. I promise. Even if you were adopted or brought up by not your blood dad/mum, whoever raised you clearly loves you...and to give them a bit of family time is a great way to keep stable, happy and balanced through your teenage and young adult years.

SOCIAL/EMOTIONAL – The reason I say emotional too is because your family can give you a tremendous amount of emotional support if you are open to their help.

EXERCISE

Now I have been lucky/unlucky enough to live a few kilometres away from the train station. My parents were big on 'being independent'. Most of my friends were getting dropped off and picked up at places and the biggest walk they did was from the house to the car. For me, I was that silly person running late, sprinting down to the train station, slipping on the wet grass only to miss the train thousands of times and be late, to almost everywhere I was going. I remember thinking at the time, 'Man, life would be so much easier if I had a car' orrrrr 'if my parents took me either to the station or even better the destination to which I was going.' (Now in saying this, I'm not cutting them any slack.) They did pick me and drop me off many times and I'm so thankful for that although in comparison to most of my friends it felt like hardly ever... But I now look back on it and am actually super thankful for my walks from and to school because I got physical exercise. It was basically a 'do it' or 'don't do it and never get home' sort of thing. It had to be done...there was no choice. When I was walking home, I really, really wanted to get home but I also actually enjoyed my time with my iPod and the kangaroos which were up my road. I chose the music that I liked and screamed it at the top of my lungs...my neighbours (and the kangaroos) must have thought I was so annoying but I just loved my music way too much to shut up and contain my singing, which was teamed with awkward, embarrassing arm dance moves. Another plus to this was I got a chance to think and have some alone time. Exercise can help your mental state as well as being good for your body. When I am ever feeling low or down, a good old walk in the bush by myself will always bring my mood up. You always hear people say, 'I'm just going on a walk to clear my head'. So now, remember next time you complain that you have to walk home to look at the positives:

you get to do some exercise (no choice, therefore has to be done). Who needs a personal trainer when all you need is no lift to where you are going? PHYSICAL/EMOTIONAL – walking releases happy endorphins.

ALONE/RELAXATION TIME

I greatly enjoy my alone time and practically need it to survive. For me alone time is something that I must have to keep a balanced life. When I am alone it gives me time to relax, and time to calm down, unwind and practically do/think about whatever I want. Music is also great for alone time as it helps me to calm down and take a break from life. But as we know, everyone is different and some people don't enjoy any alone time...they would rather be with someone all the time. What we need to understand is that everyone is different and that we should respect others' choice/s. For instance, if someone is pestering you to hang out with them when you really need some alone time, you may try to explain that you need alone time, but they may not understand as they are different and alone time to them is 'boring time'. They may think, 'No way. How can anyone actually WANT to be alone?' or say something like, 'I hate being alone; doesn't it make you lonely?'.

EMOTIONAL – Each and every one of us is different and we must work it out ourselves if we are drawn to and enjoy our alone time/relaxation time a lot by ourselves or prefer to spend our relaxation time with a friend/family member/boyfriend or even your dog.

STUDY

Now I know what you're thinking. Please Megan, we hear enough about how we should study from our teachers, parents, adults and practically anyone we talk to. We don't need to hear it from you. And yes, I understand you hear it a lot, although I'm going to take a little bit of a different approach to it. I'm just going to question you. I'm not necessarily going to tell you to study.

- Now if you are thinking about leaving school or school is not for you, just remember employers love to see a year 12 pass on your résumé. Even if you stay at school and get a below-average score, a year 12 pass is still a year 12 pass whether you got 99.9 or 15.3. Both are still accepted as a year 12 pass (in Victoria, Australia). Now if you and someone else were going for the same job with all the same skill sets and similar qualities and the employer can't decide who they want to give the job to, if you have a year 12 pass on your résumé and the other person doesn't, it shows a lot more than just a year 12 pass. It shows that you can be dedicated, punctual, don't quit when things get hard and even hardworking (they don't need to know your score, haha.) When the boss considers both of you, your year 12 pass will mean the difference between you and the other candidate, who possibly can't demonstrate those skills at this time. YOU will most probably get the job.

BOTTOM LINE – DO YOU REALLY WANT SOMEONE ELSE TO STEAL YOUR DREAM JOB JUST BECAUSE YOU DIDN'T STAY IN SCHOOL?

Might not happen, but could easily happen.

- Say you did year 12 and passed getting an average score – not really good, not really bad – mainly because you didn't know what you wanted to do after school finished. Then early in your first year out of school it clicked, and you decided you loved maths and physics and wanted to study engineering at university. You excitedly jumped up to see if you had the score to get in, but unfortunately you were about five points off. You called every uni but none would let you in because you needed five more points. You were shattered and kicking yourself because you knew you could have tried harder and got there but because you had no direction or goals, you sailed through, then regretted it once you left school. I know so many people who say, 'Oh, I wish I tried that little bit harder in year 12.'

ONLY 5 POINTS OFF!

BOTTOM LINE – do you really want to be that person who regrets not giving it their all when they could have? NO WAY. Try your best to make the most out of every opportunity!

- Now here is a very true and real story for

me which I believe has a HUGE message. I really want people to try and learn from my mistakes and try not to make them themselves. So when I was in year 12 I had the 'No boys to distract me rule' and as much as I logically wanted to not like a guy, my emotions had other plans. I was going really well all year until it hit September when I fell head over heels for this guy who ticked every box on my checklist. I hardly knew him at this stage but was already practically dreaming of our honeymoon. Even though I did really try to keep studying, my mind would just drift to thoughts of him and BANG, before I knew it, I was distracted by a boy. (As I said earlier in the book, when I really like someone, I swear, no joke, so many of my thoughts would revolve around that person.) I remember clearly trying to study for my art exam and thinking, 'Okay so I'll study for a bit, then think about Dylan (the guy I liked) for a bit, but eventually a lot of my study was overtaken by thoughts of Dylan. Damn hormones! Why don't you come AFTER exams like on Schoolies or something? But that's not how it worked. I sat my exams to the best of my ability but knew deep down if Dylan wasn't in the picture I would have done better. I tried my best to push him out, it worked a bit but never completely. Anyway, about a month

after exams we got out scores and I was shattered. If I had got six more points I would have got into a course that I really wanted to do. But I didn't…now I know it's not Dylan's fault. It was completely my fault, but this is how easily a little distraction can alter your future. My message in this story today is please **try not to get crazy over boys so that you forget about your future…** After you're in your course you can think about your crush whenever you like, but if you are in your final year atm, please give it your all and try to stop wandering boy thoughts before it's too late.

DO YOU REALLY WANT TO GET SO DISTRACTED BY BOYS THAT YOU DON'T GET TO FULFIL YOUR DREAM OR DO YOUR DREAM COURSE? Trust me; learn from my mistakes.

REMEMBER THAT ALTHOUGH IT'S UNFAIR, YOUR CHOICES NOW GREATLY AFFECT YOUR FUTURE.

- Even though you may want to go out and celebrate all the 'eighteenths' with everyone, you need to first know yourself and know whether you can afford to do that with your study load. I know some people (one of my best friends) who could easily go to all the parties and study and still manage to ace school (I swear she was just lucky/a genius) but really it was because she knew herself and her capabilities. As for me there is absolutely NO WAY that I could have gone to all the parties while studying and still pulled out awesome test and exam results. It just wouldn't happen. I know myself that if I want to succeed academically I need to put 110% into the task that I am doing and in this case study. For me it's like put in no effort, fail, put in half effort get a low pass mark; if I put in 100% effort I get average and if I put in 110% effort I get good marks. Everyone is different though. It's important to work out your radar – if you need a lot of time and effort to study or if you are one of the blessed ones who can whip out A+s and 100% with very little work. We are all wired differently and it's super important to know yourself and how your mind and body work, especially in relation to study. Remember that VCE is only a few years of your life and if you are like me and need to put the time and effort in to get results, you should, because at the end of the day we should be making the most of the fact that we have a great education system in place. Some countries don't even have the privilege to study. So look on the bright side and get your head down.

BOTTOM LINE – KNOW HOW YOU HANDLE YOUR STUDY. EVERYONE IS DIFFERENT AND IT IS SO IMPORTANT TO WORK OUT YOUR STUDY RADAR. WHAT'S YOURS?

And if you are like me and it takes more effort to get results, don't feel as though you're 'dumb' or destined to fail because what you should know is that every negative has a positive. You just have to open your eyes to see the good. And what do I mean by good? I mean if it takes you longer to study than others, you are **without a doubt good at other things**! This could be being creative, being a 'people person', art, drawing, English, sports –ANYTHING! I know that you have some things that you are good at and/or that you feel drawn to, and enjoy. I spent the majority of my primary and high school years thinking that I was a misfit and pretty much a dud who was bad at everything and good at nothing. It was only that I stepped out of my comfort zone, joined the school play and joined the art and drama classes that I realised that I love and enjoy being creative and with work I got better and better. You can do this too. It's just a matter of finding what you enjoy/are good at and once you are good at something, believe me, you will enjoy it even more.

YOU DON'T SUCK !

WHAT ARE YOU WAITING FOR? DO WHAT YOU ENJOY AND YOU WILL SUCCEED.

DO YOU REALLY WANNA SPEND YOUR LIFE DOING SOMETHING YOU DON'T ENJOY? NO WAY; NO ONE DOES.

Now back to a balanced life.

ACTIVITY

Something I believe that is really important to ensure that you have a balanced life is an activity. The activity obviously has to be chosen by you because YOU, not your parents or your friends, are the one that must enjoy it. Sit here right now and think what activity you already enjoy, orrrrr, even better, start to think about what NEW activity you think you will enjoy. I have always been a huge fan of tennis, and I also enjoyed swimming, but yours could be ANYTHING YOU WANT. The activity that you choose to do doesn't have to be in the line of sports. It could be painting, yoga, writing, reading, youth group or scouts. (Don't not join scouts coz you think it's 'loserish'. One of my regrets was not staying in scouts, as you learn many life lessons from it.) It could be rock climbing or an abseiling club or even actually sailing (boats), or ballet (girls, a lot of Victoria's Secret models do ballet, and who doesn't want to be them/do what they do?) It could be music (you could start a band). The list goes on. But some kind of activity that you enjoy is a great way to keep a healthy and balanced life. When you are feeling low, get out there and do your activity! If you enjoy it, it should automatically lift your mood. Having something to look forward to can be great, especially when all you feel like you do is study and work your part-time job. Try to use your activity to take you away from the stresses of real life and enjoy and cherish the moment when you are doing your activity. Channel your stress into this activity.

Certain activities are also great in assisting you with some life lessons and skills, e.g., tennis obviously can't be played by ourselves and therefore it is social as well. Also scouts will teach you so many life lessons, such as how to get along well with people, how to not be shy/get out of your comfort zone, how to do orienteering and also how to survive with very little camping gear: having to catch your own food, cook it and eat it. Ballet can show you how to be graceful and poised. Yoga focuses on your breathing and can be a great natural remedy for anxiety. The list goes on, so really think about an activity that you will enjoy, and go out and enjoy it! Have some fun! But whatever you do, choose the activity based on what YOU want, not anyone else.

The enemy of your potential is your comfort zone... Although it may feel good, it is a dangerous place to be.
– Unknown

PART-TIME WORK

Now this one can be quite difficult as you can't entirely do it on your own. Some may disagree with me on this (especially some parents) but I'm not writing this book for them. I am writing it for you! If you are under the age of 14 and 9 months (In Australia) you are not legally allowed to work so disregard this until you are old enough to work. Having a part-time job while in school could seem annoying, boring and unnecessary-or you could see it as an exciting new experience via which you will meet some new people, learn some new skills and get paid some real money (besides the pocket money you've been getting since you were like ten). It's so important to have a positive attitude towards work. I'll never forget once my friend and I, when we were about 13 years old, were catching the train home from the local shopping centre and we were talking about how excited we would be to get our first ever part-time jobs. The man behind us actually turned around and gave us ten dollars and said to split it between us, because he was happy that people were so excited to start work and he wanted us to keep up that attitude! We were very happy as he was so kind, while also scoring ten dollars to spend on raspberry bullet lollies at the local milk bar. But the bottom line is being enthusiastic about work is very important. So try to keep a positive enthusiastic attitude especially when trying to find a job. As my favourite, Henry Ford says, *Enthusiasm is the yeast that makes all hopes rise to the stars.* – SOCIAL, EMOTIONAL, PHYSICAL.

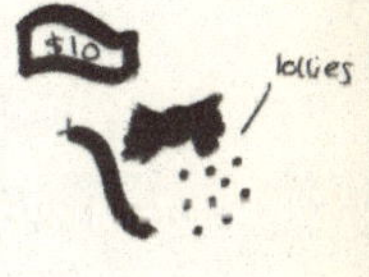

Now that you are excited to start work you have one problem-NO JOB!

SCORING A PART-TIME JOB

Getting a part-time job can actually be quite difficult. ('But seriously, who wouldn't want to hire me?' you may be thinking.) But because you don't have any experience, and a lot of places hire on experience, you may struggle (although how are you going to get experience if you can't even get a job to begin with?) Well, that's where I have a few suggestions, I believe when trying to find your first job, you need to step up and look outside the box.

- Hand your résumé out EVERYWHERE! Don't be too picky about where you work. Remember, it's your attitude towards the job which will have a huge impact on how much you enjoy working there or not. And keep in mind you might not even get ANY call-backs. Be prepared for rejection.

- HAVE CONFIDENCE. It's amazing how many opportunities are given to people who show confidence within themselves; even if you don't feel truly confident, you sure as anything can fake it. If you feel/act confident when applying for jobs, along with displaying a positive attitude and an excitement for work, you'll no doubt be successful.

- SMILE. I learned this one from Dale Carnegie's book, *How To Win Friends and Influence People.* Its basic human psychology that people like to see other people smile. The more you smile, the more liked you will be. Obviously don't go around smiling like an idiot with a giant grin ear to ear all the time but try to be happy, cheerful and smiley as often as you can. This also relates to dating. You love it when your crush smiles. Guys love girls who smile too. If you are a little bit insecure/don't have perfect teeth or have a big mouth or something like that, it doesn't matter. Smiling is what people do when they are happy and if you are smiling/happy around someone, they will usually be smiley and happy towards and around you. I remember when I first started working at a popular juice bar, one of their main things they asked you to do at work was smile! :D This is because smiling creates happiness and happiness is contagious – so get smiling.

A smile costs nothing, but gives much.
It enriches those who receive,
without making poorer those who give.
It takes but a moment,
but the memory of it sometimes lasts forever.

None is so rich or mighty that he can get along without it, and none is so poor but that he can be made rich by it.
A smile creates happiness in the home,
fosters good will in business,
and is the countersign of friendship.
It brings rest to the weary,
cheer to the discouraged,
sunshine to the sad,
and is nature's best antidote for trouble.

Yet it cannot be bought, begged, borrowed, or stolen, for it is something that is of no value to anyone until it is given away.

Some people are too tired to give you a smile.
Give them one of yours,
as none needs a smile so
much as he who has
no more to give.
– Unknown

(Pretty random but I found that quote on the back door of one of my besties' toilets. And have loved it ever since.)

- EYE CONTACT. I know it can be quite difficult, especially if you have tendencies to be shy, but eye contact is a big one when trying to get a job. Have you ever had a conversation with someone who doesn't properly make eye contact? It's awkward and you feel as though they are not interested, shady and even not trustworthy. If people, especially employers, can see that you can make eye contact, not only does it show your confidence, but it makes them feel as though they can trust you, and therefore they will hopefully hire you.
- ACT INDIRECTLY. I learned this one from one of the cutest boys I know (overheard him on the bus in high school). If you are applying for a job in say, retail, don't go in directly and say, 'Here have my résumé.' Talk to the person who works there and almost try to become their friend. Ask them for their help and, especially, opinion. Everyone loves it when their opinion is asked for. I learned at a clothing shop I used to work at that you need to 'build a relationship' with the customer. It's the same when applying for work. You need to build a relationship with the employer or, even better, the manager.

> Now once you two have built a relationship, casually slip in a 'Your job looks awesome. Hey, are you guys looking for people at the moment? Working here would be like not even working', or something along those lines. (Put your own personality into it, and say it with confidence.) Often you will get a 'No we aren't', BUT sometimes if you have made such a good impression, they will say, 'Hey we aren't, but you seem like a great person, so bring in your résumé and I'll see if I can get you an interview or even a 'Yes sure, come to this interview'. AND YAY YOU HAVE SCORED YOURSELF AN INTERVIEW! Now I'm not saying this will always work BUT it definitely does put you in a better position than the people who just said, 'Hey, here is my résumé'. When I was working in retail I had so many people just walk in and say, 'Here is my résumé'. Nothing more or less. I thought, 'Boy, if you took the time to have a chat get to know me even though I'm not a manager, I'd defs put in a good word for you TO the manager'. Don't underestimate how far networking can get you.

With getting work you HAVE TO HAVE TO HAVE TO stand out from the crowd and with your exceptional social skills you will learn from reading this you are already 100 steps ahead of everyone who hasn't.

- Sincere compliments and making someone feel special will also get you far (again I got this from Dale Carnegie's book, *How To Win Friends and Influence People)* BUT don't give a fake compliments as people can see straight through them. I remember learning this when I was about 16…when I was nice to people and paid them a compliment they seemed to like me more. Pretty obvious the reason why. It's because people like people who like them. In some way or another everyone wants approval and by giving people a sincere compliment you are giving them the much wanted approval that everyone seeks. Mind you, the majority of people can see straight through fake compliments so don't just go throwing compliments around everywhere. Unless you genuinely mean them.

CONTACTS

Sometimes when you are not getting any call-backs from jobs, you can apply one of my favourite sayings: *'It's not what you know; it's who you know'* – name of article on Psychology Today's website. Your mum may have a friend who needs a hairdressing assistant, your dad may know a lady who is looking for a part-time receptionist, or the man at the local fruit shop you speak to every time you go shopping with your mum may need help when it's extra busy

The biggest risk is not taking any risk. ***– Mark Zuckerberg (creator of Facebook)***

on Saturdays. A friend's part-time job may be looking for another casual. You just need to think outside the box and ask anyone and everyone if they know of any jobs going or if they may need a part-time worker in their business. *Ask and it shall be given to you; seek and ye shall find; knock and it shall be opened unto you*– Matthew 7:7. The worst thing you can get is a no and that's exactly where you started anyway, so really **what have you got to lose?** I've always tried to live my life like this as I get more annoyed at myself if I don't try than if I do try and fail.

- VOLUNTEER. Volunteering is a great way to get work experience especially when you are young. I know you don't get paid for it but 1. You are helping those in need and 2. It looks awesome on your résumé. My mum does some volunteering work for a disabled man who is in a wheelchair. He has a dog but can't take his dog for walks. She absolutely LOVES it and feels so happy that she is helping someone in need. If walking dogs isn't your thing there is always CFA – the fire brigade, the Salvation Army op shops (this is one I've always said I'm going to do but haven't actually got around to it yet.) and many others. There is also a company that can connect you with an elderly person who just wants to chat for a bit every day because he or she is lonely... I think this is a great idea because not only are you volunteering your time to someone in need but you can also learn so much from the elderly. Remember that they have been here much longer than us… And even the Cat Protection Society. Just Google volunteering jobs around your area and you should easily find a few that you would love to do.

- **SLEEPING**. The last person I want to sound like is your mum BUT I am telling you this as throughout my teenage years I made the mistake of not getting enough sleep. I'm not going to lie. It was so hard when I got in from lunchtime and had to try to concentrate on my class and learning when I could hardly even concentrate on keeping my eyes open. Sleep is super important, not only for learning, but for your body's entire health. The recommended amount of sleep is eight hours a night. Your body requires this to regenerate itself into working motion, as you would know if you have ever stayed up all night until the sun rises. Then you sure as anything know how you feel the day after you get no sleep…CRAP. That is your body's way of saying, 'Hey dude, I don't like this…don't do it to me anymore. Remember that I can make you feel even worse next time!' Plus it's also embarrassing to almost be falling asleep in class. I mean imagine how embarrassed you'd be if the

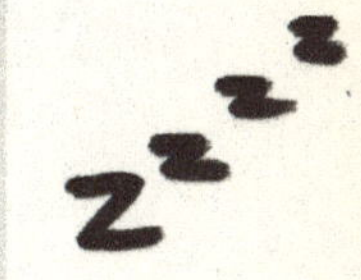

teacher asked you a question and you not only were asleep but you had no idea what the answer to his/her question was coz you were too busy with your head on the desk in dreamland. Way to make yourself look stupid in front of your crush. Bottom line is make sure you get enough sleep for your body and again assess yourself – some people feel fine after seven hours; some people need nine/ten hours to feel tip-top. Work it out and stick to what works for your body. PHYSICAL, EMOTIONAL

LAUGHING

Sometimes

Laughter is the best medicine

– Unknown

What's an alligator in a vest? Think about it...an investigator!

What did one volcano say to the other volcano? I lava you!

Hahahahaha. Now that I've told you a few jokes, let me tell you how important laughing is to your health.

Laughter relaxes the whole body. A good, hearty laugh relieves physical tension and stress, leaving your muscles relaxed for up to 45 minutes after.

Laughter boosts the immune system. Laughter decreases stress hormones and increases immune cells and infection-fighting antibodies, thus

improving your resistance to disease.
Laughter triggers the release of endorphins, the body's natural feel-good chemicals. Endorphins promote an overall sense of well-being and can even temporarily relieve pain.
Laughter protects the heart. Laughter improves the function of blood vessels and increases blood flow, which can help protect you against a heart attack and other cardiovascular problems.
http://www.helpguide.org/articles/emotional-health/laughter-is-the-best-medicine.htm
So, what are you waiting for? Hang out with funny people, look up jokes online, watch 'The Big Bang Theory' – Sheldon is bound to crack you up. Even just laugh at how much of an idiot you can be sometimes. (The ability to laugh at yourself is a really great trait to have.) Do anything to make you have a good chuckle. EMOTIONAL/SOCIAL – if done with other people e.g., watching a movie.

PRAYER/MEDITATION (optional)

If you are not into this kinda stuff/not interested in this, that's absolutely cool. Just skip onto the next section, but personally it's been a great help for keeping my life balanced over the years. I enjoy yoga a lot and meditate during yoga and before I go to bed every night. I have found that it helps me to relax and not worry about life in general and helps me to appreciate everything I have. Gratitude is a massive key to happiness, guys! As for meditation, it's the simplest thing to do because you literally just sit there and relax. You can either do it by yourself if you just Google a meditation video on YouTube and it will guide you through it orrrr if you go to group yoga at almost any gym, meditation will happen if you're in a relaxed state while doing yoga. Prayer is also a type of meditation where you calm your body and you go into a completely relaxed state. So if you have a strong belief in something, whether it be God, the universe or Buddha, you can pray to wherever your beliefs take you! EMOTIONAL/PHYSICAL.

GOALS

Goals are really important whether they are big or not so big! Having a plan and goals to live up to is a great way to live. Although having goals is great it can also be disheartening if we don't reach our goals as suddenly or soon as we thought we would. Don't beat yourself up if you don't reach them as fast as you might think. *Patience is a virtue – Proverb.* Often it takes a long time to do and achieve things, but try to remember, *Take the first step in faith; you don't need to see the whole staircase, just take the first step* – Martin Luther King Jr. Having any goal is better than having no goal. It is also important to realise the goals that you set may be more time/work than you may think, but you know how to get through that. Persistence. If you come across failure and setbacks, remember that Rome wasn't built in a day. A great way to set goals that I have used is with the trusty 'New Year's Resolution list'. It's a really

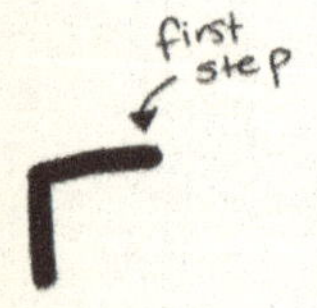

good way to keep and do your goals for the New Year. Write them all out on a piece of paper (have as many goals as you want). Make some big goals, such as getting into your dream university course/dream job, and also include some smaller goals like having at least two pieces of fruit a day. And what if you don't achieve all of your New Year's resolution goals for the year? All good. Just roll them over to the next year's list! And most importantly have a goal to reach your goals. I promise you it feels aweeesoooome when you can cross off a goal on your list. Also stick your list up in your room so that you are looking at it often to remind you how much you wish to achieve these goals. Happy goal setting. EMOTIONAL

And last but not least one of the most important things for a balanced happy life...refer to the chapter 'Something Anyone Can Do to Instantly Be Better.'

Incorporate these things into your life and you will be well on your way to achieving an optimum state of health, physically, socially and emotionally. And how's that not something to smile about!? :D

Shyness

Say goodbye to being shy!
– Megan Street

When I was about three years old to about 13/14 years old I was **ridiculously** shy. When I was in kinder they even thought that I had autism or asperger's due to the fact that I was such a shy introverted kid. If you were to meet me now you'd think no way was I shy ever, as now I can be quite extroverted and shyness is almost the least of my worries. But for me growing up was so hard. Being shy, in primary school I would cry every time the teacher asked me a question. I wouldn't answer; I would just cry and have to leave the room with a friend, who would calm me down. Teachers told my mum that I didn't push myself to the fore enough and would never be able to. Although I'd like to believe that it was entirely me who changed my shyness

I have to say that it was a lot to do with Mum, in conjunction with my mindset.

As you know my mum sent me to a high school where I did not know ANYONE. I swear I cried in my room for about a week straight when I found out that I wouldn't be going to a high school with my friends.

When I was told this I was very shy and always depended on my best friend in almost every way (I literally couldn't do anything myself), and when I was told that I wouldn't know anyone, I was VERY upset to say the least. But sometimes the things you think are bad at the time actually turn out to be the best things that can ever happen to you. I still remember my mum driving me to school on my first day. I was as scared as anything. The very first friend I made was a girl who came up to me and said, 'Hey, we have the same shoes.' It's crazy how some friendships can start. After that I made a few more friends because we were all going to the disco that weekend (Bluelight). If you want to know how I made friends when I was younger and how I do even now, check out my guide to making friends in the 'Friends (Bitches)' chapter. But anyway when I got to high school I did everything I could to give me confidence, I did my nails hot pink; I styled

my hair in a way that made me feel confident; I even remember buying some cool new jewellery so that I felt pretty, which boosted my confidence. It was never to impress anyone but it was to ensure that I had the confidence to make new friends. I made a goal that at high school I would NOT be shy. I figured that no one at high school knew me and knew that I'd always been shy so I thought I'll just put on an act that I'm not. I set small goals for myself and said that I would talk to as many people as I could and not get intimidated by them. I cried on my first day (in class, mind you), after my first day and even after orientation day. If you haven't already realised yet from reading this book, I'm a pretty big sook. But I made it through. **Setting goals for myself not to be shy really helped me a lot in overcoming my shyness**. Although it took a few years, I did eventually get over my shyness and actually turned into a bit of a loud mouth/show off. My mum still jokes that she may have got me out of my shell a bit too much.

Another goal I specifically remember setting was on the first day of year eight. Throughout year seven (first year of high school) I was still too shy and embarrassed to ask the teacher questions in front of the class. I said to myself that I was not going to be shy about asking questions in class. I remember sitting there in English on the first day of year eight and the teacher had just read the bulletin (school's daily news) to the class. He was a new English teacher and I believe he had no idea that I was and always had been quite shy and introverted, but as he asked after reading the bulletin, 'Does anyone have any questions?' I shot my hand up, voice shaking, butterflies in my stomach, even feeling red in the face and asked, 'Do we have any excursions coming up?' I did genuinely want to know this because I really loved excursions but the main reason I asked this was to help to overcome my shyness. It was a lot more of a goal for me rather than actually caring if we had any excursions coming up. I was super scared about what the other people in my class thought of me because in the first year of high school I would never put my hand up to ask anything/answer questions and then suddenly I did (we had the same people in our class as the year before). But honestly now that I look back on it I'm sure almost all of them wouldn't have even noticed that suddenly I'd asked a question. (People are often too busy with their own thoughts and life problems to even notice a lot of little things about you.) Most of the things we worry about are usually all in our own heads; the actual thing we are fearing is not usually as bad as the fear and worry itself, and what we think people are thinking is often entirely untrue. You may think, 'Oh no, he's looking at my giant pimple' when really he's actually enjoying your boobs. Another example is if you think you are fat. I'm sure 1,000,000 other girls will think you have an amazing body. We often worry too much about what people think of us (which is usually a negative trait/quality) when in reality PEOPLE DON'T NOTICE/WORRY ABOUT YOUR FLAWS NEARLY AS MUCH AS YOU DO.

Setting small achievable goals is extremely beneficial when conquering your shyness.

Over the years I set small goals to overcome my extreme shyness.

When setting goals I remember what I learned in business class was **S M A R T** – by George T. Doran

Specific – Goals should be written in a simple way and clearly show what you are going to do.

Measurable – Goals should be measureable so that you have tangible evidence that you have accomplished the goal.

Achievable – Goals should be achievable; they should make you feel challenged, but defined well enough so that you can achieve them.

Results focused – Goals should be able to show the outcome.

Time bound– Goals should be linked to a timeframe that makes you think it needs to be done ASAP, or at least soon. There should be a need to change your current reality to the reality you desire.

When and if you are shy it can literally be the hardest thing to talk in front of the class, make new friends and even just sit on the bus. If you enjoy/like being shy, by all means stay as shy and introverted as you wish to be. Many, many successful people, such as a lot of authors, are shy and introverted but if you do WANT to overcome your shyness it is important to set small achievable goals. I suggest you set and/or start with one of the below goals (or create your own.) Remember you can start at any point depending on what you already feel comfortable doing.

YOU CAN DO IT!

- Answering/contributing to small group discussions
- Stating your opinion in a group
- Talking to people without being shy/embarrassed
- Maintaining eye contact when talking to people
- Not being embarrassed by sitting by yourself on a train, tram or bus
- Not being embarrassed when around your home group class or any class for that matter
- Not being embarrassed in front of year level for example at the school locker bay
- Not being embarrassed to participate in sports in PE class (this was a huge one for me as I used to not like sports/PE class because I felt really exposed and embarrassed when participating).
- Doing oral presentations: my best friend, who was also really shy, literally could not do them. She got severe anxiety, panic attacks and stomach cramps, and would always somehow get out of them. I remember her telling me that she would rather fail the entire year of English than have to do her two-minute oral presentation. Don't be like this. YOU AND I BOTH KNOW YOU CAN DO THEM!

We need to remember that people are scared of different things, and to not make fun of, tease or bitch about these people. Many have severe fears and anxieties about certain things, such as public speaking/ shyness.

Everyone is scared of something. Try to think about how scared you are when experiencing your worst fear and then think about the other person's worst fear (which may be what you are teasing/bitching about). Imagine that the fear that you feel for your biggest fear is at the same level as the fear they feel for their worst fear. Now you may begin to understand how scared this fear makes them and that you shouldn't be mocking them and calling their fear 'silly'. It's just a different fear to yours. So try to be understanding. If you don't have their fear, don't be mean to them about it. Just put yourself in their shoes and try to understand it from their point of view.

You may be scared of your crush rejecting you in front of your whole class or you may be scared of an oral presentation...different fears...same level of the fear feeling.

WE MUST LEARN TO ACCEPT EACH OTHER'S DIFFERENCES.

One of the times when I was at my shyest was in my PE class and while playing sports. I don't know if it was because I never considered myself 'good' at sports or because I felt overexposed while running around chasing a ball, or because I was scared that no one would pass me the ball because THEY thought I was bad at sports.

I was self-conscious about my lanky body and to see me chasing after a ball practically tripping on my giraffe legs would have given the boys another thing to tease me about. They already made fun of me because I apparently walked/ran weirdly, I didn't want more teasing! But now that I look back I **so** shouldn't have cared, because *Any reaction is better than none* – Gavin Rossdale – and to have my crush / boys notice me in any way was better than them ignoring me. (Positive mindset of a 'negative' situation.)

Here are some of the many things I was very shy of in school - Which you can turn into goals:

- Talking to new people.
- Talking to friends.
- Talking to boys.
- Talking to teachers after class.
- Talking to teachers in general.
- Having to say 'here' or 'present' on the roll (my stomach would do flips).
- CATCHING THE BUS.
- Another thing with the bus was that it was like a runway where everybody checked everybody out as each person walked down the aisle, putting your ticket away. Let's be honest we all do it when people get on the bus. It gives bullies the prime opportunity to look you up and down and whisper to their

friends about you. Everyone is facing the same way forward, looking the same direction and looking at the oncoming traffic, which, in this case, is YOU walking down the aisle. Another thing I didn't like about the bus was when I first started in year seven. I was so scared that the older kids would bash me (I look back now and think how crazy 12 year olds' mindsets can be). There was probably only a very slim chance that it would have occurred. But this was something that I seriously thought would happen... I thought they would all want to bash me for no good reason (maybe being a first year high school student was a good reason). The first years (year sevens) at my school used to always cop it. I don't know why. It's the same with first year uni. At uni they call you JAFFYS (Just Another Fu*king First Year Student). It's probably because first years have no idea what they are doing, both at high school and at uni. But, trust me, guys, I can almost guarantee that you won't get bashed on the bus by the older kids. Take it from someone who thought they would and was pleasantly surprised when I was able to get off the bus in one piece.

J A F F Y

Now if you want a smooth sailing bus/train/tram ride here are my tips.

- Listen to your iPod; you can almost block out everything with music.
- Same goes with your phone; just sit on it,

preoccupied with that rather than what's around you.

- Have some bus/train/tram buddies you can rely on to catch the bus with you. Almost everything's easier to do with friends. Even people my age would prefer to start something new and/or do something with friends.
- Remember that even if your bus ride sucks, it's usually over quite fast.
- You will be driving one day (hopefully soon).
- Try not to think up crazy things like me – like, 'Oh, I might get bashed on the bus'. There is a slim to none chance of things that you worry about happening.

Other things that can trigger shyness (Remember to twist these situations into goals!)

- Talking to the guy you like.
- Standing near the guy you like.
- Hiding behind the bushes checking out the guy you like.
- Talking to other people's parents
- Calling up someone else's home phone (probably don't do this anymore as most people have mobiles).
- Catching the train and/or waiting at the station by yourself.
- It's easy to rely on your friends being around you to not make you shy but at the end of the day we need to learn how to do things on our own, without our friends. You can't have the

same friends by your side with everything you do.

- Reading in front of the class.
- DRAMA CLASS…
- Especially when you have to talk and act in front of the class.
- Walking into class late. Everybody will stare at you. Don't do what my friend did and wag the class because she was too scared to walk in.
- I used to be scared of even just walking through an older year level's locker bay.
- Remember that shyness can often be misinterpreted as unfriendly and stand-offish.
- I know one thing I used to do when I was shy was hesitate to try something new. E.g., try out for sports teams, aerobics, swimming carnivals; not once did I participate in swimming carnivals because I was too scared and shy.

I'm telling you these so that if you feel any of them you are defs not alone. I felt them and still do sometimes.

Remember that overcoming shyness takes practice. It's not going to just happen overnight. It took me a good two years before I got over my shyness and it still sometimes came back to haunt me in certain situations.

They do say though that people who are shy often make the best friends as they tend to be especially caring and considerate towards others and are interested in how others feel. Apparently people often consider them the 'finest friends'.

Take slow and steady steps forward. One situation at a time.

Try not to feel awkward when with others. Others are most likely not even aware of your awkwardness. Try to chillax.

- AND KNOW THAT ALTHOUGH IT IS HARD, YOU CAN DO IT! Take it from someone who has!
- In time, with patience, courage and practice, you CAN overcome extreme shyness.
- DON'T GIVE UP if you want to be more confident and less shy.

Personally I, without a doubt, have enjoyed life so much more and taken so many more opportunities when I haven't been shy. And although it was extremely hard at the time getting past my shyness it was one of the greatest things I ever did.

chill
+
relax
=
chillax

FAKING IT TILL YOU MAKE IT CAN WORK.

I remember once when I'd almost overcome my shyness I did an oral presentation to the class and although I felt nervous and still scared, afterwards I was told by a girl in my class that I seemed super confident. I remember being so shocked. I was like, 'Really? I was so nervous.' I faked my confidence and it really worked.

- You never know how much faking confidence can work in your favour.

Or if you enjoy being shy and don't feel any need to get past it, you could simply change your mindset:

I'm not shy. I am just holding back my awesomeness so that I don't intimidate you.
– Unknown

I'd suggest if you are serious about getting over your shyness, take on board a few of these (if not all) steps that I have suggested

- Set goals. Start small then increase bigger and bigger until you reach ultimate confidence!
- Don't give up at after setbacks; use them as motivation to push on further.
- Write a list of things you are shy and scared of and want to overcome (I've listed a fair few of mine in this chapter.)
- Conquer the goals on your list, crossing them off as you go. This way you feel completed and effectively making steps towards your final goal...and every time you cross off a situation you don't feel as shy anymore as you know that you are getting closer and closer.
- Try not to care about what others think of you – this will only keep you being shy.

- Know full well that you WANT to overcome your shyness
- Ask yourself, 'What's the worst that could happen?'
- Imagine and visualise yourself NOT being shy.
- Try your very hardest to do things on your own, not always needing/relying on your friends.

BELIEVE THAT YOU CAN DO IT.
BECAUSE YOU CAN!

But, I'm Still A Virgin!

V
I
R
G
I
N

As someone who kept her virginity long after high school, I know all too well what it's like to be called a loser, dork, frigid, or 'the girl who won't put out'. It's hard because, literally everyone, especially in school, is talking about sex: who they slept with on the weekend, who they fu*ked, who they horizontally banged bodies with...and I'm not going to lie, it's hard to 'walk the road less travelled'.

These days almost everywhere you are/look, there is sexual content, e.g., I'll be driving and on the back of the bus there is a pic of a model who looks like she's been photographed mid-orgasm, you sign onto Facebook and girls have their tits out in photos (well, you know what they say: if you've got it, flaunt it). There is also sexual meaning underlying almost every song on the radio too. On billboards these days, there are even premature ejaculation ads. Now, I'm not actually implying that these things are 'bad' because at the end of the day 'sex sells'. But what I am saying is that if you are already feeling like a bit of a loser because you've never slept with anyone, these things can remind you that you may not feel hot enough and ultimately make you feel even crappier than you may already feel.

These things can also give you the nudge to make you curious and sleep with any guy who will take you... pun intended.

You think that once you sleep with someone you may feel more desirable; you may feel as though you can go out and sleep with heaps of guys now that your first time is over. At the end of the day after all, it's supposed to feel good; you can even have sex talks with your friends rather than sitting there awkwardly twiddling your thumbs trying your best to fit in with the convo until someone says, 'How would you know? You haven't even had sex.' Or after sitting there in silence, do you feel as if you want to go and grab the first guy in the street and tell him that you just want to play 'hide the sausage' simply so that you can fit in with your sexually experienced friends? This would give you the ability to join in their convos with your 'Oh, it feels sooo good', 'I know exactly what I'm doing in bed', 'The guy who I slept with was literally the hottest thing to ever exist', and that he 'banged you so hard you couldn't even walk the next day'. (These are all terms people I know and friends have used during convos about sex.) But... deep down you would know that you didn't lose your virginity for yourself and that you did it to 1. Know how it feels (were curious) and 2. To fit in with everyone.

I've heard many reasons why girls I know have lost it...here are just a few:

- Wanted to lose it by a certain age.
- Was curious.
- Wanted to fit in.
- THOUGHT IT WOULD MAKE HIM LIKE ME MORE.

- Tip: guys don't necessarily associate sex with attachment, but girls do. Guys can easily have a 'f*ck buddy' but as for girls this is a little bit harder. This is actually due to science as when we have sex, 'oxytocin' is released, which is the 'cuddle hormone' which will bind you to him emotionally...that is why when women sleep with men they usually get attached. Whereas men manage to more easily remain neutral and emotionally detached because the main hormone released for them during sex is the 'pleasure hormone' Dopamine. – Biology class 101.
- Couldn't restrain any longer.
- Wanted to feel wanted.
- Wanted to feel desirable.
- Wanted to feel sexxxyyyy.
- **We love each other (Better Reason).**
- He had earnt it and I like him...don't give it to guys easily as they actually like the resistance. As I say, be like a football – unpredictable and exciting. Boys love sports – especially football (AFL) and when you are a football that can bounce in any direction when thrown to the ground, you will be able to keep his focus on you, almost as much if not more than when he is watching footy on the TV.
- One word – 'sexcercise'.
- Wanted to become his girlfriend and by having sex with him will automatically make me his gf... unfortunately in this day and age just sleeping with someone does not mean that you

two are bf and gf. He could easily be sleeping and 'hanging out' with four other women/girls at once. The same goes for girls. Just because a guy is hanging out with a girl, doesn't mean that she is with him exclusively. She may be doing the 'four-man plan' by Cindy Lu and rotating dates with different guys. You are only his gf when you are officially his gf. Don't set yourself up for pain, by giving up everything for him (including other guys) when he only sees you as 'one of his options'.

- I wanted to join in with all the sex talks.
- I wanted to make my boy happy.
- I'm not going to tell you how to live your life and what you should and shouldn't do, but what I am recommending is that if you are going to sleep with a guy (maybe even let him take your virginity) make sure that you are doing it for the **right reasons**. You and I both know that you have respect for yourself, and the guy you end up sleeping with should have respect and treat you with respect before he gets lucky enough to get in your pants.

Respect: a feeling of deep admiration for someone or something elicited by their abilities, qualities, or achievements
– English Oxford Dictionary

Respect is a feeling you have about someone else.

Having respect for someone means you think good things about who a person is or how he/she acts. You can have respect for others, and you can have respect for yourself.

You should treat others with respect.

Showing respect to someone means you act in a way that shows you care about their feelings and well-being.

– Talkingtreebooks.com

Urban Dictionary:
Respect
A quality seriously lacking in today's society
Respect? What the hell does that mean?

Respect
Something that no one has for one another nowadays.

So many of my friends say that they totally regret who their first time was with, how old they were and so many other details about the occasion, e.g., 'I wish that I hadn't been so drunk'. This was one of the most prevalent answers when I asked a lot of my friends what they would have done differently when talking about losing it. Most of them used one of the reasons I have listed previously although none said that she had loved him. These girls without a doubt regret it and wish that they had waited for the guy they are with now, or at least someone who shows them respect. Some even said they would have slept with a guy they actually liked. Yeah, that's right. Some people even lose it to someone they don't even like.

Although you may think it's 'cool' to sleep with someone now, when you look back on your first time about five years later (most of my friends' ages after they lost their V card) but, as they all say, it's actually really not cool to look back and not have a positive memory of their first time. In saying that, even though they may not have liked him, he may have been really good in bed – so maybe it was actually a good first time, but with little to no emotional component to it.

They call sex 'making love' for a reason.
Physical and emotional = great sex.

It's entirely up to you though...if you wanna lose it to a guy you met that day through your Tinder app, go ahead, but I'm just warning you that once your virginity is gone, there is no undo button. You can't backspace that shit. For the rest of your life that is your first time memory of sex.

just because you are sleeping with him, doesn't mean he's your boyfriend.

Make it a good one!

I'll never forget when I was in my final year and there was this horrible Facebook page that someone created, which was called 'Hursty (abbreviated name of the town I grew up in) Goss'. On this page's Inbox, people submitted girls' names and ratings out of ten on both their ability in bed and how likely guys were to 'get some' in bed with this girl. The page posted it with the girls' last names and all, for everyone to see. One night, my friend inboxed me the link to the page (which I had no idea about) and said that there was one on me! I still remember my stomach dropping as I thought they'd call me a slut (coz at that age I practically lived in short skirts), so I followed the link and read on. It said, 'Megan Street 0/10, no points; don't bother, she's just a massive frigid cock tease. We can't give you a rating on her ability as no one knows it.' After reading this, I immediately felt like I had to prove this 'Hursty Goss' wrong. I was soo close to just messaging the guy I liked at the time to let me come over and he could have sex with me. SO CLOSE, but then I decided to sleep on my decision (by myself). The next day I realised and said to myself: 'No, I'm waiting for the right person', so I just ignored the post.

HURSTY GOSS

FRIGID!

This is an example of how easily you can make a decision that you can never take back when you are young. Remember that you only get to use your V-card once.

Now as I said earlier it's super hard (stop having a dirty mind) when all of your gfs are chatting about their sexual experiences and you are just sitting there like a nun (nothing wrong with being a nun, mind you). But the crazy thing is the even harder part (only funny first time) is when boys actually make fun of you.

If you are one of the girls who is waiting for the

'right person', I'm sure you have probs heard all the lines that guys will use to go all the way with you.

What we need to remember is that guys really want sex. Like more than really want sex. They really really, really, really, **really** want sex. They will say almost anything to get it. Some of the lines I've heard over the years from guys attempting to go all the way are:

- It will feel really good.
- It will be fun.
- You'll love it.
- You're missing outtttt.
- Don't be frigid.
- Loser.
- I'd break you anyway (referring that his penis would be too big for a virgin).
- Dork.
- You nun.
- You're beautiful.
- Baby, you're amazing.
- Don't be a sook.
- I'm hard.
- My blood is bursting.
- Come over and 'watch movies'.
- My parents are away.
- Please let me be your first time.
- You're so pretty.
- Let's cuddle.
- I've fu*ked other virgins before… I know how to do it.
- You're scared aren't you? There is only one way to conquer your fear.
- We'll put in 'just the tip'.

- How about we just have anal; that way I'm not technically taking your virginity.
- It's fun up the bum.
- You'll have fun letting me pop your cherry.
- I love you. Yep, one of my guy friends told me that this is one of his fave tactics to getting girls into bed. Appaz we are 'suckers for words' and this one 'works like a charm'.

So anyway you get my point. Don't fall for boys'/men's crap. Sometimes they are being truthful; sometimes they are not.

If he is trying what you may believe are lies on you, assess his actions and the way he treats you. See if they match up to his words. *Actions speak louder than words.*

Respect yourself and others will respect you.
– Confucius

It is difficult to keep your virginity in a world where so much relates to sex and everyone is always banging on about it. Be sure to know yourself, know who you are and know that you will make the decision to lose it for whatever reasons you choose. Hopefully these will be the right reasons, it's your choice entirely.

Remember that insecurity is not a good reason to lose it, especially if you are using the person you are sleeping/have slept with to increase your self-confidence.

Just because a guy sleeps with you doesn't mean he 'wants' you. Most men would pretty much fu*k anything with legs (not literally) but they're pretty much always 'down for a root'. As one guy once told me: 'Pretty girl, lights on, ugly girl, lights off'.

Now let's not forget that just because you may not be having actual sex yet, you are not completely depriving your um needs. There are other ways you can get sexual satisfaction. Just because you may be a virgin this doesn't mean you are missing out on all the fun. I know a few virgins who do everything but...and are just waiting for the right guy.

Something I strongly believe that should be invented is a warning label like alcohol that says 'Enjoy responsibly', stuck smack bang on them somewhere when their clothes are off. This would ensure that you know what you are doing; you are sure you want to do it; so that you practise safe sex; and that you won't do something you'll regret in the morning. I know how it feels to be caught in the moment and not thinking straight when things are getting heated. As for protection, something my mum always says to just tell him, 'It's not on if it's not on' or 'Can your worm before you squirm'. Keeping safe is so important.

So your virginity is something that can only be taken from you once...it is entirely up to you who it is with and when it happens. Don't let anyone, despite his dreamy eyes, force you into it and especially try not to get smashed and let him take advantage of you (unless you like it like that, that is).

But at the end of the day, *Treat your body like a temple* (Jim Rohn)...take care of it.

Take care of your body.
It's the only place you have to live.
– Jim Rohn

Teachers

Bitch, please. You've got more issues than Vogue.
– Unknown

If the teachers never give you awards...not to worry.

Awards are merely the badges of mediocrity.
– Charles Ives

You all know now that when I was in high school I was never the kid who got the highest grades. I didn't succeed in many tests/exams/projects unless it was in art, drama and sometimes, if I was lucky, English. Now before you close the book and say, 'Ew, why am I looking at advice or even reading a book created by someone who probably has a brain the size of a pea?' I promise that what you get from this next chapter will help you be so much happier **for the rest of your life.**

So back in school I would try very hard to receive higher grades in the other subjects but hardly ever actually achieved them. I was known as 'dumb' not only by my peers but also by the teachers. I know it's crazy that the people who are grown adults, and who should be there for each and **every** student, were actually just as bad, if not worse, than the kids at underestimating me.

But...something we need to not forget is that although the teachers at your school are professional, qualified, adults, more experienced in life, leaders and ultimately people that we look up to, they are still human. Most will still judge you as a student. It took me a long time to realise that just because someone is older/more mature/had more life experience/highly educated/in a high position at the school or anywhere, this does not necessarily mean that they will act how they should, provide support, be nice to you...and even treat you with respect. Each and every person in life is dealing with life problems, insecurities, financial struggles, losses of things, broken marriages, inability to find the love of their life, unrequited love – the list goes on. And sometimes, as much as it sucks, you can be the teacher's outlet – yes, it's unprofessional and wrong but it unfortunately happens. We all know that a lot of teachers have their 'favourites' and if someone has favourites you can bet they will also have 'unfavourites' – kids they don't like for whatever reason. Don't blame yourself. It may not actually be anything you have done to them at all. I had a girl in my class who was a grade A student (in every subject) and all the teachers LOVED her except for my English teacher; he hated her, with a passion...and we will never know why.

It may be as simple as that you have the same hair style as the girl that bullied your 50-year-old male teacher when HE was in high school over 30 years ago.

Therefore he hates you, and takes his past emotional issues out on you. He may even enjoy embarrassing you in front of the entire class. As I said earlier in the book, no matter who you are, not everyone is going to like you in life. Even if you are very popular and one of the most well-liked people there will be someone out there hating you.

If you know that you have been a truly nice person – polite, nice, not a brat, rebel or smartass, never rude towards the teachers, I can almost guarantee to you that the meanness that they are showing you is THEIR unresolved emotional issue/s, not actually anything you have done wrong at all! So stop racking your brain about what YOU have done wrong to this teacher. It's their problem not yours. Feel sorry for them that they have to treat someone so poorly and meanly in life to make themselves feel better and/or deal with their own emotional crap that they have to live with, and move on. My suggestion is that if worse comes to worst, ask your coordinator to change your classes. You don't even need to mention this to your parents unless you want to. Some parents will be great, believe you and call the school to organise the class swap, although other parents won't believe that the teacher is being this cruel without you deserving it and not help you at all. Judge how your parents would react to the situation and act accordingly. If you are too scared to ask the coordinator to do the swap for you without your parents, just think that 1. You'll be happier to be in the other class and 2. When you get out of school you will be on your own. You will do things yourself and you won't rely on Mum and Dad to get you out of tough situations. I know people even my age who still rely on their parents so much (at 20 they get their parents to call their work for them). You are better off learning early that **if you want something done, you do it yourself.**

WHAT IF THEY ARE TELLING ME I CAN'T/ WON'T SUCCEED AT SOMETHING OR IN GENERAL?

Let me tell you a story about a boy I know. He was what most people would call a rebel, a ratbag, a little shit of a kid who never did his work and mucked around almost allllll the time at school and outside of school. One day he had an interview with the careers teacher the year before his final year at school. She told him that he should drop out of school and that he would not be able to achieve any good grades so he may as well leave. He knew his capabilities and took the insult. The next year he put his head down like there was no tomorrow. At the end of the year after exams he pulled out an in-the-90s ATAR (final schooling year score), which is really high in Melbourne, Australia, got into a law degree and is now a lawyer. He proved everyone wrong and used the criticism from teachers to succeed and help him to become a better person...and not only is this kid a lawyer, all throughout university he ran his own successful business. He was an awesomely smart person who used doubt and negativity to push him further to succeed.

Just because a teacher or anyone doubts you, that is what THEY think, not what YOU think... You know you are capable of whatever you want if you put your mind to it... ANYTHING IS POSSIBLE.

Tips to remember

- Genuinely happy people are not mean to others. They love, care and respect other people.
- People who are unhappy within themselves are normally the first to take it out on other people.
- People are insecure – in fact, scrap that, EVERYONE IS INSECURE in some way or another.
- Try not to bite back, it's not even worth your time!

I learned long ago never to wrestle with a pig. You get dirty, and besides, the pig likes it.
– George Bernard Shaw

Don't let their negativity towards you make you stoop to their level and do it right back – that makes you as bad as them. Simply smile, feel sorry for them (in your head; if you say this it will most likely anger them more) and move on.

When people are insecure they jump at offending

others as it makes them feel better about themselves. Some people will actually realise why they are doing this and stop. Some people may realise they are doing this and NOT stop. But most people will not realise that they are doing this and continue to do it because the bottom line is that **it feels good to be mean to the people we don't like.**

Jealousy is also another emotion which will sure as anything bring out the worst in someone.

Don't let their green eyed monster get to you!

One story that I remember vividly regarding teachers is this one. So when I was in year 12 (final year) I wanted to apply for school captain, I knew within myself (or so I thought) I would make a great school captain, despite my 'rebel reputation' and the fact that I hardly got to school on time. In my defence I did try my hardest to make the school a kinder, happier place and always chatted with almost anyone in the schoolyard. I believed that it was really important for the school captain to have the ability to converse and get along with other students, because at the end of the day, the students are what make the school. Anyway, I knew that my writing skills were not going to beat the brainiacs of my year who were practically married to their textbooks (mind you nothing wrong with that), so I had to take a different approach. I thought really, really hard about how I, Megan Street, could get the prestigious, most sought after role of all of high school – School Captain. I was SO determined to make the school the best place ever for students and to be a super fun and exciting school captain. I wanted to share my out-of-the-box ideas to make the school an awesome place that students would LOVE going to while also learning at. So it hit me: I would ASK MY MUM TO HELP ME WRITE MY SCHOOL CAPTAIN APPLICATION SPEECH. She's a genius in almost every way and is a qualified agricultural scientist who used to pretty much be the dux of everything when she was studying. (Mum, I wish you'd passed on a little more 'mathsy sciencey' brain to me. Not because I'm not grateful for how my brain is but it defs would have bumped up my maths and science tests and exams from my average, which was about 30% despite how hard I studied.) So I remember running in the door home from school super excited to ask Mum if she could help me write my speech annnnndddd...SHE SAID YES! But there was one condition... that I would help her with how and why I would make the school a better place. She specifically said, 'I'm not writing the speech for you, you know.' I was like, 'Yeah, awesome, sure, anything to get you to help me.' I remember writing about focusing on different types of learning – hands-on, kinesthetic, sporting, peer support, anti-bullying programs, social skills programs and most of all making the school an enjoyable place for students to be at while learning. Mum helped me write up the three-page long speech

(they called it a speech but really it was just a paper that we submitted to the teachers. Pfffffffft, a proper speech is a way better idea because you can see who has the ability to connect with the audience...in my opinion anyway.) But I wasn't worried. This was because, I'm not going to lie, the 'speech' turned out aaaaamazing! I was like, 'I'm SO gonna be rocking this school soon'. Positivity and confidence are the keys, guys! I was jumping round, so excited to hand it in, get an interview and then become the SCHOOL CAPTAIN. I prayed and prayed and prayed to God to let it be me who got it. But then the school rained on my parade, shut me down, crushed my hopes and dreams. They didn't quite admire my positivity and enthusiasm because I didn't even score an interview. ☹ In my eyes getting rejected before anyone has even given me a chance is way worse than giving something your all and best shot and then failing. (I discuss this more in the Unrequited Love chapter) When I found out, I cried...actually 'cried' is an understatement. I was practically a walking waterfall. I was so shattered because I would never get that opportunity again in my life. (I suggest if you get the opportunity to be school captain make the most of it and try to get it. I even tried my best at persuading, trying to talk my way into an interview, asking every teacher I saw if they could pretty please try to score me just one five-minute interview. They didn't want a bar of me, and told me to buzz off and accept defeat. But they didn't know me...nice try, teachers I don't give up *that* easily. So I decided to go by the motto, 'First is the worst, second is the best'. (Sorry to the girl who really did get school captain because she did do an

awesome job of it and really deserved it.) Anyway, so it was VICE CAPTAIN HERE I COME. ☺ And to my utter disbelief I didn't even score an interview for that either. Hmmmm, something was up. If my paper was amazing (thanks Mum), it must have been ME they didn't like… All good because if you fail, try try, again. That wasn't the last they'd hear of Megan Street trying for a big role at the school, so it was 'HOUSE CAPTAIN COME AT ME.' I was so pumped because I was the only girl in year 12/final year who applied for house captain in my house (Blue was the bessstttt). It was pretty much guaranteed that I would become a house captain (as they say third time lucky) but this time I had learnt from my mistakes not to get too excited too soon, so I played it cool AND ACTUALLY SCORED AN INTERVIEW! Weeeeehoooo, persistence really does pay off! I was like 'Awesome. The rules for house captains was that there has to be a boy and a girl captain and I'm the only girl going for it in my year (only final year students get to be house captains). This baby's mine.' I remember looking in the mirror before my interview, practising my charisma – like on The Sims video game. I was ready to smash the interview and score house captain. When I walked into the room of the interview, I walked past a girl who was leaving the interview room. At that moment my stomach dropped. This girl was super sporty and I knew the teachers LOVED her BUT SHE WAS IN YEAR 11 (not her final year of school), unlike me. She wasn't even in year 12! They had never ever, ever given a house captain role to a year 11 before and the fact that they were even interviewing her hugely decreased my chances (again before I was even given a shot). But I didn't let this get in the way of my confidence and charisma during the interview. Although I was into exercise, I was more of a dancing, yoga, tennis, walking, sort of girl while this girl was the typical running, super fit, crazy amazing at sport, even did the great Vic bike ride, sort of girl. So again I felt like she had another one up on me, on top of the fact that the teachers already thought she was God's gift to this world. I finished the interview and had yet another sook...and prayed to God (I really wanted this) but I pretty much already knew the outcome...and a few days later, the house captains were announced and she got it (congrats girlie, coz she did a great job of it).

After all that work they (teachers) managed to crush me. Well done to them. They got what they wanted the whole time...to not have me as a school leader and ultimately not even give me a chance to succeed. In fact, considering my reputation, I probably didn't deserve any of the three positions anyway.

Surprisingly the hardest part about this was not actually the fact that I didn't get any of the roles or even that I didn't get a chance at an interview for school or vice-captain. It was because about a year and a half before my mum had had a brain tumour right in the centre of her brain, which by miracle was successfully removed. (If they left it one more day she would have died the doctors told my dad and also if she hadn't been as fit and healthy she wouldn't have made it.) Because of this she was absent, recovering in rehab for the majority of the first year of my (her first child's) VCE (two final years at school). As a result of everything going on and Mum not being well, I even failed two of my six subjects in year 11 – Legal Studies and Food Tech (yeah, I know, how do you even fail food tech unless you set the room on fire?).

So when I didn't even score an interview for school or vice-captain I was not only disappointed in myself but felt as though I had let down my mum who had gone through so much over the past few years too. It was such a big deal to both her and me, because in primary school my mum wanted me to apply for school captain but I was too shy to do it (I was the only girl in my year who didn't). I wanted to make her proud in high school to show her that I had overcome my shyness (mainly thanks to her – I talk about this in the Shyness chapter) and was ready to take on the role of school or vice-captain. When I didn't even score an interview, telling my mum was so hard as I first of all was shattered myself, but also shattered because I felt like I had let my mum, who had just successfully recovered from a brain tumour, down. I so badly wanted to do her proud by getting school/vice or even house captain but sometimes not everything goes your way...which ultimately teaches you resilience.

So anyway I got over it and listened to the teachers' advice and 'accepted defeat'...there was nothing more in my power that I could do. I wish they gave the students a chance to vote coz I was friends with so many students over all of the years and I would have had a good chance of getting one of the three roles I applied for.

After my own negative experiences as a student, I am now aspiring to become the best, nicest and most considerate teacher out there and **will always give**

students a chance. Most of all, I will try my absolute hardest to never be mean to a student, as I know how upsetting it can be (despite how hard they hide it), and how low it can make someone feel. As my grandma says, 'If someone is mean to you, feel sorry for them that they have to treat you badly to ultimately make themselves feel better.'

If you truly loved yourself, you could never hurt another.
– Buddha

Remember that quote next time a teacher treats you unfairly. It's THEIR problem with themselves not your problem with yourself.

WHAT YOU AND I CAN LEARN FROM THIS STORY

- Sometimes despite how hard you try, things won't always go your way. Just like sport – sometimes you win; sometimes you lose/learn.
- It can be hard when other people not only don't believe in your greatness but actually try to step on you and keep you down. Don't let their opinion of you make you think negatively of yourself though. Believe in yourself…ALWAYS…despite others' opinions.

- If you fail, try, try again…persistence is a key trait to being successful in anything in life. Although it failed in this story, it has worked in many, many more.
- Be nice and give people a chance. As shown in my story, you don't know the motivations of someone and how much you are not only hurting them, but other people, when they are not even given a chance.
- In case you were wondering, my mum made a full recovery and is living every day like it's her last. Life is so precious and can be taken away from us at any time. Live life to the full; be kind and show love to everyone.
- RESILIENCE – When you are knocked down keep going. The difference between a successful and less successful person is resilience.
- You don't know what people are dealing with…be nice to everyone.

Let your haters be your motivators.
– Nikki Carter

- Reputation is important…once people have formed judgments about you, it's difficult to change them.
- HEALTH IS SO IMPORTANT! – If my mum hadn't maintained a healthy lifestyle throughout her life she was told she almost definitely wouldn't have made it through her

brain surgery alive. Keep healthy because you'll never know when you'll need it.

- Despite the crap you have gone through, try not to get into the 'poor me' mindset. Be grateful for what you have and give everything your best shot.
- If you feel like a failure, turn to my 'Failing' chapter...many successful people fail many times before they are a success. Don't stay on the ground – get back up onto that horse!

When people hurt you over and over, think of them like sandpaper. They may scratch you and hurt you a bit, but in the end, you end up polished and they end up useless.

– Andy Biersack

Social Media

The reason we struggle with insecurity is because we compare our behind the scenes to everyone else's highlight reel.
– Steve Furtick

What happens on social media stays on Google forever...
– Unknown

Now let's not get distracted from this chapter by just reading the words 'social media'. I know what you are thinking: 'Ohhhhh, thanks for reminding me, I need to check my Facebook/Instagram/Snapchat/Kik/Twitter and every other form of social media I have an account with right now to see who is trying to contact me via cyberspace. My advice right now would be to check it all so that you can read this chapter without distracting thoughts such as: 'Oh, I wonder if my crush liked my photo' or 'What if I need to snapchat my best friend back?' or 'I wonder what so and so is eating right now.'

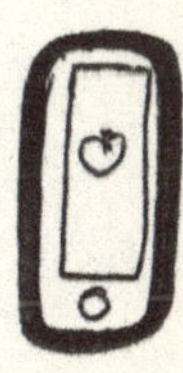

Check it NOW, then come back to this chapter with a fresh mind.

So now that you have checked it all I can begin the chapter.

As you most definitely know, social media is a HUGE part of our lives today, especially when you are in high school. It's super crazy and hard to believe that for the majority of people, the first thing we do in the morning and last thing we do at night is stare at a screen, whether it be our iPads, iPhones (phones in general if you are part of team Samsung/Blackberry), computer/laptop screens or whatever it may be. People these days check their phone like it is the morning newspaper. I also know a lot of my friends and people I know who can't even get to sleep without some form of screen playing in the background (either a laptop playing a movie, a TV, or their phone screens).

- Now don't get me wrong. I LOVE social media and all the amazing electronics and the world wide web that we have such easy access to with the click of a finger or the touch of a button (or, I should say, touch of a screen). But what we need to realise is that our screens are not real life. I'm sure you have heard this many times before and are probably thinking, 'Oh shut up! I know you are just going to tell me to get off my screen and go 'play outside''.
- But seriously, hear me out, because I am almost exactly the same as you...practically glued to my phone/screens.

Now I'm going to start with Instagram as I've had

an extremely interesting experience with it myself (Instagram is a photo sharing app mainly just used for posting photos; unlike Facebook on which statuses are written and people talk to you as well as photos being posted.)

I gave in to the Instagram trend (Sometimes I try to see how long I can hold off a social media app/account just to see how long I can last without giving in.) about two years ago. I also didn't want to get it because I want to try to stare less at my phone and more at my actual life. But I gave in. My like/dislike relationship with Instagram continues to this day, so here's my list of pros and cons of Insta, which also can apply to Facebook and other forms of social media too.

Pros

- Exciting
- Makes keeping up with friends easier
- Style and fashion inspo
- Great recipes
- Amazing motivational pages such as quotes and mottos (we must remember there is a huge difference between knowing/posting inspirational quotes on your page and actually LIVING by them). We need to understand that just because someone posts a quote/motivational words, this does not necessarily mean they live their life according to their quote; they may just WISH that they did!
- It's also the same with you. Just because you post something, people may think that you

live by it. If we are fully serious with ourselves some of us don't actually live by those quotes at all. Of course some people have posted these to truly reflect their value systems. You may also get fake confidence boosts from how many likes you get...as much as I don't like it I'll admit it happens to me too.

How many likes did I get?

- Body inspiration: looking at girls with 'hot bodies' motivates us to eat clean and go to gym/do more exercise.
- Able to keep up with what famous people do with their lives.
- Show your life through pictures/statuses to everyone else.

Cons

- We should be getting out and living our lives, and seeing the beauty of the world rather than looking at someone else's photos of the beauty of the world.
- Comparing yourself to 'fitspo' and other people and other people's bodies/boxgaps which is more than likely a photo shopped image of a stunning girl with an unrealistic photo shopped body shape (unless you are one of the many that follow Victoria's Secret Models. They are most likely not photo shopped but have awesome bodies due to their intense workouts and diets and genetics. Some amazing people actually are real).

- If we don't get any/many LIKES we can feel down, the reverse of getting 'fake confidence boosts'.

Insecurity

- I know that I was definitely affected by this. I've always been quite content with who I am as a person. Yes, I have flaws but I have accepted them and moved past them. But I'm not going to lie to you as when I followed some models on Instagram I began to feel insecurity creeping in. 'Oh why don't I look like that?' 'Why doesn't my stomach look like hers?' I need more asssssss. And after never really being a hugely insecure person I started to develop some insecurities. I'm sure most girls do when they follow amazing models and people on Instagram. That is why if you are feeling that who you follow is creating insecurities within yourself that you don't normally/wouldn't normally have, I'd strongly suggest to 'un-follow' them (don't worry I'm sure they won't even notice so you won't be hurting their feelings).
- Realise that your confidence is so important and withdraw from following such amazing people IF you feel they may have a negative impact on your confidence.
- Most of us already have a negative view of

ourselves and we don't need hot models and 'fitspo' girls on Insta to rub it in.

- We must understand that our confidence plays such a HUGE part in who we are and who we will be in the future. The most successful people in the world have large amounts of confidence and have a great ability to believe in themselves. How else would they get as far as they have?

Love yourself completely.
– Unknown

Some people say I have attitude – maybe I do. But I think you have to. You have to believe in yourself when no one else does – that makes you a winner right there.
– Venus Williams

If anything or anyone tries to shatter my confidence I will either deal with it or use it to make me better ...

E.g., if a workmate constantly puts me down I'll TRY to use that as motivation to become a better workmate and work harder and focus on my job rather than being negative and spiteful towards them (which ultimately would waste my time and energy). I will also TRY to use it to teach myself that I don't ever want to hurt anyone the way that that person hurt me and will ultimately become a better person through their negativity and mean remarks. The reason I say 'TRY' in capitals is because I don't always succeed; I'm not perfect and sometimes I can and do fight back when I should be shutting up and moving on.

Insta wasn't making me any better other than I gained fake confidence from the likes/comments and followers I got. I assessed the situation and realised that Insta was bringing me more harm than good.

One thing to remember from Miranda Kerr's *Treasure Yourself* (book) is: *A rose can never be a sunflower, and a sunflower can never be a rose. All flowers are beautiful in their own way, and that's like women too. I want to encourage women to embrace their own uniqueness.*

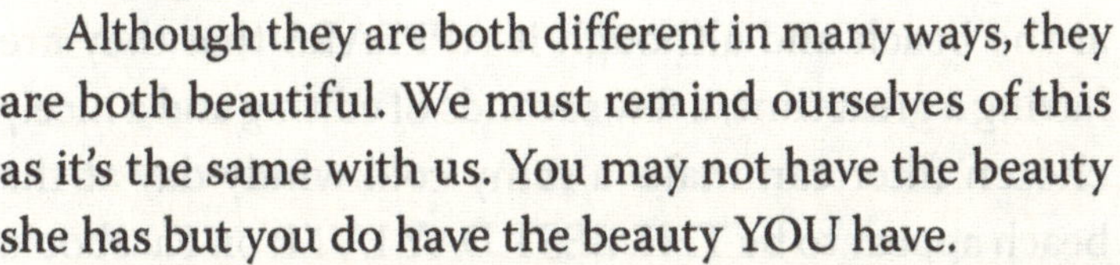

Although they are both different in many ways, they are both beautiful. We must remind ourselves of this as it's the same with us. You may not have the beauty she has but you do have the beauty YOU have.

Now I'm not saying I don't have Instagram, which I do (come say hi! @meganxstreet Haha), but I think it's so very important to keep in check what and who you look at on it. If you are beginning to feel insecure in day-to-day life because of what you see on Instagram, I strongly suggest to stop following the people whose photos make you feel like this or just withdraw from Instagram completely. I know it may be super hard because social media is so very addictive (I'm totally addicted), but you need to remember your health and view of yourself and most of all confidence. It's difficult but just remember as I said earlier, one of the top traits almost every guy looks for when he begins to like a girl is CONFIDENCE. Don't let yours be ruined by some confidence crushing app called Instagram (or another social media app's name here).

Facebook

Now although Facebook has many great things about it, it can also have a very negative effect on our psychology and overall self-esteem. Yes, you may just sign on, check your notifications, scroll down the newsfeed and check out a few people's profiles BUT what you may not realise is the majority of people on your Facebook will only present HALF of who they really are to you.

E.g., you see pictures of friends partying, people at the beach and although it APPEARS that they are having a great time, a few seconds of editing and a nicely chosen filter can make a rainy cold windy day at the beach appear to be THE BEST DAY EVER on Facebook.

Another example is people posting pictures of their travelling overseas. Yes, it may appear that they are having the times of their lives in Bali or wherever they are travelling BUT what most people will usually purposely fail to mention is that they've actually had a terrible headache or back pain the entire time overseas. Another thing is, although you see all the amazing shots of friends at overseas festivals and living it up in Europe, you don't see it all. There are the tired nine-five days spent at work; the breakdowns people have had from working so much; and the hard times of not going to certain events and missing out to save money for their trip over to Europe – or anywhere for that matter.

What I'm getting at is what you see on Facebook is not everything. **Don't compare someone's Facebook life to your real life.**

Seeing everyone else having an amazing time on Facebook can make almost anyone feel insecure about their own lives. Why aren't I doing that? Why haven't I finished my degree yet? Why am I not at Tomorrowland partying? Why am I not in Japan right now?

Another example of this is: you are sick in bed with tonsillitis and you see all of your friends going out on Saturday night in your Facebook feed without you. You could be thinking, 'Damn, I wish I was with them', considering how much fun they seem to be having at that new club you were SO excited to go to. These photos make it LOOK like they are having an amazing night now. Let me break this down

- One of your friends is having an awesome night although tomorrow will be a different story when she is vomiting all day from all the alcohol she had.
- The friend who looks amazing and all the boys love her may actually have social anxiety that you have no idea about and actually hates the attention she gets from guys always looking at her. You may think this is crazy and would love that attention yourself but some people are like this. They don't actually want the attention they get.
- You don't see that one of your other friends actually chased the guy she's had the BIGGEST crush on for years to the club, only to find him

eating another girl's face off while she stands and watches them heartbroken, with tears welling up in her eyes.

So there you have it. Maybe staying at home in bed with tonsillitis was actually a better choice than going out with your girlfriends. Although from their photo filter and hashtags they are #havingthetimeoftheirlives #bestnight #lovinglife #nightoutwiththegirls. There are always a lot of things people are dealing with that you actually have no idea about. You never know what someone is going through until they open up and really trust you.

Words can really build someone up or break someone down. Be nice, this includes online too. Just because it looks like they are having an awesome night and you comment something mean or inbox them being mean because you THINK they are happy with life, they may actually be upset inside and just trying to hide it on social media. I've seen girls who look completely happy on social media the day they were in hospital for depression; a lot can be hidden online... Be kind.

REMEMEBER: once you say something it may never be forgotten by the person/people who heard it.

E.g., if you call another girl fat she may never forget that comment and always be insecure in not only her bikini but her everyday clothes. She could even develop an eating disorder. All because one person said one negative comment.

If you say someone has an 'ugly' feature it can stick with them for years.

E.g., when I was 17 (my final year of school), I said behind a guy's back, 'He would be hot if he didn't have such a big nose.' This may be one of my biggest regrets in my life so far as he came up to me almost four years later and said, 'MEGAN, why did you say that? It really hurt back then.' It was crazy that four years later this boy brought up such a hurtful comment that I'd forgotten I'd even said.

The axe forgets what the tree remembers.
– African proverb

WORDS REALLY CAN HURT SOMEONE DEEPLY AND MAY NEVER BE FORGOTTEN.

Your tongue is a weapon. DON'T use it as one.
– Megan Street

My final example of this happening was to ME at a 21st birthday party. There was a boy who was drunk and hitting on me (drunk people hit on almost anything with legs) although I wasn't interested and at the end of the night he walked me to my car and told me I had an ugly feature. (Talk about my karma from the nose comment). I'd never been insecure about this feature in my life but ever since then I have been insecure and more self-conscious about this – it has been two years now. (See, I'm not even telling you because then you may notice if you ever look at me.)

WORDS REALLY CAN HURT SOMEONE DEEPLY AND MAY NEVER BE FORGOTTEN.

From this day forward let's begin to use our tongues for the POSITIVES we see in people, NOT the negatives, because whoever you say it to may never forget your words, either good or bad.

One thing I now live by is:

- If you have something nice to say, SAY IT! Good words and compliments should never be bottled up. Don't be embarrassed to be nice. You may just make someone's day or even someone's life.

We must remember that **we are all in this world together**!

BACK TO FACEBOOK – GEE, I GET DISTRACTED SO EASILY!

Now not only will people mislead you with photos but sometimes even their whole online 'identity'. E.g., jobs, where they live, what they study, where they are heading in life. Many people will have jobs up on their Facebook about which they may actually be stretching the truth or even lying so that they appear better. Someone may only do a few shifts at a certain high-end clothing shop and really dislike the job and quit after three shifts BUT because it is such a well-known high-end clothing shop she decides to keep it up on her Facebook as 'Works at ____' or even 'Worked at ______' so that people see it and think better of her. This is also the same with study. It may say that someone is studying 'Bachelor of ____' and therefore it appears that they are smart, well accomplished and on the road to success (if you believe getting a degree is successful), when in reality they may have deferred their studies for the year as they may have to work full time to pay for their family, rent or even food. You just never know.

So next time you look at someone's online profile, try not to compare yourself to someone's online identity

There is almost always more than what you see to someone's life than they make out online. No one leads a perfect life as much as someone makes out that they do, either in real life, or online. They don't. No one does. So please try to remember that not everyone and everything you see online/on someone's Facebook, gives the entire picture and may not be the truth. It may not even be that person at all (fake profiles are made SO often, where frauds pretend to be other people).

If you ever see or feel yourself comparing your life to someone else's 'life', which you are only viewing as an online profile, think back to this chapter and remember that online is NOT real life. If you sat down and spoke to the girl, I can almost guarantee you she will be fighting problems you have no idea about. I always try to remember the quote:

If we all threw our problems in a pile and saw everyone else's, we'd grab ours back.
– Regina Brett

You may think that what you have/have to deal with is bad but just wait until you hear about the problems 'the girl you wish you were' online has.

When we realise that OUR problems aren't nearly as bad as the ones other people have, we begin to reassess whether our problems are even bad at all.

We're all in the same game, just different levels dealing with the same hell just different devils.
– Unknown

Everyone's problems are different but everyone has problems that DO exist.

Bottom line of this is that online profiles can misrepresent the truth and lead you to believe that other people live better lives. Don't fall into the trap of comparing yourself to other people's online identities, and try to remember that everyone has problems: even though you may not see them/know about them, they do exist.

NOBODY IS PERFECT even if you think they are. This includes the fact that nobody's BODY is perfect either.

If you want to read an awesome article on body image and social media, follow the link below. The writers of this blog post are models (Laura Henshaw and Steph Smith) who share a great point of view on social media and body image. Their website also has some winning healthy recipes too, seriously take a look! http://keepitcleaner.com.au/blog/view/23/

And if someone LOOKS perfect (as in stunningly physically) attractive, just download the app 'Photowonder' and see how deceiving edited photos can be on social media. On this app you can smooth skin, enlarge eyes, whiten teeth, put make up on yourself, even 'thinnify' yourself (make yourself look thinner). There are also the usual filters and cropping. This just proves my point that people are not always what and who you think they are, especially online.

Another thing that you may find annoying (and with

fair enough reason) is if someone decides to steal YOUR Facebook/Insta (any social media site) photos and use them for THEIR personal use, pretending to be you or pretending that they look like you. THIS IS NOT OK... and should without a doubt be reported. BUT instead of complaining about it, try to take it as a compliment... someone wants to be like you/be you and actually admires you. (It's kind of sweet that despite all the insecurities you have someone still wants to be like/be you.) Try to see the good in it while reporting it and taking it down.

Now if you are someone who finds it tempting to do this, I won't judge you, I know what it's like to want to be like someone else. You may be jealous of her or she may have stolen your ex-boyfriend. Whatever the reason, just stop for a second and ask/say to yourself:

- What will I gain from this?
- Do I really want to waste my time trying to be someone else?
- Put yourself in THEIR shoes...would you like this done to you?
- What I should be doing is getting out there and improving myself (whatever it might be – exercising, trying a new hobby, catching up with a friend, enrolling in a life drawing class, getting a new piercing or even dyeing your hair blue! Basically, anything would be more productive and useful than stealing someone else's photos and/or pretending to be them on social media.
- Wouldn't you rather work towards being a better version of yourself?
- Even if you do get attention from your new page by using other people's photos you are

tricking other people and most importantly you are tricking yourself into thinking that you would be better off being this person.

DON'T WASTE YOUR TIME...there are so many awesome things you could be doing in this world and pretending to be someone you're not should be the LAST thing you want to do.

Seriously, **BE YOU**!

Always be a first rate version of yourself and not a second rate version of someone else.
– Judy Garland

There is only one you in the world. CELEBRATE YOU BEING YOU.

A quote I try to live by is: *Play the hand you're dealt.*
– C.S Lewis

I read this previous quote on a boy's chest at a nightclub one time but since then it's stuck by me. My interpretation of the quote is: take the circumstances you have and try to make the best out of them even if you feel that they may appear worse than other people's; stay strong and remember to try your best with what **you** have.

Online Dating and Dating Apps

A few of my close friends have met guys that they have fallen head over heels for online, so in my mind there is no doubt that it is a good idea.

Personally I have mixed emotions about online dating and dating apps such as Tinder.

PROS

- I think any way to meet and interact with new people is great.
- I also think that distance is a factor, as some people would not be too keen on a long distance relationship. Travel costs can be high, they can't take the time off work or they may need to babysit their siblings, but for whatever reason, a long distance relationship just isn't going to work for them. The app tells you how close you are to that person geographically.
- Another good thing is that you can easily find people with the same interests, hobbies, values and beliefs as you and therefore you already have a bit of common ground to get the ball rolling. These things can be very important to many people when looking for a relationship.
- It's also good as people can only portray good and appealing aspects of themselves and photos that they know they look hot in. (This is similar to the previous page on Facebook

– only showing positive and attractive qualities online.). This is a pro because you may score a date from your hot pics; then when you meet in person you may not be as physically attractive but your charm might capture his heart.

- It can also cover up your not-so-positive traits and score you a date before the person finds out about your not-so-positive-traits. #winning #datesallround. But at the end of the day a relationship isn't about hiding your negative traits from people. It's about the other person falling for your positive traits AND you're not-so-positive traits too.

The next one is one of my main points and it may be short… but sometimes short and sweet is the best way to go:

You can't feel a 'spark' online.

The 'spark', 'chemistry', 'feeling' – whatever you want to call it – cannot be found unless you are actually with the person in real life.

Now you may be thinking: 'Oh but Megan, the physical chemistry has to be there too'; 'I have to find this person physically attractive before I even want to meet up with them', Yes, this is true to an extent. Most people will decide if they want to take things further purely by the looks of someone. (As much as it sucks, we all do it.) You don't look at someone over the bar who doesn't physically attract you and think, 'Oh, I feel like he has a good personality, I should date him.'

Beauty attracts the eye but personality captures the heart.
– Unknown

BUT have you ever found someone not attractive in photos but extremely attractive in person? That is 'the spark' at play. I believe that we all judge people on looks way too much, when really if we gave people who were not our 'type' a chance or got to know someone who on first meeting we didn't find physically attractive, we would be so much more lucky in love. What can happen sometimes is that initially the girl/or guy doesn't find him/her physically attractive, but as she gets to know him/her and he/she is funny, kind, sweet and witty, he/she realises that he/she is actually falling for him/her. If each had not given the other a chance because there was initially no attraction, BANG, opportunity for a true love would have been lost. You can go sit on the couch on Saturday night eating your ice cream while watching re-runs of *The Bachelor* as you sulk in your single state, while the love of your life may be driving away thinking, 'Damn, I wish she at least had given me a chance...'

A dating point to remember:
Something girls have is their checklist, which lists all of the qualities a man she dates/marries must have. E.g., before I stopped going by my list, the traits on mine were blonde/brown hair, blue eyes, tattoos, smartass, fun, muscles, six-pack. If he doesn't check enough points on your list he doesn't get a chance or is put in the friend zone, full stop. What I'm going to say right now is a massive thing – I think all girls SHOULD GET RID OF THEIR CHECKLISTS. You close your mind to soooo many people if you only date people who match up to your check list. If you want to find the love of your life, give the next guy who tries with you three dates. (My friends know this as 'Megan's three-date rule'.) If you don't feel anything after three dates, sure leave it but we need to start giving guys we don't 'think' we'd be attracted to a chance. Most of the time the love of your life is not who you think but who you actually least expect it to be.

So what are we waiting for? Give that lawyer a chance if you are usually into bad boys; give the computer programmer a chance even if you think you'd rather stare at a brick wall than listen to the smallest thing about computer programming; and what the heck, give that neighbour who's been hitting on you for years a chance. You honestly never know where giving someone a chance will take you. ☺

Cons

- A lot of guys (and girls too for that matter) use Tinder for a 'quick root'
- People can easily fake who they really are. Have you seen those t-shits that say 'you looked better online'?
- I personally believe that the actual human connection is so important.
- It can be dangerous...often some of us forget about the safety of things when our head may be clouded by the guy with 'the hottest tinder photo ever'. All you want to do is meet up, hang out, get to know him and whatever else. But we do need to remember that going to a random guy's house by ourselves CAN be dangerous (there was a recent murder of a young 17-year-old girl in Doncaster, Melbourne), especially if this is done at night. If you want to meet him, **most definitely** stay on the safe side and try to meet in daylight in a public place, say for coffee or something and have several dates in public places before you go to his house. But this may not work, as he may just want you to go over to his house straight away (from what my friends have told me and my experience of Tinder this is usually the case). So if you must, must, must go and pretty much can't say no to the super-hot guy whose short Tinder bio shows that you both have so much in common and you have stalked him on Facebook, and thought

about how your name sounds with his last name, then go, but, if I was you, I suggest you:

1. Drive yourself in case you feel uncomfortable and want to leave right away
2. Bring your mobile (with battery); this one shouldn't be too hard as the majority of us these days have our smart phones pretty much glued to us 24/7.
3. TELL SOMEONE WHERE YOU ARE GOING and what time you are expecting to be back. If you don't wanna tell your mum that you are just going to meet some cute guy you swiped right on Tinder, who lives only three kilometres away, that's cool (and understandable), but at least tell a few trusted girl/guy friends or even siblings. Your safety is super important and you don't want to end up like that girl who was locked up in the basement of some man's house for ten years.

4. Stick to your word. It is so easy to get caught up in the moment with a guy, especially if he is subtly (or not so subtly) trying some sexual advances on you. He wants it…you are unsure but kinda want it. But you just don't know if you want it enough to go there. Decide as you are on your way there how far you are willing to go tonight AND STICK TO YOUR WORD. You have respect for yourself and just because he is like an 11/10 in hotness this doesn't entitle him to do whatever he wants with you. Stand your

> ground and decide how far you are willing to go. And please try to remember that boys will say ANYTHING to get in your pants, even if it is lying through their teeth. When they want something most of them will twist every word they say correctly to get it. But seriously as I have said like 1000 times in this book so far ACTIONS SPEAK LOUDER THAN WORDS. If his actions don't match up to his words you know which to go by.

He may try the 'Oh babe, you can come to my family do this weekend', or 'Our babies would look really cute', or 'I can't wait to introduce you to my mum', sort of lines. (This is not just for Tinder; this is dating in general.) Maybe he means it all but probably he's putting those thoughts about the future in your head so you will think that you are the 'One' for him but ultimately he only wants to get in your pants. If he thought all of that about you and was serious about it, don't you think he would be picking YOU up for dinner, taking you to a nice restaurant downtown and paying for your meal? This would all be to try to impress you, rather than having you drive to HIS house, to lie on his bed in his messy, smelly room 'watching movies'? I'm not trying to dull your sparkle/burst your bubble or anything but I sure know that if he was planning to be my future husband, I would be expecting a lot more than a movie in his room for one of our first dates.

You know what you deserve, don't settle for less, especially if you think he's amazing. The more amazing he is, the LESS you should be settling for anything but the best. Amazing guys generally get girls falling at their feet and doing whatever they want whenever they want. That is exactly how you are going to stand out. NO, NO! I'm not saying by doing whatever he wants whenever he wants. I'm saying you are going to do the opposite and make him work for you. He's going to say, 'Hey, this girl's really cool. She's different from the other girls. If I want her I'm going to have to lift my game to try to impress her.' Haven't you heard the saying,

If she's amazing she won't be easy; if she's easy she won't be amazing; If she's worth it you won't give up. If you give up, you're not worthy.
– Bob Marley

why does he deserve you?!

Make him prove himself to YOU; why is he lucky enough to be your boyfriend? Not what can I do to make him like me. Change your psychology/mindset; change your life.

- People can easily not be who they say they are. I know of a guy who actually Googles photos of 'hot guys' and puts them up on his Facebook as his profile picture and gets younger girls to talk to him. I know – pretty messed up hey? But that's what's out there these days, and we really have to make sure we stay on the safe side. It's a crazy world...be careful.

I also know a friend who was asked by a guy to send pics of her. So what did she do? She Googled 'hot ass' and sent that to him. Remember that people can and will trick you...not everyone is as honest as you in this world.

If I am ever asked to send a nude, I respond with 'Wanna see my pussy?', then send them a picture of my cat. Haha. That way 1. He finds it funny. 2. He doesn't get annoyed because I didn't send him an actual nude and 3. He sees that you can be witty (which is a trait a lot of guys like in girls). Then 4. He realises he's not going to get one from you and gains respect for not only your choice but you.

Nude Pics

As I said earlier, in this day and age most boys/guys will do anything: 1. Try to get in your pants and 2. Try to get you to send them nude pics of you to them and 3. Basically anything that stimulates them sexually they will try for with you. With nude pics if you are wondering what they are, it's where a girl takes a suggestive photo in little/no clothes and sends it to a guy...even photos with clothes on can be considered raunchy. This could potentially cause the same harm to your reputation as a nude pic.

Anyway, it is entirely up to you if you decide to do/send them. Some people enjoy sending them a lot and get a lot of satisfaction out of this. I know a few of my friends and a lot of girls I know have, and when I say 'know', I mean I 'know' them because of the nudes they have sent to people that have circulated around the towns I live near, and almost everyone knows them now for the few photos they have taken and sent. These pictures can really get out of hand and may be something you could regret for life.

DON'T EVER feel pressure or compromise your own values to make a guy like you.

If it's against your morals and beliefs to send one but some guy who you really like is pestering and begging you for one, don't give in. Stand by what you believe and don't budge, despite how many times he's called you 'beautiful' and 'the only one for him'. As I said earlier, boys can and will say anything to get what they want from a girl...especially if it can increase the blood flow to between their legs.

Being a guy's slave and doing whatever he wants will not make him like you more. What it will do is make him take you for granted and maybe even use you for what he wants until the girl he really likes and wants to be with comes along, and he'll drop you.

> *You can cook with diamond oil and do back flips in bed but if he has no respect for you, he has no respect for you.*
>
> ***– Unknown***

You'll most likely end up being a time-filler and it won't be too long before some other girl replaces you.

Now it can be really difficult when the guy you have the BIGGEST crush on asks you to send him nudes and you agree and send them. It's really easy to think 'I do so much for this guy... I'm so nice to him...why doesn't he like ME and he likes her?' (There is a reason one of the most popular dating books is called *Why Men Love*

Bitches and a reason why men like to play football/sports. It's because they like a challenge.) How would you feel if the next thing you know, you overhear him saying to his mates, or worse, the girl he likes/has heaps of respect for, 'Oh, (insert your name here), she wants me so bad, I have her wrapped around my finger; she basically begs me to look at her naked in nude photos'. YOU DON'T WANT THAT.

One of my guy friends told me that he categorises girls. He decides whether the girl is a 'root and boot' girl or a 'keeper'. What puts a girl into the 'keeper' category you may ask?

How much respect she has for herself.

I remember when I was in school and one of my close friends sent nudes to a guy (mind you, he was the hottest guy that everybody wanted) and they literally got around the entire year level, not only on guys' phones but girls' phones as well. She was humiliated. I remember when she was too scared to even come to class as she was SO embarrassed. What we need to never forget is that people can be cruel and not everyone has the same morals as you. Once a photo message is sent to even just one person it can be sent around so easily. He may have just sent it to his best mate and then he could have sent it to a few of his mates from other schools and then next thing you know everyone could have seen you naked/partially naked.

BUT when you are in the moment, even the fact that your crush is texting you drives you a little bit crazy, you can't stop smiling. Your brain feels like mush while you also feel on top of the world. It is VERY hard to think logically in this moment. We have all heard

the song *Crazy Little Thing Called Love* by Queen. Even scientists have proven that when you are in love with someone, you experience a similar rush to what you get when you do cocaine. It's addictive and you want more... Love is addictive. And therefore when you are in this state of mind and on your 'lover's high', it may seem like a great idea to take a hot/nude/partially naked snap of yourself thinking, 'Oh, what's the harm? I want him to like me', hashtag it with #foryoureyesonly then regret sending it the second you click 'Send'.

Now the last thing I want to sound like is a mum here, but when you do get older/even just old enough to work, if an employer or even a part time/casual jobs boss sees or even hears about your nude snaps, you can almost definitely kiss away your job. It looks terrible for the company and therefore no job for you.

Also at the time, you may not know what career you wish to pursue when you get older. You may want to be a school teacher, a lawyer or even a psychologist, a police woman or work with kids in any way. If the employer sees or hears about your naked snaps he/she would find it inappropriate to hire someone who was to work with kids, who has naked photos of themselves floating around all over the internet.

Now I'm not trying to ruin your fun here but what I am trying to do is to make you think twice, even three times, before potentially ruining your future career/reputation/life just because you want to impress some guy you have a crush on in high school/when you are younger.

YOU NEED TO THINK LOGICALLY AND CLEARLY IF AND WHEN YOU ARE ASKED TO DO THIS.

Remember that being a slut or at least acting like one will not get him to like you more. You don't want to be seen as a piece of meat; you want guys to treat you right. It will be worth the restraint.

In our younger years and even all throughout our lifetimes, reputations and judgments can be made so easily. School is practically a battlefield for this to happen and sending/doing nudes is a surefire way to get a bad rep fast.

Even though your hormones are nuts, please pinky promise me that you will 2nd 3rd and even 4th think before you send a nude snap. This also includes if you have any of other people. Put yourself in their shoes. Would you appreciate it if someone was sharing YOUR naked body with their girlfriends/cousins/guy friends? No way, so think before you send any sort of nudes, even if it isn't of you/you don't even know the person you have the naked snap of. If you do decide you want to send one to someone (of you) don't put your face in it or any distinguishing tattoos/piercings/dermals that you may have, because if you do, most people will straight away click that it's you.

'Did you see the pic of her? She was literally naked!'

A few points to remember – READ THIS IF YOU ARE CONSIDERING SENDING A NUDE PIC. (Don't just think it won't happen to you either, because I know so many people who have sent them and think, 'Oh that won't happen to ME'... two months later their pic is viral.) Maybe even highlight this so when you are in the moment of being asked you can quickly turn to this page and read these points:

- Be prepared for bad things to happen.
- Be prepared for the photo to circulate.

- Be prepared for even your parents and teachers to see it.
- Be prepared for not only your girlfriends to see it but many girls who you don't even know.
- Be prepared for your managers/future managers at work to see it.
- Be prepared for the world to see it; if it goes online that's what you are in for.
- Be prepared for your grandparents, aunties, cousins to see it.
- Be prepared for your pastor at church to see it.
- Be prepared for the children at the local primary school to see it.
- Be prepared for virtually anyone to see it!

The exact same things that I have mentioned about nude pictures also apply to videos that you may want to record with a guy too. Yes, it may seem 'fun' and 'naughty' at the time but it may not be so 'fun' when you never hear the end of 'Oh (insert YOUR name here), the girl from the sex tape'.

Back to Social Media

Whether it be on Facebook/Insta or whatever the social media craze at the time, remember that people will probably at one time or another comment/talk badly about you. As hard as it is, when people hit a nerve and say something mean/nasty about what you may be already insecure about yourself, we must remember that happy people are not mean to others. Being mean to you makes others feel that they have power over you and also makes them feel better about themselves. It's actually a reflection of THEIR insecurities they have themselves. As I read in the article 'Beyond Happiness: The Upside to Feeling Down' found in *'The Upside of Negative Emotions'* issue of *Psychology Today* magazine, we can actually use the envy we feel to push OURSELVES to become more successful. *'Envy – even more than admiration ignites our ambition to overcome a sense of inferiority and achieve future success.'*

Let's use our envy we feel for good not bad!

Being mean to her isn't going to make you any better.

Overall, I do admit that I love and am obsessed with social media, but I hope that this chapter has opened your eyes as to how easily bad things can come from it. It could be negative self-esteem/body image, jealousy, nude pictures, comparing ourselves to others and stalking people as you can always see where someone is tagged in and go to where they are. (I shouldn't be putting ideas in everyone's heads). If all of this gets out of hand it can pretty much lead to sadness and even depression. Try to remember that the people you stalk on social media are not perfect in real life, as much as they appear to be on social media. Try not to compare yourself and your life to only the good half of someone's real life. It's only going to make you feel like crap. REMEMBER PHOTOSHOP EXISTS. Next time you jump on social media, realise that, yes, it is great for contacting friends and sharing information but try to never forget that it's not real life. It's a carefully constructed illusion which makes other people appear better than they really are.

Don't let others' illusions make you feel crap about your own life because if you really knew their problems you'd want your own life back ASAP.

- *Posting on social media while socialising is antisocial.*
  – Unknown
- When someone gets their phone out and replies and goes on social media when I am with them I think, 'Aw, are they more important than me?'
- *Focus on how to be social...not how to do social.*
  – Jay Baer
- *May your life someday be as awesome as you pretend it is on Facebook*
  – Unknown

Social media is more about sociology and psychology than technology.
– Brian Solis

Boys/Heartbreak

Your heart isn't plastic, and it isn't a toy,
but if you want it broken...
give it to a boy.
– Unknown

Now I'm going to start with my first, biggest, most painful story of my teenage heartbreak. Just so that we all know, most people will go through a sucky as heartbreak. There was this boy who I used to see at the train station on my way home from school almost every day. He was a super cute blondie/brown-haired surfer looking guy with big blue eyes, who was always either holding a footy or kicking it around the station while waiting for the bus/train with his mates. You may remember 'the guy I saw at the station' from previous chapters. He was that boy every 16-year-old girl in the local area wanted. After checking him out religiously every day after school, one day my dream came true and he came and asked for my number! I was so ecstatic. We messaged for a bit but then I ran out of phone credit, lol. About a week later I was on the bus to school. I looked out the window (I was on the early bus for some reason so I was by myself on the bus) AND HE BLEW ME A KISS... At this moment after all the idolisation (admiring him from afar) I'd done I was beginning to like this blonde surfer dude who was always holding his footy, and I wanted to get to know him more.

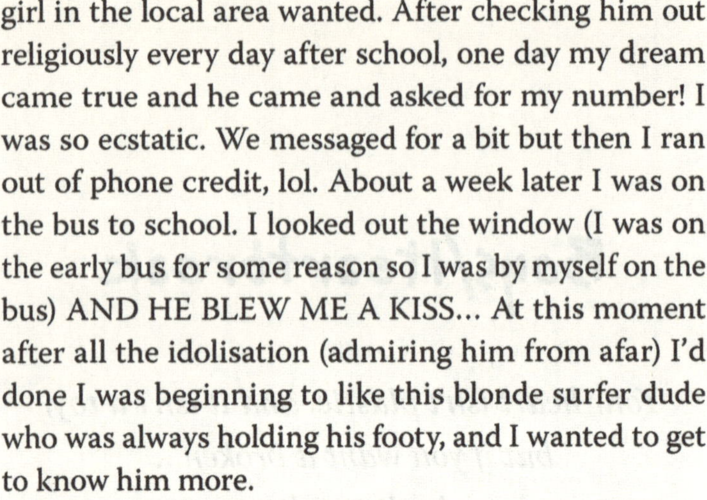

When I was at the station we would always look over at each other, until one day he started throwing rocks at me. I knew it was just games. It wasn't like he was throwing boulders at me, so I took it as a compliment and secretly enjoyed it. I loved boys (especially him) even when they were being mean. There was a difference between this playfully throwing rocks at me and actually throwing rocks at me to hurt me. And I came to the conclusion that it was just to get my attention. (Maybe he genuinely DID want to hurt me but I was deluded by the fact that I thought he was doing it to get my attention, but I guess I'll never know.) Then suddenly, I don't even know how it happened, the tables quickly turned and I was the one chasing HIM. He was acting not interested anymore and I had NO idea why. So what did I do?

I took matters into my own hands and added him on MSN (which was like Facebook chat-instant messenger) and I was that girl who spoke to him ALL the time. He spoke to me first, no joke, once. And at the station I was suddenly the one who was always going up to him.

He wasn't trying with me anymore, so I, being young and ignorant, tried even harder...not having what you want drives you more to want it. According to Helen Fisher in Cupid's Comeuppance *article published on PsychologyToday.com* it's called 'frustration attraction', which means 'wanting the person more when barriers are increased'. https://www.psychologytoday.com/articles/200409/cupids-comeuppance

I honestly wasted SO much time trying to get this boy to notice me again that I was acting waaaaayyy too keen and as much as I hate to admit it even desperate for his attention. And this is what scared him off. (Now that I think about it, if a boy was acting as keen as I was acting towards him I would be running for the hills asap.) But we all learn from our mistakes.

One night I went to a deb after-party I knew that he was going to be at...I was so excited coz I was like 'Oh yay, finally we are going to kiss'. :D Anyway, to my surprise I got there and ten minutes in, I saw him hooking up with another girl in the corner of the room, hands on her ass, in her hair and everything. Ten minutes later he was kissing another girl, and no joke, another ten minutes later he was kissing ANOTHER girl. Man, words can't even describe how hurt I was that night. I came to kiss him and there he was hooking up with so many other girls right in front of my face. Ouch. He held my hand for a little bit around the deb after-party but never actually kissed me. I guess I should have been happy with that. I shouldn't have even wanted to kiss him anyway, coz I'd be tasting the 1000s of other girls he'd kissed that night. But I still wanted to. I was crazy. I know. At the end of the after-party I went to say goodbye to him and we had this forced peck on the lips (which mind you was SO awkward). I initiated it and most definitely should not have. He invited me to stay the night at his house that night and I was thinking, 'Yeah, right buddy, you've kissed like a million girls tonight and you think I'll come back to yours to do you know what...keep dreaming.' I was interested and super keen on the guy but I wasn't going to give up my boundaries. I knew my boundaries and I knew that he wanted one thing from me. As much as I absolutely adored him I wasn't going to have sex with him until he treated me right, was my boyfriend and wasn't kissing thousands of other girls at after-parties.

Having respect for yourself and knowing what you will and will not take from a guy is so important when growing up.

- I know so many girls who have thrown away their virginity trying to get a guy to like them.
- Be warned. Guys will often leave once they get what they want from you, either sexual stuff or sex. (This is not entirely the guy's fault. Guys' brains are different to ours and they can separate emotions from sex whereas

girls' brains are wired so that when they have sex, oxytocin fires in the brain. Oxytocin will help/make you fall emotionally for the guy especially after you sleep with him, so if you have just slept with a guy, watch out, because as much as you THINK you aren't emotionally attached to him, it's hard to beat the science of your brain chemicals.)

- Don't just throw it away because you 'want it gone' or 'everyone's doing it'. There is nothing wrong with being a virgin despite what people say or if they tease you. You are ready when YOU are ready. Wait for the right guy. (See But, I'm Still a Virgin! Chapter.)

Anyway back to the story. So I would go to work and every single shift I would hope that he would walk past, come in and say hi. (He lived near the local plaza that I worked at.) He used to only ever walk past and wave, which kept a little bit of hope still in my mind that he was still keen. I know it was just a wave but that was enough to keep me still interested. He seriously had me wrapped around his little finger.

As you know, I even caught the early train in the morning so that he could wave to me from the other side of the train station in hope that he would come over and say hi. We do absolutely insane things when we like someone. I guess it's just all part of growing up.

I did this for a while and realised that he wasn't coming over to say hi. All he would do was wave. I wanted things to move faster so I took this situation into my own hands. I got my best friend at the time to come over to my house (on a school night, ohhhhh naughty) so we would catch the early train together and catch the same bus as he and his friend did, in the hope that they would come and talk to us. This seemed like a brilliant plan at the time.

So it turned out that we missed the train. (This is a recap of the story I told earlier in book.) But we were two 16-year-old (desperate) girls on a mission to get these boys to love us. So waiting for the next train would have meant that we would miss seeing them and we were NOT going to let that happen. So what did we do? WE CAUGHT A CAB at 7.00am to the train station (mind you, only two stations away). It cost us $20. We could have paid the same amount of money and actually got to school. But that wasn't the plan. The plan was to catch the bus with them. And once we got out of our cab at the station, the bus was waiting there and we got on. The whole bus ride was SOO awkward. We didn't even talk to them. We were too scared to. We just pretended that they didn't exist and they kept yelling at us, trying to talk to us. MAN, NEVER AGAIN.

After the bus trip I realised that there was not much more I could do to get him to like me properly back. So what do you think I did? Nope, I still wasn't ready to give up yet. So I decided I'd do one more thing to see if there was any hope left. I know what you're thinking – Megan, stop, please don't embarrass yourself anymore! As I said I used to work at the local shopping centre (plaza) and he worked at a video shop which was right near the plaza. One day at work when I was supposed to be taking the rubbish out I sneaked up to his video shop when he was working. He was busy with customers so I had a quick look around at the new to-rent movies. It was weird because the first movie I noticed was *He's Just Not That Into You*. I should have taken this as a sign, but I just shrugged it off. I finally got to chat to him at work and, ahhhhhhh man, I'm actually embarrassed to even tell you, but I had a heart-shaped post-it note from work that I took up to him. I asked if I could borrow a pen and wrote 'To Dale I like you' and drew a love-heart. (I thought the word love might be a bit full on. Haha. Not that the note wasn't anyway.) I signed it 'Megan' and stuck it on his chest. In my head it was a cute thing to do. He didn't really say anything back. Then I left the shop and tried not to think about it. I didn't take it as complete rejection…yet. So the next night he was on MSN and we started chatting (obviously I started the convo) and I asked him what he had done with the note in hope that he'd stuck it on his bedroom wall. The convo went like this:

Me: So what'd you do with the note?

Him: Oh, I chucked it in the bin.

Me: Oh, okay.

Him: Look, I have a girlfriend. Sorry.

AHHHHHHHH CRAP! I thought, while my heart broke into 20,000 miniscule pieces.

It was time to get over him once and for all. It took me about a year to properly get past him but I did eventually get there and I am so happy that I did.

He did say sorry and was nice about it...but even though he was nice about the rejection, that doesn't stop heartbreak. I deleted his number and MSN and we honestly have not spoken since.

A few years ago I did see him at a nightclub but I wasn't interested... I'd changed, he'd changed, and yeah, we'd moved on. Although when I saw him at the nightclub something I did want to do was actually THANK him (I didn't though) because, as crazy as it sounds, he did teach me about love and life, like not being so desperate, to focus on school/study and not get distracted by boys.

Although it was really hard, I never did hate him, or the girl he was with. What I hated was the situation.

My studies were greatly affected due to my huge crush on this guy, who mind you wasn't even my boyfriend, and frankly wasn't ever going to be my boyfriend. At this point I was in my second last year of high school. I failed two of my six subjects and the only thing I really cared about was looking hot so that Dale would like me. I wasted hours in front of the mirror doing my hair and makeup before school only to see this guy for maybe max ten minutes at the train station. I would get up at 6.00 to catch the 7.00 train when I could have been catching the 8.30 bus to school just so that he could look across to me at the station. (Trust me, I am NOT a morning person.) It was crazy. I was crazy and that's what your first huge crush will most likely do to you. Don't worry, you're not alone. I let my hormones of my first crush literally take over my life.

Sometimes goodbye is the only and best thing you can do.
– Megan Street

I was even planning on leaving school to study hairdressing just so that I could be at the same TAFE campus as him. I look back on all this and realise that yes…I was an idiot.

But, after the heartbreak, I really sat down and thought about what I wanted to do and decided that I was going to stay in school and go to uni to study teaching, as I loved and enjoyed children and have a huge passion for helping people through education. And to this day I am so thankful that I did.

This leads me to another heartbreak story: When I was 12 (yeah I know realllllllly young), my first year of high school, I was quite shy and nervous and still trying to even just get used to the whole new high school life. Although I was what you'd call 'popular', I was like the queen bee's sidekick who did everything for her. One day after school, I went to my primary school friend's house. I'd kept in touch with her because she went to a high school ages away from where we lived. She'd got her school photos back and decided to show me everyone in her class at her new private high school. There he was, standing in the back row, tall, wearing a bottle-green school shirt, wind blowing in his hair.

He was an 11/10 guy who was literally SO amazingly attractive. I had to immediately know his name. My friend told me it was Wilson Green. She told me that he was a troublemaker who was a massive jerk... but that didn't stop me. I was a 12-year-old with a fast developing schoolgirl crush. Apparently he would wag school all the time, throw things at people and basically bully almost everyone in the class. She had him on MSN, so I asked her for his MSN address and added him (kind of like adding someone on Facebook). After that we started talking and he was **so rude**. I asked him if he was going to the Bluelight disco (the cool place to go when you were 12). Even though he went to a school ages away he actually lived in my local area as well – and he said yes! Obviously I was going to go and meet him. I was soo excited. I went out to my fave clothing shop when I was 12 (Supré of course) and bought the hottest most 'in' ruffle skirt and halter top in pink, as pink was my favvveee colour. I already had my pink and white sk8r shoes ready – Gallaz, which were a sort of punk/Avril Lavigne style. So now I was set and ready to meet this 11/10 boy...on the night I felt a million bucks! I was set and ready and prepped myself to dance with him (dancing at the Bluelight was where you had your arms around the guy's neck and his around your waist/hips. Depending how intimate and close you were, bodies were either touching or spread apart, in my case usually spread apart because I was 12 and all boys, except for Wilson, had cooties). So when we got there my friend and I searched everywhere for Wilson; then *to my horror* we found him dancing in the middle of the Bluelight disco WITH MY BEST FRIEND...the queen bee of my school. I wasn't annoyed at her; she had no idea I liked him (well liked who I thought he was anyway. I hardly even knew the kid). But that moment broke my heart. Those two were dancing together in the middle of the disco and instead of his hands being on her hips they were on her ass ☹, with crowds circling them, disco lights flashing, music blaring and then me, just an innocent heartbroken bystander. Even writing this over ten years later it hurts to think about that moment.

But just you wait – it gets even worse:

Later that night, I thought that I'd still try my luck and dance with him. So we went to find him around the Bluelight. By this stage, I'd even folded up one of the ruffles on my skirt as I thought if my skirt was shorter he might like me. (Trust me ladies, dressing like a slut won't work, and if it does it's only short lived attention.) Then my friend saw him, tapped him on the shoulder, and said to him, 'Will you dance with her?' and pointed at me. There was a long pause. Then he looked me up and down (very obviously mind you) and said, 'nup,' and walked off. My heart broke into 10,000,000 tiny little pieces. I could feel tears welling up in my eyes. It literally felt like my heart was getting ripped out of my chest... like in this video. LINK HERE https://www.youtube.com/watch?v=z3Ef1WhfBzo or simply YouTube 'Bart

getting heart ripped out of chest'. It's the first one, and goes for about 20 seconds.

Then Wilson got kicked out of the Bluelight for starting a fight (I told you he was trouble). In saying all this he looked so cute in his light blue shirt and with his pouty, plump red lips. Even though I was shattered I didn't give up...not that easily anyway. We spoke a bit more on MSN and he was actually unaware that he'd rejected me at the Bluelight. So my friend and I thought that it'd be a good idea to go to the local festival, which we knew he would be at just because I wasn't going to give up this amazing guy THAT easily. We found him and his mates watching the skateboarders. We sat down near them. I was wearing my hot 'flared jeans', a cool flying eagle jumper and my hair was in plaits. He saw us and I blew him a kiss as I'd seen models and my best friend the queen bee do it and guys seemed to like it. So I assumed it would be a great flirting move, but unfortunately for me it wasn't. His friends and he all just pointed and laughed at me. I was humiliated and soooooo embarrassed. After that I gave up on him. He clearly wasn't interested so I stopped trying.

Two years later:

It was my first day of year nine. I remember getting on the almost empty bus and there he was – that 11/10 boy Wilson Green, dressed in a new school's uniform ON THE BUS THAT I HAD TO CATCH EVERY DAY TO GET TO SCHOOL! He was a new kid at another one of my friend's school. I will never forget thinking, 'Oh man, he's going to make soooooo much fun of me and laugh at me now that he's on my bus.' I really thought he'd make my bus trips to and from school living hell. But luckily for me he didn't even click to the fact that it was me who used to chat to him on MSN, me that he laughed at when I blew him a kiss and me who he refused to dance with at the Bluelight disco. (Plus side to getting rejected!) So school went on, life went on and I had to look at this boy I literally wanted to marry every day at the bus stop and on the bus. Damn he had the cutest smile ever. I even had the front row seat to watch him actively chat up other girls in my year at my school while on the bus. I was SO jealous. He even made one of the 'popular' girls at my school his girlfriend. The years went on and I still saw this guy every day on the way to and from school. (I even thought he was hot when he had heaps of pimples and was a horny 16 year old who actually attempted to hump the seats on the bus a few times. He was apparently showing his mates how hard he would 'bang his gf on the weekend'.) Luckily by this stage I liked other guys, had other boyfriends and he had other girlfriends. He went to a few parties that I went to. We got along but hardly knew each other and there was absolutely no way in the world that I was going to tell him about the past. It was way too embarrassing for me!

As we approached our final years at high school, groups were no longer seen as popular or unpopular and I wasn't as unpopular as I had been when young (after being popular I turned into a bit of a loser – I discuss this in Friends [Bitches] Chapter); in fact, people were calling me 'cool'. (I have no idea why – maybe it was because I knew a lot of people outside school.) It was weird coz I thought that I was a dork! I was being asked to almost every party every weekend where there was drinking and boys, no parents and sometimes Wilson!

Then something amazing happened. Wilson asked if I would catch the connecting train to the local shopping centre with him (just as friends). Now I know it's such a small thing but I thought it was a miracle that the guy who'd rejected and hurt me so much in the past actually wanted to spend time with me. I was so happy, not because I liked him, but it just felt great for someone I used to want SO badly and had the hugest crush on to want to hang out outside of school with me ☺. So we caught the train together and have been in love ever since. No, I'm totally kidding! He ditched me as soon as our bus got into the train/bus station terminal to hang out with some other people.

When I got to my final year, a lot of my close friends dropped out of school to study at TAFE (similar to university but more practical), but I stayed at school as I had a goal to finish year 12. A lot of people bullied me and I hardly had any really close friends. I'm not going to lie. It was really hard. I often got called names such as slut, dumb, and idiot. Even though I had my good friends out of school, the bullying in school got to me and really upset me a lot as I felt as though no one was truly there for me. I also sucked at standing up for myself.

Some of the things people said didn't bother me as I knew the truth, but some things really did hit a nerve and I would go home and cry about it. There are two things I remember about when I was being bullied in my final year. Wil (Wilson) got along well with the guys at my school as they all caught the bus together. They bullied me so he joined in too. He had just got on the bus in his prissy private school uniform and said to me (I didn't have ANY sort of crush on him at this time), 'Why do you even bother studying? It's not like you'll ever be smart enough to get into university.' (I was at a public school that he looked down on.) I was insecure about not being academic enough and this comment really hit a nerve, especially when I was already feeling down from the bullying I'd dealt with during school that day. The other time was when Wilson and his mate, trying to be funny, poured a whole packet of cocoa they must have stolen from their school food tech room all over me when I was waiting for my train at the train station after school. It went in my hair and all over my clothes and I was completely covered in cocoa. Now that I look back it was kind of funny, but at the time I couldn't stop crying. It was physical bullying that I couldn't get away from. This boy reallllllly did know how to push my buttons.

Anyway, so school finished and I was looking forward to the future and was actually so excited to get away the bullying I'd dealt with in school and Wilson and his mates who gave me more crap on the bus. The next year (first year out of school) I went to a few gatherings and I saw Wil. He looked different but still attractive. We exchanged a few 'Hi, how are you?'s. I was dating other people; he was dating someone else.

Three years went by and I decided to start working at the local gym and was told that Wil worked there too. I was like yeah cool it'd be good to see him, see what he's up to and also to show him how happy I was with myself and my life at that point in time. I kind of had a 'success is the best revenge' mindset. I also decided that I would tell him how much he broke my heart when I was 12 when he didn't dance with me at the Bluelight disco, as I was wayyyyy over it and was casually seeing/hanging out with a famous sports star at the time. I thought it would be funny to tell him as I've been too embarrassed to speak out my entire life. (We were both 20 at this stage.) After a few shifts I saw him talking to a hot girl at the gym but I knew her and knew that they were just friends. We all said 'Hey' and he said I looked good and he flirted a little bit. I didn't think much of this because that's just his personality, a fun, easy-going flirty kind of guy. As the night went on, it was actually kind of weird – Wilson was acting really strangely, almost like a little boy who wanted attention: throwing a rag around that he was using to clean, trying to whip me with the rag and basically just being silly. It was really strange. I actually thought to myself that I couldn't believe I used to have the biggest crush on this guy. I know it's mean, but he had a massive beard in which I genuinely thought the entire cast of '*A Bug's Life*' was living and he also really needed to wash his hair. However, he was definitely still super funny and had an awesome personality. We kept working and he kept trying to distract and flirt with me. I didn't flirt back at all. I just thought to myself that this boy who used to be so cool, mean and tough is now a bit more of a loser who loved to smoke weed like all the time. We both ended up finishing our shifts and I was walking up to the tea room with Wilson and another guy we worked with and Wil kind of joked about taking me out on a date. I laughed because I thought, 'This guy cannot be serious. He was a bully to me in our bus days, not to mention rejected me in the past'. We walked into the tea room and after eight years I spilt the beans. I told him that I'd had the biggest crush on him and that he refused to dance with me at the Bluelight disco. I even mentioned that I hitched my skirt up for him. He laughed and said, 'That would have been hot but no way would I reject you.' I just replied, 'Haha, well you did.' He didn't bother me at all or make me fall back into liking him. This bully/heartbreaker wasn't going to shake me, no matter what he said/did.

Or so I thought.

After work you sometimes sit down with workmates and have something to eat that's on the communal table while chatting. It was really weird because the only one I was interested in talking to was Wil, even though there were other people I knew who worked at the gym too. We all spoke about life, what we were doing, who was pregnant, who was on drugs – that sort of thing and somehow it was brought up that Wil had had depression for a while for many reasons. But he said the main reason was because someone close to him (his mum) had committed suicide about a year ago. I sat shocked at what I'd just heard as even though this boy had been mean to me in the past, I did still care for him. For a second, I tried to put myself in his shoes, but honestly I couldn't even begin to imagine how hard that would have been for both him and his brothers. By this stage everyone was packing up our food and leaving the communal table. I said to Wil, 'You need a hug and despite how mean you have been in the past to me I always thought you were a cool person.' (Well of course I did. He was one of my first biggest crushes.) Then he asked me what I was doing the next day. I was flat-out busy with uni work that I'd left till the last minute. He said, 'Let me take you on a date.' I was shocked. I didn't know what to feel. Part of me wanted to laugh in his face, part of me wanted to say no way, but what I did say was, 'Yes.' I told him not tomorrow but maybe next week. He got my number and went from there. I didn't actually want to go on a 'date' with him at all. Physically I didn't find him my 'type' but he has this charm about him that draws you in.

You can resist beauty but you can't resist charm.
– Audrey Tautou

After chatting to my bestie about it I decided that I was going to see him as a friend as I wanted to make sure he was okay especially after everything he'd been through pretty recently. I am also a massive believer in forgiveness as well so I was interested to see if he was truly sorry for what he'd said and done to me in the past – especially the cocoa thing. We also have the same taste in music, know so many of the same people and have a lot of similar interests. I knew that we'd get along well. So basically I said yes because 1. I always had respect for Wil and did think he was a cool person and never followed the crowd and 2. Because I was put on the spot.

As I drove home, I'm not going to lie, my ego was quite high as I thought, 'Yeah, I can pick up boys at work.' We messaged a bit over the next week or so, just friends' stuff, no flirting. After I got back home from hanging out with the sports star, Wil messaged me, wanting to hang out. I decided that as soon as I hung out with Wil, I would tell him that we were hanging out as **just friends** – nothing more. I messaged him with 'Sure, let's go on a cruise.' (If he was a guy I was dating I wouldn't have settled for a cruise. I would have wanted him to properly take me out, but seeing we were just going to be hanging out as friends, it didn't really matter). When he picked me up I met him at the bottom of the driveway because my house is hard to find and he gave me the biggest hug hello. I actually thought he looked kind of cute in his trackies and ugg boots that were for two left feet ☺. He opened the car door for me and I got in and told him to drive really carefully because I'd been in a car crash and still freaked out a bit when in cars, especially because sometimes boys can be hoonish drivers. And I said to him, 'Wil, don't try and kiss me or anything. We are hanging out as just friends.' So he ignored that and took me down to the local oval and I lost my virginity to him. JUST KIDDING! But we did go and park down at the local oval and talked. We talked for a while and I literally had the best time. Hanging out with Wilson was actually heaps of fun. I was so interested to know about him and his life since his 'I'm the best; I go to a private school' days, especially about his depression, his mum's suicide, what he studies (believe it or not, Law, mind you.) and what he was doing now. He asked me a lot about my life too. It was insane how much we got along. Things were great between us and I thought, 'Awesome. I've found myself a new friend.' But then he goes 'Megan, I really want to kiss you.' I looked at him and said, 'Don't even think about it.' I was standing by what I had said earlier and I wasn't going to let him, although I did say to him that it felt 'different' with him than it did with most other guys... it was a weird feeling. I can't even describe it but a good weird. Then he said to me, 'Megan, I feel it too.' (He said my name so many times I thought he was reminding me that my name is Megan.) At that point I know it sounds silly but I looked into his eyes and gave in... Yep, I let my bully, the guy who shattered my heart into pieces and the guy who poured so much cocoa on me I could hardly breath, kiss me. It was strange. I felt a lot of things during the kiss. First of all, I felt annoyed at myself for giving in to him. I also felt kind of happy that I'd finally got the boy who'd broken my heart, while I was also feeling good because he actually wanted ME not the other way around. It almost felt like some kind of goal conquered. But then I realised what I was doing and pulled away (part of me wanted to keep kissing) and said, 'This is weird...we should stop.' I continued, 'Why is it different kissing you?' and he answered, 'Megan (yep again), we have good chemistry.' (If you want to have a positive influence on someone, use their name. People love hearing their name, and it helps them to warm to you and like you more. Again, thank you to Dale Carnegie's book *How to Win Friends and Influence People*.) We apparently had 'the spark'. We kept hooking up for a while after that...the strange thing was that I actually wanted to keep kissing. It was crazy. I went from thinking, 'Ew, you are so not my type' to 'Willllll, don't stop kissing me.' It was like he was an addiction... Let's not read in to this too much though, as it could have easily been the leftover nicotine in his mouth (he was a smoker). I mean, I'm not going to lie to you, I'd dated and kissed a few other guys before (not heaps I promise!), but had almost never felt anything like this. The next day I was on my high horse walking around uni with a massive smile on my face, not because I was casually hanging out with a sports star and was hopefully going to travel the world with him but because of Wilson. It was a weird feeling, like a new-found confidence, and I also couldn't stop thinking about him. I was like, 'NO WAY NO WAY NO WAY. I CAN'T BE BEGINNING TO FALL FOR WILSON GREEN – for the second time only eight years later....' Anyway the day went on and nothing more happened. The next day he messaged me with, 'Hey, let's hang out again.' I was super-duper looking forward to it so I went and I remember sitting there in his car with him thinking, 'Wow, I'd actually rather be with no one else right now other than you, not even the guy I've liked for three years. It was so crazy – not even my celebrity crush! We kissed again and yet again we couldn't stop. He tried to go further but I said, 'No way. Don't even think about it.' (This was super hard to say at time coz I was keen...if you know what I mean.) I kept pulling away and saying, 'This is weird and I don't even know if we should just stay friends.' (Clearly my actions were showing otherwise.) He was just telling me to relax. I'll never forget about when he dropped me home and we just couldn't stop kissing. (THIS IS SO EMBARRASSING AND I CAN'T

BELIEVE IM EVEN TELLING YOU GUYS THIS.) We both knew how silly we were being but we both also knew that it felt right. I let him kiss me for the final time, then left and said, 'Good bye Wilson.' He replied, 'My blood is bursting.'

Now as annoying as I'm going to be, this story actually doesn't go any further than this... I had a lot going on in life, both good and not so good, and wasn't ready to keep hanging out with Wil. It's been about two years now and we have drifted our separate ways. He's a great guy who I'll always love and have respect for, but both he and I are not ready to take anything further at this point in our lives.

I wanted to share this story as it just shows that things can change in a matter of years. People can and most likely will come back to you...especially boys when they realise what they lost/threw away in the past. The hard thing to do is to focus on improving yourself and not let other people bring you down, especially boys that you have crushes on. If someone doesn't like you right now, it's his/her loss and in a few years (or eight) they'll be back and it's up to you if you want to give them a chance or not.

A few lessons I have learnt from this heartbreak/love are:

- Whoever wronged you in the past can always come crawling back...especially boys when they realise they threw away someone like you!
- Show people that they should want to come back to you by living a great life, following your passions and dreams. Go after your

dream course, buy your dream car, work your dream part-time or full-time job. And don't ever give up on improving yourself...life is about learning and creating yourself.

- Try your very best to not get discouraged by what one person may say. That's their opinion and for all you know, they may be stepping on you to make themselves appear better and to ultimately feel better about themselves.
- Remember to try your best to forgive people
- *In this African tribe, when someone does something wrong, they take the person to the center of the village where the tribe surrounds him and for two days say all the good he has done. The tribe believes each person is good but sometimes makes mistakes, which are really a cry for help. They unite to reconnect him with his good nature. (So Beautiful).*
  – Unknown
- *If you want to see the brave look at those who can forgive, if you want to see the heroic look at those who can love in return for hatred.*
  – Bhagavad Gita
- *If grass can grow through cement, love can find you every time.*
  – Cher

What we need to remember is that if someone is mean/nasty towards us it is often almost always because they are upset with their life and/or themselves, or they feel jealous in some way or another. I have done this in the past and even sometimes now too. If I was a little bit jealous of a girl I would bitch about her and find one of her negative qualities to make myself feel better. It's crazy and stupid and whether we realise we do it consciously or simply do it unconsciously, the reasoning behind why we do it at the end of the day is we have all put other people down either to their face/behind their back out of deep-sown insecurity and unhappiness. I'll never forget when I walked into a party and girls I didn't even know/had never talked to me or even met me before started to bitch about me and give me a hard time. It used to upset me so much. And I used to think, 'What have I done to these girls to deserve this?' But now I've got to a point where I understand the psychology of other people to a greater extent and can see through meanness because *'What Suzie says of Sally says more of Suzie than of Sally – Remember that* – Unknown'. If negativity comes out of someone's mouth it shows more about them as a person than about you.

So anyway back to Willy: After many years of him making me cry and be upset and heartbroken, I have realised that this boy was simply troubled. Those who are nasty are actually the ones who need the most love. Now in saying this, and after getting to know Wil properly, and after we have both grown up a bit more from our bus days, I have to admit that I have the hugest amount of respect for him and consider him one of the most fun people to be around ever! He has overcome almost all of his meanness now and has become such an awesome person. I truly look up to him as he has gone through some pretty hard adversity and is still smiling...and best of all he always knows how to put a smile on everyone else's face. :)

Darkness cannot drive out darkness; only light can do that. Hate cannot drive out hate; Only love can do that.
– Martin Luther King Jr.

Try to not forget that it is important to try to love and understand those people who hurt you... I know it's very hard but whatever the reason, they are the people that actually need it.

Overall it is important to try to understand someone's situation, rather than just being mean back. There is almost always a reason which explains other people's behaviour.

So now that you have listened to me crap on about my teenage heartbreak you might be thinking, 'YEAH, you got your heart broken. Most of us have or will in our lives too. YEAH, we feel sorry for you and YEAH you acted like a huge idiot. But what's your point, girl? Is there actually any reason I just wasted the last say twenty minutes of my life reading about how your pretty little heart got broken by some hot guys?'

Now for the point of the chapter.

LESSONS LEARNED FROM A HEARTBREAK

Are you serious, Megan? What can I learn from getting my heart broken other than that boys suck – and boys are mean; they have no feelings; I'm never going to love again or I may as well just prepare myself to be a crazy cat lady and die alone!

Well, look at it like this. You can wallow in your own sorrows and feel sorry for yourself when you get heartbroken or you can learn lessons from it to make yourself better at dating, better with boys/men and overall a better person in general.

Only in darkness can you see the stars.
– Martin Luther King Jr.

Troubles are often the tools by which God fashions us for better things
– Henry Ward Beecher

(If you don't believe in God simply change it to *Troubles are what fashion us for better* things.)

Every cloud has a silver lining.
– Proverb

- Being/ acting/looking like a slut isn't going to get him to like you. At the time you think this will work and it may for a little while but he most likely won't respect you and do you really want to waste your time and years of youth with someone who doesn't respect you?
- Now as silly as it may sound, I am SO thankful that surfer/footy boy (Dale) broke my heart. It

helped me realise that I should NOT base my life on seeking the approval of not only men but other people in general.

- No matter how hard you try, sometimes who you like won't like you back. You can't change people and you can't force them into liking you.
- Don't act desperate...it will only push him further away
- Focusing on yourself and living a happy life that you want to be living will almost definitely make him second think letting you go.
- Following your passions and dreams is more important than any guy.

Some women choose to follow men, and some women choose to follow their dreams. If you're wondering which way to go, remember that your career will never wake up and tell you that it doesn't love you anymore.

– Lady Gaga

- At the time it feels like the end of the world... Trust me, it's not and you WILL get past it.
- Heartbreak gives you the motivation to be the BEST person you can be. Prove to that person that they lost someone amazing.

The best revenge is happiness, because nothing drives people more crazy than seeing someone actually living a good life-
– Unknown

- If he's not talking to you or trying with you, chances are he's not that interested. Try not to twist things around in your head like, 'Oh, he's just shy', or 'Oh, he's just playing hard to get'. If he likes you he will usually show it... I'm not saying this definitely though. Some guys will play the head games and make you think they are not keen when they really are... and sometimes he may like you but the timing is not right or he has other stuff in life to deal with in life. So just to contradict what I just said, sometimes even when he's NOT trying he still may be into you...but don't hold too much onto that hope. If he's not trying, the chances are high that he's not THAT into you.
- Let your heartbreak teach you lessons about what you could have done differently. E.g., for instance in my story I should not have acted so desperately for Dale's attention.

LEARN FROM YOUR MISTAKES

- Try to remember what is important (big picture) in life i.e., study, career, family, friends, you-time.
- At the time you may think he is the only guy who is so amazing and that you could never

love anyone as much as you do him. Trust me it will pass. There are others and most of all (and I know it's waaaaay overused but I'm saying it anyway), ***there are PLENTY more fish in the sea* – Proverb/saying/phrase.**

- Ask yourself if this will be important in five years.
- He will most likely come crawling back either sooner or years later. Boys realise what they've lost when they meet you again or run into you and see the amazing life you lead without them and the cool (not desperate) person you have become. They can't help but beg you for a date. Just imagine the boy who broke your heart begging you to give him another chance to take you out, wining and dining you at the most expensive restaurant. Sounds pretty good, huh? With the right mindset, goals and focus on the important things in life, all of your heartbreaks and crushes that didn't want you at the time can come crawling back.
- Remember to try not to hold grudges.
- Life isn't fair.
- Without heartbreak love would not be so great.
- We realise that it is important to find happiness within ourselves NOT through others (this is really hard but it is so important to remember). Try to not place your happiness in someone else's hands. It's not theirs to have…it's YOURS.
- LIFE GOES ON.

- The end of it makes room for the start of another guy... At the time you may feel that he is the only one out there for you...but if he was, he would like you back. Do you really want to spend your time with someone YOU think is amazing but who thinks that you're mediocre? No way! You deserve someone who thinks you are amazing and who you also think is amazing.
- *Boys are often like lollies – the best ones are bad for you.*

  – Megan Street
- You have been saved from the wrong person.
- At least you know you are not a psychopath... they can't feel love. You are lucky as some people don't even have the privilege to feel love.
- This is not the end of your love story.
- *Sometimes the hardest thing to let go of is actually something you never really had.*

  – Unknown (More on this in Unrequited Love chapter.)
- Someday this pain will be useful – **I know it**.
- Every instance of heartbreak can teach us lessons about the kind of love we really want.
- *One day someone will walk into your life and make you see why it didn't work with anyone else.*

  – Unknown
- *Sometimes it takes us love that doesn't last forever to show us lessons that will.*

  – Unknown

- *Sometimes cupid shoots the arrow at only one person instead of two.*
  – Unknown
- *You fall for one they fall for another; sometimes it's like dominoes.*
  – Unknown
- Most people will fall in love with someone who doesn't love them back, at some stage in their life. Don't worry you are not alone.
- SOMETIMES THE BEST PERSON FOR YOU IS STANDING RIGHT IN FRONT OF YOU.

When one door of happiness closes, another opens; but often we look so long at the closed door that we do not see the one which has been opened for us.
– Helen Keller

- The right guy may easily be the one you least expect.

HOW DO I KNOW IF HE'S SERIOUS ABOUT ME? (A quick and easy tip to work out if he's serious or you may just be 'on-the-side fun'.)

How you find out whether they are serious about you or not is through working out if your guy's **actions match his words**. E.g., he doesn't speak to you all week and only contacts you on Saturday nights/early hours of Sunday morning when he's drunk. When you ask him to hang out in the daytime say for lunch, he is always 'busy' or worse doesn't even respond to your text and when you guys finally do hang out the only offer he has is 'movies' at his place. But yet he's telling you that you are the 'most beautiful girl in the world', or 'so amazing he can't even deal', or you are 'the prettiest person to exist'. Then you sure as anything realise that his actions DON'T match up to his words and you can almost be sure you know exactly what he wants from you. Although it is sometimes disappointing, at least you have saved yourself some heartbreak.

If you do want him treating you with respect and actually meaning the words that come out of his mouth you can easily turn around the situation, if he is even worth your time/if you really do like him. You can do this by simply demanding the respect you deserve. No, no, no, I don't mean demanding as in going up to him yelling at the top of your lungs saying, 'I READ THIS BOOK AND IT TOLD ME YOU DON'T RESPECT ME BECAUSE YOUR ACTIONS DON'T MATCH UP TO YOUR WORDS. I NEED RESPECT FROM YOU ASAP.' What I mean is, pretty much in a nutshell, don't be so nice to him...even ignore him if he tries behaviour on you that you don't like/doesn't portray respect for you. *Men respond best to no contact* – Why Men Love Bitches. If he calls/texts you Saturday night wanting you to come over...don't even respond to his texts. If he asks you over for movies at his house, say ever so politely, *'I can't come round for movies at yours but I'd like to go out for lunch with you one day...you seem really cool.'* Remember to slip in the subtle compliment so he knows that you ARE interested in him but only interested in him if he treats you with the respect you deserve. It's also best to try to keep your hangouts in the daytime for the first few dates. That way, it makes him put you in the 'girl I respect' category rather than the 'girl I want to root and boot' category.

What we do sometimes need to remember is that there ARE exceptions to the rule...not very often but yes, they do occur. So if one of your girlfriend's guy was playing the not respectful card on her and his actions didn't match his words, but then three years later they are still together and engaged, you CAN go around thinking that if you let your guy treat you with little respect it will work out like that for you too. BUT my advice would be to follow the *Actions speak louder than words* policy and highly increase your chances of getting the guy you like. It's almost like if you were to buy a lottery ticket every week for a year you would spend about $800 but there is the slim chance that it may work and you may hit the jackpot. At the end of the year you assess that you have just been losing your money on the slim chance that you will win big. It's kind of like that. You can hope and hope and hope that it will work with the guy who's not treating you with respect but then time and time again you are disappointed after you don't win the guy's heart and he doesn't take you seriously.

Wouldn't you be better to not take the chance of the lottery and save yourself the $800 and disappointments?

Wouldn't you be better to put into practice that a*ctions speak louder than words* rather than getting your heart broken time and time again when you listen to the friend whose experience has been the exception to the rule?

I know what I'd pick...a boyfriend that loves and respects me and an extra $800 dollars in the bank.

Well done is better than well said.
– Benjamin Franklin

Being You – Everyone Else Is Taken

Beauty begins the moment you decide to be yourself.
– Coco Chanel

Just be yourself. There is no one better.
– Taylor Swift

In the end, people will judge you anyway, so don't live your life impressing others – live your life impressing yourself.
– Eunice Camacho Infante

- If you like something, EMBRACE IT

As I went through school I always enjoyed a certain genre of music. I would always keep it a secret and hide away the fact that I secretly loved this music. This was because I didn't want people to judge me on what I truly enjoyed listening to. I know, I know, silly, because there is absolutely nothing wrong with enjoying what you truly enjoy and not apologising for it or trying to hide it. When people were around me I used to make sure that I was listening to Top 40 music. (Don't get me wrong. I did enjoy some of the Top 40 stuff, but I would have MUCH preferred my other music over that any day.) Then as soon as I was by myself (usually when I jumped off the train and was walking home) out came my '25 most played' / enjoyable playlist to which I screamed my lungs out. I grew up in a pretty bushy sorta area so no one (that I know of) heard me screaming lyrics at the top of my lungs. Haha. It was awesome. I swear to you that certain bands got me through my years of school, I don't know where I'd be without those bands and their music. But the whole point of my story is to go out and enjoy what YOU enjoy/like, not only in music but in everything and anything! Don't make my mistake and rob yourself of the pleasures of what you like and enjoy, just to 'fit in'. The younger you realise that you shouldn't care so much about how you appear to other people (which is hard in today's world), the better and happier you will be.

*Life is very, very short, and you can choose to live it how you want. You can choose to dumb yourself down and not express yourself just so you can fit in, just so people don't dislike you. Or, you can f**king live."*

– Gerard Way

Be proud of who you are, what you do, what you like, who you listen to, who you hang out with and pretty much anything and everything that makes you…you.

- Don't let other people influence you about something you know YOU want to do.
- If you like chess, join the chess club.
- If you like soccer, join the soccer team.
- If you like footy, join girls' footy – even if people think you are a high maintenance princess.
- If you are religious – EMBRACE IT.
- If you like punk 'emo' music but are a girly girl, by all means listen to it and don't be ashamed.
- In fact, don't be ashamed of anything you love.
- Don't change who you are. BE who you are!
- If you don't know what you like to do and what hobbies you enjoy, the only way you will find out is by trying. Try a few classes in whatever you think you might enjoy. If you love it, GREAT. If you don't, keep searching. :D If you don't try, how are you ever going to know?
- Make a goal, for example, say to yourself maybe once or twice a year that you'll start or at least try two new activities or you'll try a few new genres of music, just to see what you're into and to see what you enjoy/like. For almost everyone, they don't know until they try things and work out what they love and are passionate about in life.
- How do you think Michael Jordan worked out he liked basketball? He tried it.

- How do you think Einstein found out he liked inventing? He tried it.
- How do you think Maria Sharapova found out she liked tennis? SHE TRIED IT.

You don't have to be great to start,
but you have to start to be great
– Zig Ziglar

Finding an Outlet

Those qualities that separate us are often ridiculed by others or criticised by teachers. Because of these judgments, we might see our strengths as disabilities and try to work around them in order to fit in. But anything that is peculiar to our makeup is precisely what we must pay the deepest attention to and lean on in our rise to mastery.

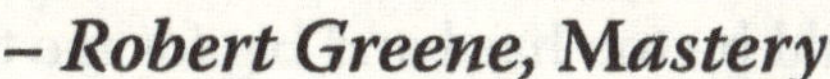

– Robert Greene, Mastery

What are you good at?

If your answer is: 'I don't know. Nothing', don't fret. I was in the same boat and I promise you that you ARE good at something, if not MANY things. You just have to work out what.

For a long time, in fact, all of primary school and about five years of high school, I had NO idea what I was 'good at'. I used to look at the other kids and think, 'Oh, he's good at science', 'She's the really good basketball player', 'He's a superstar on computers'. I think for most of us we don't even realise or it takes a long time to realise what we are 'good at'. Although I felt as though I wasn't good at anything, I always did enjoy certain subjects more than others. I played sports here and there at school and tennis outside of school but I'm not going to lie, I was never amazing at any of them. It was almost frustrating to see other people go so well at things, while I was that person who sat as a sub for the majority of the games we played, whether it be netball, footy or basketball. I did always enjoy art and drama and the more creative classes but it was only in year 12, after five full years at high school when I was 17 that I actually found a huge passion for art. My school didn't offer a drama class so it wasn't until first year uni that I realised how much I actually loved drama. I honestly pretty much just fell into it. I began to look forward to my art classes and actually enjoyed doing my artwork/project.

I took on this giant art project that everybody, including the teachers, (except for my mum), said that it would be too hard and big for me to do. They didn't know me well enough to know that the second someone tells me that I can't do something, I'm not listening anymore. I TRY to use the 'No' as more motivation to push me to achieve my goal.

It got to a point where I was staying back after school till 6.00 (school finished at 3.20). Even all of the teachers had gone home and I just sat by myself and painted. I remember another time when I was in health class and was thinking, wow, I wish I knew what career path I wanted to pursue when I left school. I was always drawing on my paper in class, and love art. The other thing I absolutely love is other people (I have a natural curiosity about everyone I meet, I just want to know more... As you probably already know from reading this book!) Then it clicked...being a teacher would be amazing. I could incorporate everything I love into a job and get paid for my passion. And at that point I realised that I love being creative. So, as I was studying over the holidays, I adapted a new study method. I would draw pictures next to things that I needed to remember and to my surprise it actually worked AMAZINGLY! After years and years of reading notes and going over them in my head (thousands of times over, mind you, still hardly remembering the information), I realised that I learn best VISUALLY. It all fell into place.

- I loved beauty and anything that looked nice.
- I always had a crush on the hottest boy (physically).
- My room was always immaculate. I can't stand it if it doesn't look nice.
- I loved to look beautiful, hair and make-up.
- Going to art galleries was my idea of fun.
- I had a HUGE motivation and passion to do my art project.
- I was always drawing on the side of books and everything. (I swear if you leave a pen/paper with me, I guarantee that I actually can't help but draw on it.)
- I saw beauty in the world. I still will pick up something like a single leaf or a melted candle and see the absolute beauty in it.
- AND THIS IS HOW I FOUND OUT THAT I AM A VISUAL PERSON – I applied this to

my study techniques and I swear the results that I was getting were amazing!

Trust me, studying is SO much easier when you find out how you learn best.

Now it took me a long, long time to realise how I learn best. For you, an easier way to find this out is to Google 'What type of learner am I quiz' (especially the ones based on 'Howard Gardner's Multiple Intelligences theory'). Here is a link that you can follow.

http://www.edutopia.org/multiple-intelligences-assessment or you can simply find your own on Google by typing 'Multiple Intelligences Howard Gardner Quiz'.

working out how you learn best will increase your marks with little to no more study time!

Maybe do more than one just to see if you are definitely that type of learner. Or you can do a 'me' and try and work it out yourself but this may take years... why not make the most of our awesome internet and find out RIGHT NOW! :D Aren't you curious?

Once you realise what you enjoy you can use it as an outlet to help get you through struggles and the hard times that you may be going through or may go through in future.... Wait Megan, so you are saying that if you enjoy maths, get out some tricky maths problems when you have just broken up with your boyfriend, are going through a family struggle or are just feeling down? And as crazy as it sounds, YES – if you are one to enjoy maths that is. ;)

Using your passion as an outlet not only will improve your skills in what you are passionate about but if you can channel your emotions into your passion, practically nothing can stop you from becoming amazing at it. :D

For instance, like when I was being bullied in year 12. (I swear I'm just talking so much about myself to help you guys, not because I'm some self-obsessed narcissist.) I would always come into the art room, either by myself or with a few friends and I would focus on my passion and let out my feelings into my artwork. Luckily for me, it was an abstract sort of whirlwind artwork, as sometimes I felt like I just needed to slap on paint and mess it around to try and express my emotions. One thing that my art teacher did say to me was that she admired how much I just 'did what I felt like' with my artwork and didn't think through to how it would turn out in the end.

I think that 'just going for it' is so important. Just do something and don't think too much about the outcome...obviously within reason. Don't go scratching someone's car just because you feel angry and aren't thinking about the outcome. I'm talking more about situations in life such as making friends. Don't think too much ahead like, 'Oh, this person will be my best friend now'; or regarding boys: 'Oh wow, he SO needs to be my new boyfriend'. Also with simple things like catching the train, 'Oh no, what if I am by myself and have no friends?'; or when starting a new activity, 'Oh crap, what if I fall over and embarrass myself in front of everyone?' Just go with the flow as Buddha says: *Do not stay in the past, do not dream of the future, concentrate on the present moment,* and Nike, *Just do it.*

I know it's hard but try to worry about the problems when and **IF** they even happen.

What you are most scared of probably won't happen. And if it does you'll have a good story to tell people.

But the more you worry about it the more it probably will.

Your mind holds a LOT of power.

Overall the outlet to turn to when times get hard could be anything. Everyone's outlets are different and that is what makes each and every person so unique and exciting! :D

My only tip is to make it a positive outlet...

Here are a few suggestions of what you could try... but honestly the best outlet for you is probably the outlet which you enjoy most.

- Art
- Drama
- Sports (even not so common ones like ice hockey, ice skating, dodge ball).
- Music both playing and/or listening
- Reading
- Being with people
- Volunteering
- Charity work (They say that when you are sad one of the best things you can do can be to help someone else.)
- Construction
- Woodwork
- Mechanics
- Gymnastics
- Writing
- Yoga (Yoga is great not only for flexibility but to help you stop worrying and stressing

out. Also makes your pelvic floor muscles stronger… You'll thank me in the future. ;)

- Gym (My brother deals with issues by channeling his emotions into going and working out at the gym.)

As I mentioned earlier:

Another story of an inspirational person who puts her emotions into an activity is my friend Casey, who is the marathon runner I mentioned earlier in the book. She is a very successful sports/athletics fanatic, who is legit a pro at almost every sport she tries! She also recently completed a 100 kilometre run (I know she's crazy. I complain when I just have to walk to the letterbox from the house and here one of my besties is running 100 kilometres.) But anyway, as you know I asked Casey how she does it and what motivates her and she said that when she is in the moment, either playing sports and/or running, she feels as though she is close to her dad who passed away when she was really young. She channels all the emotions she has regarding her dad's death and converts it into motivation to achieve amazing things. I strongly believe that when we channel our emotions into an activity we can succeed in it with no boundaries!

With such a deep rooted interest you can withstand the setbacks and failures, the days of drudgery, and the hard work that are always a part of any creative action. You can ignore the doubters and critics. You will then feel personally committed to solving the problem and will not rest until you do so.

— Robert Greene, *Mastery*

Escaping Life

You can easily get addicted to anything that takes the pain away.

Instead of wondering when your next vacation is, you ought to set up a life you don't need to escape from.
– Seth Godin

Almost everyone turns to other outlets to escape throughout their lives and it does not necessarily mean that these outlets are bad or not good for you. For instance I'm sure you or someone you know may enjoy a good fantasy book or an action thriller novel. This by no means is 'bad' or 'negative'. Video games and movies are also great ways to escape reality. It's when these seemingly fun and harmless activities become full-blown addictions that is when we need to examine why we are carrying them out to the extreme. We need to do these in **moderation.**

There is a huge difference between escaping reality for a little while and escaping your own reality because you dislike it so much that you just NEED to escape it.

Alcohol

A lot of people turn to alcohol to escape the reality of their lives. I loved a drink (before I quit drinking) on the weekend and I'm sure many other people do too. Alcohol can calm you down and loosen you up to have a good time with your friends. It's just that problems may occur if it is used too much/too often and for the wrong reasons. You may be using it only to escape facing the reality of a situation, e.g., a broken relationship. If you are a regular drinker of alcohol you need to assess WHY you are using it. Is it just for a bit of fun when you go out with your friends, or is it because you feel like you need to escape your problems and the feeling of drinking gives you that feeling?

Don't let alcohol become an addiction for you and don't depend on the feeling you get from alcohol to bring you happiness. If you allow the feeling you get from drinking to be the only way you can feel happy, you can bet yourself that soon enough you will be addicted. You will believe that the only way you can feel happy and have fun is if there is alcohol around. I can completely relate to this as before I gave up drinking I was one of those people who literally could not have fun without alcohol. I remember going to a party when I was 19 and saying to myself, 'Nope, I'm staying sober tonight,' and about half an hour into the party I was begging people to give me drinks as I was not having a good time without them. It's okay if this happens to you but just rethink whether you want to be someone who can only have fun with alcohol when they go out? Or maybe giving up drinking would be a good idea (I know when you first start it sounds crazy) but I promise you I love not drinking now, and love even more that I am so much healthier because of it. Most of all I still have an awesome time when I am out and I am completely sober… I know its extreme but it's well worth it. Well, for me it is.

Drugs

Another way that many people try to escape their reality is drugs. I can't personally give you my experience with drugs (illegal) as I have never done them, although I can tell you a scary story that may make you reassess your thoughts on using or even just trying drugs. As for illegal drugs it can be a little bit different to alcohol, as in Australia drugs (except for tobacco and alcohol) are illegal. So literally one day as I was scrolling through my newsfeed on Facebook, one of my friends who I used to party with (house parties we used to go to when we were like 16) almost every weekend was checked into the psychiatric hospital – I briefly mentioned this story earlier in the book. I had known that since we were about 16 he had been heavily into weed. I'm not really too sure if he was doing other drugs and what drugs they were but I knew he was always one of those boys who enjoyed them a lot. So I shot him a message and asked if everything was okay. He gave me a call. I missed it and then I shot him a call back. We spoke on the phone and it wasn't quite our normal conversation. He struggled to get his words out and he wasn't making a lot of sense. He told me that he is improving. It's just that it would take a bit of time. I asked him if they had diagnosed him with anything and he told me he was diagnosed with Schizophrenia (drug misuse increases the risk of schizophrenia) but I wasn't too sure what exactly it was at the time. I Googled it and it's 'a serious brain disorder that distorts the way a person thinks'. Then what I read next made my heart sink. 'Schizophrenia is a lifelong disease that cannot be cured'. He is such great guy, he really didn't deserve this.

I just want to you to remember that if you are thinking about taking up drugs either for enjoyment or to escape the life that you are living, think back to this story the second you are about to put the substance into your body. So many people think, 'Oh, it won't happen to me', or 'I'm not addicted so I'll be fine', but what I want you to realise is that these things CAN happen to you...and people you love and are close to. Even if the statistics of it happening to you are low, once you have the condition, the statistics fly out the window and don't mean anything anymore to you and you are stuck with a lifelong illness. Please read the Choices/Drugs chapter if you are considering trying/taking drugs (illegal).

Will it really be worth the hit you get on the night if you end up lying in a psychiatric hospital wishing that you stayed clean and had never touched drugs?

Smoking

Heaps of people smoke. It's an activity many people believe helps them to relax and calm down. But as you know smoking is highhhhhhly addictive. I was researching about drugs the other day online and was looking at a YouTube video that was counting down the top ten most addictive drugs. It went from cocaine to heroin but then it finally got to the number one most addictive drug, which was actually tobacco. I know, I was shocked too. But it does make a lot of sense considering how many people are addicted to cigarettes.

Probably about half the people you know/see on the street are either addicted to smoking or smoke 'only when they are out' or have smoked and given up. What I learned in health class at school was that in Australia cardiovascular diseases were the leading cause of death (in 2010) – it can be caused by smoking. If you are considering trying smoking or taking it up at a young age for example in your teenage years because you may think it's 'cool', try to think clearly and thoroughly before you do. I know so many people who started young and literally just can't stop. They tell me they wish, wish, wish that they had never tried it, especially at a young age, because now they finding it so hard to give up. If you are thinking of trying smoking, realise there are many other ways that you can get that relaxing feeling that will be easier to quit and give up if you need to. Why not take up something that may be productive and healthy and good fun, such as yoga and or meditation, running, listening to music, movies or even video games? And if you still want to have a smoke, just take a good hard look at the packaging of cigarette packages in Australia... the pictures are gross!

On some level or another we are always going to want to do/use something that makes us feel as though we are escaping our lives. Honestly just try your best to make it a positive escape and also reading the 'Finding an Outlet' chapter will help too – but please remember that anything that makes you feel good can be addictive, so monitor yourself. Have restraint and look at the big picture.

Fantasy Relationships/ Unrequited Love

The most embarrassing story:

This is actually a really, really, REALLY embarrassing story for me to share with you guys, although now that I've been through it and am past it I feel that there was a reason this happened to me. It was so that I could share my story and help others to learn from my experience and hopefully not do what I did.

So, it all starts back when I was 17 and I was doing my final year of school. I was really motivated and committed to school this year and, as I've mentioned in the book earlier, I said to myself that I was NOT going to get distracted by boys, unlike the year before when I was crazy about my past crush.... Now I actually, believe it or not, did quite a good job at this until one day when I was studying at home in the September school holidays. I remember that day like it was yesterday. I was in a really good mood and super happy (mainly because I had just got my new hair extensions attached to my head). Even though I was getting up at 7.00am every day to study, I felt happy doing this and that I was finally actually getting to achieve something and I was productively working towards my goal of getting into university. Although at the time I was very motivated to do and get good results in my school work, I did have a small addiction to Facebook and HAD TO check it at least once or twice a day. (I knew I should have deactivated it that year but I didn't have the willpower to actually do it.) I kept telling myself I had to but never actually did. So anyway I signed onto Facebook halfway through my holiday study and I had a friend request. I clicked it and it said: 'Dylan Bunings has added you as a friend.' The second I went onto his profile, my mouth actually dropped. He was AMAZINGLY attractive – probably one of the best looking, if not the hottest person, I'd ever seen in my entire LIFE, no exaggeration. And I thought that he was just my type too. This, at the time, was hard to find because I was so picky with guys. I hadn't had a boyfriend for a few years so I thought awesome, this is GREAT. As soon as I finish my studies and exams are over, I'll hang out with him and become his girlfriend! :D. I was SO excited (I look back now and admire my positivity), BUT the reality was that I actually hadn't even MET this guy. I had no idea what he was even like as a person and we had like three mutual friends so I couldn't even ask them about him coz I hardly knew the mutuals. I was just judging him on his Facebook photos and there weren't many photos anyway. As I look back on this now I realise I was definitely a bit naive and silly (fine, maybe a liiiiiitle more than a bit), but at the time I was SO happy that someone amazing had come along and I was practically planning our wedding already.

MS 4 D.B ♥

I tried to go back to my studies after this but I honestly could not concentrate. I couldn't stop day dreaming about all the fun we would have when we were together. In my defence, I did think that he had added me for a reason (somehow he must have thought I was attractive), so there must have been a little bit of interest there. (I'm not completely crazy, I promise.) At this time I was also quite vulnerable because I wasn't living my life to the full, e.g., not going to parties, not seeing my friends (except for at school) because my head was practically buried in a book almost all of the time. Now I waited a few weeks and then messaged him. I was soooooooo nervous. I think it was because of the build up to me actually talking to the guy. I still remember it so clearly. But it was actually five years ago. Once I messaged him, we flirted and talked a bit and he liked a few of my photos but nothing went past that. I kept trying to study for my exams as, even though I was really excited about this new guy, I knew that these exams were important to my future. I'm not going to lie; it was pretty hard to concentrate on studying when my mind kept wandering off about a new teenage romance/crush. I actually got to a point where I had specified study time and specified 'thinking about him' time. So embarrassing. It hardly worked, and my study time eventually turned into 'thinking of him' time and my 'thinking of him' time stayed at 'thinking of him time', too.' lol. He had no idea about all this either…oh, if only he knew. Now that I understand a little more about psychology and have grown up and matured, I now know exactly what happened here. My thoughts of everything I wanted with a guy were put into who this

guy was, without actually knowing him. So therefore I created a false personality, which was my complete fantasy of who I WANTED him to be (with every personality trait my dream guy had) and I imagined that he was like that. When you think that someone has the ideal personality you have always wanted in a guy, matched with the insane good looks he/or any guy has, you have created a fantasy person. In your mind he is your everything but in reality it is just your mind creating who you want this person to be. It happens all the time when people fall in love. As they say

Absence makes the heart grow fonder.
– William Shakespeare

18

Anyway so I sat my exams and gave them my best shot. I walked out of four of my five exams knowing that I honestly gave them my all, and I was happy with that. I had my studio art exam on my 18th birthday, and I remember thinking with this one I HAVE TO smash it. But as much as I don't like to say, more importantly on this day I wanted Dylan to message me Happy Birthday on Facebook. Talk about not having priorities straight! I had a fair few birthday messages on the day (as it was my 18th) and I went through each and every message, and every person who wished me Happy Birthday, only to be disappointed/kind of heartbroken , there was nothing from him. As a 17-year-old crazy girl, my hormones were obviously raging and I was head over heels for this boy that I didn't even know! So, I finished my exams, and then it was time for

SCHOOLIES (huge party time for teenagers to celebrate the fact that they have officially finished high school). Although Schoolies was awesome fun, all I could think about was Dylan. All I wanted to do when I was both in Queensland and Lorne was get great, amazing photos so that he would like and comment on them on Facebook. (I'm sure we are all guilty of this a little…we take a super-hot selfie and post it in hope that our one crush 'likes' the photo.) Having our crush like and comment on our photos gives us their approval to help confirm that they think we are hot and thus we get an ego boost. I mean, come on; everyone wants their crush to like their super-hot selfie, which took about 100 photos and an awesome filter to make them look that good.

So, the entire time I was there I was partying so hard, and hooking up with other people, but the only one I really wanted was Dylan. I remember hooking up with this awesome guy down at the beach and he said he was from a town I knew that Dylan visited on his holidays (thanks Facebook photos.) So what did I do when I was with this guy? I ASKED IF HE KNEW HIM. AH MAN, could my mind seriously not just give the guy I was hooking up with the respect of paying attention to HIM while I was with him? It was a fantasy relationship where I had put him on a pedestal – and what we need to remember is, I STILL HADN'T EVEN MET THE GUY!

I think back now and know that I was just purely attracted to who I thought he was, not who he actually was. Time passed and I did have an awesome time on Schoolies but never properly gave any other guys a real chance just because my heart was wanting someone else. I got back from Schoolies and I was feeling so high, so happy and so on top of the world, BUT one thing was missing...Dylan. So after a lot of thought and putting up photos that he never liked, I decided to message him. I literally just messaged him my number and a smiley face or maybe it was a winking face, I can't exactly remember. I cringe, looking back now. I was so silly and now I have realised from many failed attempts that guys respond better when THEY ask for your number and pursue you. They like a chase (most guys). You don't just send it to a practically random person over a Facebook message. But anyway, he replied, 'What's this?' 'I replied, 'It's my number, boy' (why I said boy I do not know). Then he goes, 'I don't text first...you message me', and he typed his number (to this day I still know his number off-by-heart...sad). I called my friend to ask what she thought I should say back and she told me NOT to message him first because 'the more you chase HIM the more you will LIKE him'. It's the same with boys: the more they chase YOU the more they like YOU. So anyway what I actually said in the message was, 'Nah, you message me, or your loss'. (Mind you, I DID NOT want to say this but my friend said it would be the only way that would work to get him keen.) So I sent that on Facebook and what do you know, I had a message from him on my phone. I was SUPER excited. I opened the message and all it said was '.' I was like ARE YOU SERIOUS? (in my head of course) so again I called my friend to ask her what she thought I should do/say and she told me to message him back with '..' so I did. Then he replied with '...'. Then I replied

let him chase you!

with '.... I win.' and he goes, 'No way'. Then our convo stopped. Two weeks later it was a few days before my first music festival for NYE. I was really excited but still heavily crushing on Dylan. I even tried messaging other guys that I'd crushed on in the past in the hope that they could distract me from Dyl. It didn't work. They also thought it was weird me messaging them after not talking for like two years lol. At this point in time I was still obsessed with getting 'hot' photos so that he would see, 'like', and hopefully comment on them. He was liking and commenting on some of my photos, so naturally I thought things were going really well. But… it was like a few days before I was going to head to the music festival and I signed onto Facebook and it said, 'Dylan Bunings is in a RELATIONSHIP' with another girl. I looked on her profile and she was soooo pretty. And she had big boobs (and I was and still am pretty much as flat as a tack in the chest area.) I'm sure many girls go through this experience where the boy they like is with another girl. THE EMOTIONAL PAIN ABSOLUTELY SUCKS SO MUCH. But what we need to remember about why this story is different to most heartbreak stories is that I HADN'T EVEN MET THIS GUY. But in my head I thought he was a a a a a amazinggggggg. So after that I left it about three months. I was talking and hanging out with other guys but I still couldn't manage to forget about Dylan. I've realised that no matter how many new guys you hang out with, your heart is always for one (well mine was). So anyway…I couldn't take it any longer. I gave in and messaged him. And he replied, 'Who's this?' MAN THAT HURT SO BAD. I was so silly I

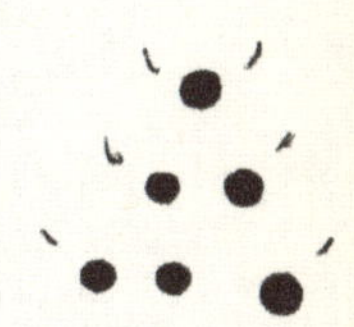

completely 110% regret messaging him when he had a girlfriend. Please learn from my mistake and don't try and hook in with someone who is in a relationship... it shows both lack of respect for yourself and for the couple in the relationship and just remember **if he was to cheat with you...when he's with another girl, what would stop him from cheating ON you if you two were together?** We talked a little, but nothing for about another three months or so. Then he invited me to his 19th birthday (it was a casual thing at a club). I tried to drag a few friends with me (most of them bailed on the day but one of them didn't and came with me.) I did have to pay for her entry to convince her to come but that was cooooooolllll coz I WAS GOING TO MEET THE LOVE OF MY LIFE (well, I thought he was at the time anyway). I saw him in the club next to his gf and, I'm not going to lie, I was a little taken back as he didn't look quite the same as he did in his photos. It's true that photos can sometimes mislead you, especially with the new Valencia filter and selfie sticks, but this attraction was too far down the line, as I was not only attracted to what he looked like but what I *thought* he was. Right now if you have a crush on someone, ask yourself if you like them for THEM or for who you think/imagine they are in your head. I think even if he'd looked like a dead frog in real life, I would still have wanted him as I had built up who he was in my mind so much. I got a drink at the bar and went right up to him to say Happy Birthday. He asked me why I hadn't replied to his messages (as he had messaged me asking if I was coming or not to his birthday). I purposely hadn't replied, to keep him wondering if I

was or wasn't coming. Attempting to 'play hard to get' I just said, 'Oh whoopppps,' when he asked why I hadn't replied. We shared a drink and then went our separate ways and my friend and I went to a new club. As I was leaving, I hit him on the ass, then smiled (my 18-year-old self's attempt at flirting; not going to lie, I still use this move). I know I've said it before but I'm going to say it again: GIRLS: if someone has a girlfriend, don't be that 'other girl' or a 'homewrecker'. Being that girl, believe me, feels like crap, especially if he chooses her over you, which he already has by being in a committed relationship with her, not you.

Trust me, you can save yourself the pain and heartache if you just steer clear of the boys that are taken. It's honestly not worth it. Focus on having fun with your friends. Remember, ***'Chicks before dicks'*** – Urban Dictionary

Anyway, to my excitement that night, he actually messaged me once we left the club saying, 'What's doin'?' I didn't reply till the night after again, attempting to flirt again/playing hard to get. We talked a bit and I thought he was flirting back by replying with a ☺. But really now that I look back, I don't see this as flirting at all.

After that we kind of stopped talking. I had sort of given up and had the mindset of 'if I really liked him I honestly wanted HIS happiness over mine', and by the way that he's been acting his happiness was clearly with her not me. About five months went on and I literally thought about him first thing when I woke up and last thing when I went to bed. I honestly believe that it was some kind of addiction. About five months later I got

home, no joke, and I remember doing my hair while thinking about him, and I got a message from him that said, 'Hey sexy' (mind you he still had a gf at this time). But as silly as I was, this didn't bother me. I was ecstatic. I called my friend screaming. I was sooooo excited. I replied and we talked for a bit...over the next few weeks I was super happy because he was actually trying with ME for once. Messaging me like once every two/three days was great. Then one day HE ASKED TO HANG OUT (the next week). I will never forget the extent I went to just to see this guy...and it really does prove that the more effort you put into someone the more you will like them. I literally got my hair done, had a spray tan, new underwear, waxing, new bras and even nails (acrylic, of course). I almost had everything organised for next week's date when he messaged me saying, 'Hey, are you still on for tonight?' I THOUGHT WE WERE DOING NEXT WEEK! I had got the dates wrong. It was a Sunday when I was hung over. I had gone out the night before and my fake tan looked like I was some kind of orange speckled monster. I couldn't see him tonight. I replied with, 'Hey, I thought we were doing next week.' Then he said, 'Oh yeah, sure, next week is fine.' Pheeeewwww. Mind you, by this stage, he and his gf had broken up, so I wasn't doing the complete dodgy and hanging out with him when he was already with someone. We didn't message all week and my friend told me that that's not really a good sign. So anyway on the Sunday (the day we were meant to be hanging out), it got to 3.00pm and I hadn't heard anything. I knew that his footy team had lost the grand final the day before, so I thought that might explain a

how my fake-tan looked

bit. I sent him a '☺' and I got nothing back and to this day I'll never know why we didn't hang out that Sunday.

After that we stopped talking. He stopped messaging me and he kept being checked in on Facebook with another girl. Now I was getting a litttttttle (in fact, a lot) worried; then a few weeks later, take #2 'Dylan Bunings is in a RELATIONSHIP' Reeeeaaaallllllllyyyyyy, again? You didn't even give me a chance? (As I said earlier, I get more annoyed if someone doesn't give me a chance than if I do get a chance and I fail/they don't like me) By this stage I'd liked him for over a year and had really only met him once. It was a huge fantasy relationship. I was so into him, it was crazy. I was always stalking his Facebook, often more than once a day, and I was so over-liking someone who was clearly not too keen on getting to even know me. When he was about four months in with this new girl, I did the dirty once and for all and I said, 'It's a shame someone as hot as you is no fun', and I got back, 'Sorry, I have a gf', and 'All the best'. This was really emotionally painful as it was all over…no more chances. I wasn't going to message him ANYMORE. I was shattered but I knew it was for the best. I just replied with a final message that said, 'Thanks you too', and at this point I had no choice but to get over him and past the whole fantasy relationship I'd created in my head.

Two years went by. I was dating other guys… guys who I thought would make me get over Dylan –actors, sports stars, tradies, models, but Dyl was still #1 and I still felt like no one could beat what I'd created him to be in my head. When I was seeing other guys, I'm not going to lie, some of them did make me feel that 'on top of the world' feeling, but with almost every one of them (I'm making it sound there was heaps… it wasn't that many.) I always had Dylan in the back of my mind. I would try not to look at him on Facebook but I always gave in…not very often but I did give in. I honestly thought that he was 'the one that got away'…and what hurt most was that I didn't even get a chance. Not actually meeting him properly just fuelled my fantasy relationship even more. Anyway, one day after about two years, I looked at his profile and it didn't say that he was in a relationship anymore. My Facebook stalking revealed that they had actually broken up. Both he and I were now 21, three and a half years after him first adding me on Facebook. I, even three years later, immediately bought a hot exercise crop top as I knew he liked girls wearing these and he loves the gym. His ex worked at a gym and I always see him liking photos of girls in exercise crop tops. (Stalker, much?) Still can't believe I even know this. By the time it came in the post, some kind of weird thing had happened AND I WAS ACTUALLY OVER HIM! I liked another boy. When we hung out, our connection was amazing and I honestly don't think that anyone could beat that connection, despite how good I thought Dylan was, or how good he actually was. I personally believe from my experience that it is realllyyyyyy hard (but not impossible) to properly and completely get over someone you like/love/are infatuated with until you find someone better. And this guy was actually better than anything Dylan could ever have been. (Here we go falling hard again.) I *almost* stopped looking at Dylan's profile. And when I did, I actually didn't care. I'd moved on. WOOO HOOOOO!

WOOOO!

Although, I'm not going to lie, every now and then I did have a cheeky stalk :P just to see what he was up to. I'm sure almost every girl does this with their ex/ people they've liked just to see what they're up to. When I stalked I didn't care and for some reason I actually started to feel sorry for him…as it appeared the only person he was hanging out with was his brother. Anyway now I was looking at the new guy I was really into/ stalking HIM on Facebook (at least I actually knew this guy). I had a friend request: Dylan Bunings has added you as a friend (he had deleted his Facebook when he was with his old girlfriend). I called my best friend at like 2.00 in the morning in shock (I felt bad coz I woke her up). She didn't mind because she knew the importance of Dylan Bunings coming back almost four years later. I didn't accept the request for about three days…then I finally did. Part of me just wanted him to like my photos so that I could get the ego boost from the fact that the guy who never wanted me now did, but then I thought to myself at the end of the day, it doesn't even matter. I knew who I wanted and it wasn't him. However, I would have liked to have met him properly just to see if he was everything that I created in my head…which he won't be as I'd created a fantasy person who he most likely wouldn't have been able to live up to. It was a complete fantasy relationship that went for almost four years. It was honestly like chasing the clouds. Now I am 22 and am pretty sure I know who I like, and I highly doubt anyone can be better than him. But who knows what life will throw at me next? The only thing I really have to say is THANK YOU to life bringing me what and who I need in my life, at the right time.

Now you may be thinking that this is where the heartbreak, nonexistent relationship story ends...but it doesn't. Four and a half years later I was out at a bar in the city of Melbourne for one of my best friend's birthdays and as I got up to go to the toilet, THERE HE WAS! Dylan Bunings was sitting on the bench thing about ten steps away from where I was sitting. I immediately realised who he was and had a mini-freak out. I called my friend and could hardly speak – I know it's crazy, even like four years later I was acting like some giggly tongue-tied schoolgirl. I asked her what I should do and she suggested to go say, 'Hey, I know you, but can't work out where from.' Biggest lie, but I wasn't going to say, 'Hey Dylan, how are you? I've had theeee biggest crush on you for like ever and its awesome to finally properly meet you. Thanks for distracting me from my studies in my final year at school; thanks for keeping me hung up on you for like ever; thanks for keeping me a virgin for so long because I was holding out for you', so I stuck with my friend's suggestion. 'Hey, I know you but can't work out where from.' He responded, 'Hey Megan Street.'

Bfhekhwfbjkebewjk,fgbkbewfkjbjk.rghker

HE ACTUALLY KNEW WHO I WAS!

We chatted for a while and we got along quite well. He seemed really cool in person but obviously I still didn't know him well enough to conclude that I wanted to hang out with him again, if he'd even give me a chance, that is. He messaged me on Facebook once I left the bar and we went from there. We chatted for about a week, then he finally asked for my number...we were texting on and off for about three weeks when we decided that we would hang out (YEP, THAT'S RIGHT ACTUALLY HANG OUT.) But I couldn't help but wonder that even though he was saying this, I kind of knew this guy and wasn't going to believe that he was going to follow through with his plans until I was actually sitting next to him in person. So what do you know? Four and a half years later, we actually did hang out. I had a lot of fun and think he's an awesome guy. It was kind of weird, because he was completely different from what I had made up in my head over the past four and a half years (he most definitely did not have the personality I had imagined him to have although he did have a strangely attractive and mysterious personality). I'm not going to lie, I was hugely attracted to him… but for different reasons to what I'd thought. It wasn't charm or wit that drew me in, or any personality trait I imagined that he'd had over the years. It was his almost shyness and reserve. He intrigued me. I'll never forget sitting in the car next to him while I was tracing my fingers on the tattoos he has on his arm when he leaned in close and was going in for the kiss.

To be honest I would have preferred a bit more of a warning, maybe five minutes before he kissed me, so that I could think about all the times over the past three or four years that I'd **really** wanted him.

You know, like the times I kissed other guys wishing it was him.

The times when I tried to take so many hot photos when I was like 18 in the hope that he'd like and comment on them.

The time when I freaked out when I was going to actually meet him at his 19th birthday party.

The times when I thought that no one could ever be as good as him.

The times I thought about him when lying in bed.

The times I thought that he was 'the one that got away'.

The times when I had dreams about him and me being together.

The times when my friend and I had to call him by the first letter of his name 'D' because saying his name hurt too much.

And now after four and a half years this guy actually wanted to kiss me... It kind of felt like a dream come true.

But a dream that I'd wanted so long ago and not so much anymore.

His timing was about four years off and I wish it hadn't been like that but the reality is that it was.

As they say:

Sometimes it's not that two people aren't right for each other. It's more like the timing wasn't right.
– Unknown

So overall I have realised, and I hope you have realised from my long and embarrassing story that the guy you may be crushing on but hardly know is not who you imagine him to be. He may still be great, but he is most likely not the fantasy figure you have in your head. And the bottom line is that

IT'S IMPORTANT TO FALL FOR WHO SOMEONE **ACTUALLY IS**...NOT A FANTASY IN YOUR HEAD.

- Unrequited love can be a hugely destructive thing for anyone to go through emotionally... It's hard because it is like you are addicted to a fantasy figure that isn't real...but in your head they are completely real.
- If someone doesn't like you, it's not necessarily YOU. They may be emotionally unavailable and not willing to (at this point in their lives) open their heart to anyone, NOT just you. But don't hold on to that false hope...as you could be waiting forever.
- Not everyone in the world will like you...even if you haven't done anything wrong to them. The sooner you realise this, the better and happier you will be.
- Try not to change yourself to get any person to like you... 1. It's silly because you should be who YOU want to be and 2. Even if you were to completely change yourself there are NO guarantees that he'll/she'll like you anyway. I know this can be really hard because when you really like someone subconsciously (a lot of people do it without even realising) you think about slight ways you can adjust yourself to make that person like you...for instance, I know a girl who liked this guy. He usually preferred brunettes but she is a blonde and loves being a blonde but she too

does still have those thoughts of 'Hey, maybe I should go brunette. He might like me more'. Then I talk her out of it and explain why she shouldn't change herself to get a guy to like her. She goes away from our convo and thinks, 'No way. If he's going to like me I want him to like me for ME not because I represent his 'ideal girl". Even boys do it too. I know a guy who found out that the girl he liked (was trying to pursue) loved guys with lip piercings so, what do you know, he went out to get a lip piercing. I do actually think that's kind of cute when a guy goes to such extent to get a girl to like him BUT at the end of the day no one should have to change themselves to get someone else to like them. If someone doesn't like you for YOU, are they really worth your time? Do you want to spend your entire life constantly changing yourself to suit the guy you like? No way. **You want someone you can be yourself around.**

You want him to like you for you!

- Unrequited love has very little to do with the person you are in love with at all.

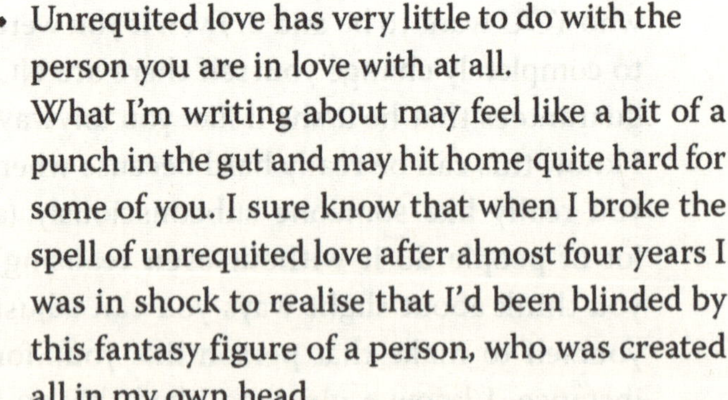

What I'm writing about may feel like a bit of a punch in the gut and may hit home quite hard for some of you. I sure know that when I broke the spell of unrequited love after almost four years I was in shock to realise that I'd been blinded by this fantasy figure of a person, who was created all in my own head.

The other really annoying thing about unrequited love is that we don't open ourselves up to meet other people (guys). And yes, I went on enough dates with enough guys only to realise that almost none of them could beat this fantasy figure, my unrequited fantasy love, even though physically I was dating other guys, emotionally I wasn't even beginning to let them in to properly give them a chance of me liking them at all. I was stuck. I honestly thought that no one could beat who he was in my head...as much as I wanted to like someone else, I actually couldn't. The way I broke the spell was when I found someone amazing. That can be one way of breaking it but don't worry, I know all too well how hard it is to find someone amazing and I also think the **best** way to break the spell is not to be finding someone else but by working through it yourself. Later in the chapter I have my guide to getting over unrequited love. By all means, it's not an easy process, but I want you to understand the importance of not wasting almost four years of your youth head-over-heels for a practically non-existent person.

- As long as we aren't actually with them, this gives us the opportunity to think about who they MIGHT be and how perfect everything would be if we were with them. A great example/analogy of this is Stendhal's theory... called crystallisation. It's where a branch is thrown into a salt mine and after about three months in the mine the same branch is taken out only to be covered in heaps of crystals.

You can't even recognise the original branch that went in.

This is exactly what happens with unrequited love...we tend to crystallise the person that we are in unrequited love with due to our distance from them (which can be either physical distance, mental distance, or both). We make assumptions in regards to who they are, what they like, what they enjoy doing in their spare time and almost anything about them.

At this point, the person becomes crystallised and idolised in our eyes, from a distance. It is similar to the branch that was thrown into the salt mine. At the start, it was just another branch; after months with distance it becomes crystallised, and extremely valuable. Now did this person begin as just a normal person to you and over time have you grown to crystallise them, not for who they really are, but who you THOUGHT they were?

- We must remember that fantasy relationships are addictions about what could be, NOT what is.
- Once the fantasy of unrequited love is broken, you look back at the person and see no idol, who is everything you have ever wanted. You see a normal person...and that's when you know that you are over it.
- Be warned; it can take a very long time. It took me almost four years to properly break

the spell of unrequited love. That is why I am opening up (even embarrassing) myself with this chapter, in hope that others learn how important it is to not close yourself off from the real people who love you, treat you right and give you the love and respect that you truly deserve throughout your youth and life in general.

ALWAYS REMEMBER THAT YOU DON'T NEED THE APPROVAL OF ANYONE TO BE HAPPY.

- HAPPINESS COMES FROM WITHIN... If you let outer circumstances/people/possessions determine your happiness it can sure as anything be easily ripped away from you. I know that it is SO much easier said than done but it's a really important thing to remember. It's the same with love. I believe that you should be happy with yourself BEFORE you get into a relationship with someone just in case you break up; your happiness will not completely depend on him/her (whoever floats ya boat) only. I have heard of and know many people who get into relationships out of insecurity 'Oh, I'll be

Love yourself first!

happy when I have a boyfriend.' 'Oh, I need someone to love me to make me feel loved and wanted.' 'Oh, I don't know if I like him but it's good to have someone there.' Why? What's the point? 1. You are wasting both your and his time when you just want a bit of approval and validation. 2. The time that you spend complaining, e.g., 'I'm so fat' and the time that he spends reassuring you that you are not you could have gone on a run/a walk and felt way better about yourself FOR yourself, rather than seeking someone else's approval to make you feel good. Don't be with anyone who thinks you aren't amazing...

Because you're worth it.
– L'Oreal Paris

- It doesn't matter what HE thinks. It matters what YOU think and how YOU feel. I can almost guarantee you if you feel ugly in the new green sweater you bought the other day and your boyfriend says he likes it on you, yes, you have got his approval BUT do you really like it yourself? If the fact is that you start to like it suddenly after he says he likes it on you, you may have a problem of seeking others' validation for your approval. Does his opinion sway you? Or even if he says you look hot, do you dislike it on yourself? You should make your own choices and believe what YOU wish to believe. In saying this, it is important to have respect for other people's viewpoints but as I quoted earlier, at the end of the day you may be the 'juiciest ripest plumpest peach' but not everyone likes peaches...

- I have a friend who has and still is in unrequited love with this guy she met at the snow when she was 16 (she's now 22). They hooked up and did stuff back then, but nothing ever went further than that and sadly she still, to this day, has never got over it. He is still brought up almost every time we all hang out and she talks about him...she questions if she is in the right relationship at the moment. The crazy part is that she has been with her (now) boyfriend for over two years. But in the back of her head is still 'Oh, I wonder what (let's call him Rick) is doing now?' Every now and then Rick will message her, just as friends, which will keep the spark alive in her head. By him talking to her, it gives her the feeling that he is still there...and something still might happen all these years later and that he is still thinking about her and this just fuels her unrequited love. This is a prime example of how someone can be in a relationship with someone but mentally with someone else. It's really sad but it's a very real situation for many girls. Her fantasy has beaten her reality and she lives with that spark of hope that one day he will fall in real love with her and they will live happily ever after... I hope for her sake

WHAT IF?

that this happens and, to be honest, only time will tell.

- Everyone gets rejected at some stage or another in their life whether it be at work, in love, by friends or family, or anything. Accepting that rejection is NOT the end of the world is a hugely important thing to remember, although it is very hard to master as no one LIKES being rejected. Although getting rejected does hurt our ego, it also strengthens our character and helps us to push harder for what we want, e.g., not getting a job that you have an interview for can make you push yourself harder to become better for the next time you have an interview. You teach yourself to learn new skills, pick up on what you may have done wrong and become more prepared. With love, you may re-evaluate your actions and realise that you may have acted a liiiittttlllleeeeee bit like a crazy psycho girl (even though at the time driving past his house to check if he was home and not with another girl seemed like a perfectly logical thing to do when he didn't reply to your text messages, right?). Rejection happens. But you can take one of two thought processes, 'Oh, I suck and always will', orrrrrrr 'Every time something doesn't go my way, I get one step closer to it going my way', or 'I get one step closer to my goal'. Two of my favourite quotes are:

We all learn lessons in life...some stick, some don't. I have always learnt more from rejection and failure than acceptance and success.
– Henry Rollins

Most fears of rejection rest on the desire for approval from other people...don't base YOUR self-esteem on their opinions.
– Harvey Mackay

- If they are not interested it is usually best to walk away. It can be hard, but you must do it for your health. You can get past unrequited love and open yourself up for the excitement that will come in the future in your love life.
- If they don't need you...you shouldn't need them. You deserve someone who is utterly obsessed with you.
- You MUST unhook your heart from this person.
- If we truly love them, we want what is best for them...even if that doesn't include us (having unconditional love for them).
- When you do find that someone special you

realise the importance of an actual connection not just a fantasy connection.

- The funny thing about love is that we are not actually scared of love... We are scared that the other person won't love us back. We were born to love but we are scared of being rejected.
- One of my mum's friends, let's call her Jane, was also another victim of unrequited love. It all started when she was young and in her first year of university when she was placed in a class with this super funny 'hunk' of a guy. They started talking and got along really well, and soon enough became close friends.

For a year or so she was dating other people, he was dating other people, and they stayed on the friendship level until it slowly crept on Jane that she was actually beginning to like this guy as in like more than a friend. They hooked up and things were going quite well but then he suddenly became less interested in her and more interested in someone else. It broke her heart. But because they were friends she continued to see this guy and she fell in 'unrequited love' with him.

By being friends with this guy it was hard to keep him out of her head. She couldn't physically distance herself from him which also meant she couldn't mentally distance herself from him to help herself get over her love for him. She kept thinking that when he stopped being interested in the girl he was with he would fall back to her and fall in love with her. This did happen briefly as he did fall back on Jane, but to her disappointment, within a few weeks, he was with a new girl. In my opinion he also liked knowing that he had 'options'. Mind you, he was a famous Rugby player (he left university to pursue rugby) and he was defs never short of options, being quite attractive as well. This was probably another trait which kept Jane hooked. I mean let's be honest. We all perve on sports stars, most likely because 1. They have a high status due to their sporting ability and 2. Because they are usually physically attractive due to the fact that they are fit and have to keep fit to stay in their career. By going back to Jane, he kept her hopes up and the fire (or should I say 'the spark') alive in her heart/head as she believed that eventually he would come to his senses and run away with her and her only. She told me that she would sit in her room at night and look at pictures of him and wish with all her heart they would properly be together and live happily ever after.

But as we know not everything turns out how we plan and she felt strong unrequited love for him for ten years...yeah, that's not a typo. I really mean ten years. Eventually she decided the smartest thing that she could do for her mental health and unrequited love was to quit her job pack up and travel the world in a little paddleboat for the rest of her life. No

10 years!

I'm totally kidding! ;) But what she did actually do was quit her job in Australia, pack up and move to America, yep, sunny California. As she did this she slowly got over her unrequited love...it did take time and also some therapy sessions, but eventually it worked out for the best and she got over him. **It can be done girls**! It may not be easy, but it can definitely, be done. Just think, if Jane can do it after ten years of being in unrequited love for someone, you can get over yours too. Now back to the story. Jane was living over there working a job she loved, meeting heaps of new people every day. One night she went to a bar with some friends who introduced her to a man. She and this man clicked like no tomorrow, got along really well and had so much in common. It was crazy as she had just finally gotten over her unrequited love and had opened herself up to finding real true love. That night he asked her on a date. They hung out and things just felt 'right' with him. After a little bit they moved in together and things went really well.

So it was time for her to come back to Australia; he was also from Australia and was just visiting Cali on a holiday. She invited him to meet her family and friends when they were back in Aus...and when she said to my mum, 'Oh, you need to meet my boyfriend,' my mum and even Jane's family all thought, 'Oh, just another one of her boyfriends,' as she had been with quite a few guys over the ten years, even though her heart was set on the one guy. As we know, girls and guys can date many different people but most of the time their heart is truly with one.

So I'm going to finish up this story with 'it's crazy how things work out' because nine years down the track both Jane and this man are still head over heels in real love with each other and have also brought three beautiful kids into the world. They are so great together and both of them couldn't be happier. As for the other guy that my mum's friend was hung up on for ten years, he actually did contact her when she was with this new man. He asked to catch up as friends as he was in Cali, so she agreed. When she caught up with him she felt nothing...she was in real love with this new man and nothing, not even her ten-year crush, could change that!

- So what we all need to remember is that things may not happen how we expect them to happen. We have this image of how things will turn out and often our thoughts don't match the reality of the situation. We do this with many things, e.g., 'Oh, yay, I have a new job. It will be so much fun', when in reality we start the job and we actually don't enjoy it at all. Or when we start high school we have this vision that all the boys will fall in love with us, when in reality they don't and they all like our best friend. Or it could be the other way around. You expect everyone to hate you and bully you at high school when actually everybody loves you! Sometimes it sucks; sometimes it doesn't. Life can be unpredictable but remember that the great way to deal with everything that happens is to adapt to the situation. Try to be like a chameleon adapting to whatever environment and situation you are in.

- *A tree that is unbending is easily broken.*
  – Lao Tzu
- *Thus the rigid and inflexible will surely fail while the soft and flowing will prevail.*
  – Tao Te Ching – *Lao Tzu*

I hope with all my heart that after you have read both this chapter and my story/stories of people I know that you realise how destructive to your mental health and health in general unrequited love can be. I can't express how much. I don't want anyone to get hung up on a guy who they hardly know or know but doesn't love them back for a long period of time. I was actually lucky mine only lasted four years – Janes unrequited love lasted for ten years and my friend's for six years so far. It's ridiculous, crazy and I hope you now know how to recognise the signs and to stop it before it sucks away your years of youth and so much of your time.

I have written a small guide on how to get over unrequited love. If you ever feel like you are falling into it, have a read of this chapter and/or this guide or you can watch one of the most awesome movies, *The Holiday*, with Cameron Diaz and Jack Black. It's a really good movie that gives a great spin on unrequited love.

(I won't say too much about it or it will ruin the movie for you!)

It's Not Rejection, It's Redirection.
– Courtney Turner, It's Not Rejection, It's Redirection

Tips That Will Help You Get Over Your Heartbreak/Unrequited Love

- Try to meet new people and make new friends…you never know where you may meet the real love of your life.
- Avoid the person you are trying to get over as much as possible.
- DON'T STALK THEM ON FACEBOOK. Or any form of social media for that matter… it will only make you worry about any girl who likes/comments on his photos and statuses. Blocking their posts or even unfriending (if you know you won't re-friend them again) would be my advice.

- Remember that
  Your value doesn't decrease on someone's inability to see your worth.
  – Unknown
- Not everyone will like you in life.
- KEEP BUSY. New activities, new friends, new interests, new music for your iPod, anything

that will keep you busy and not wallowing in your own heartbreak.

- I remember when I was 16, I was once trying to get over a guy I had a crush on, and I thought, 'Hey, how about every time I think of him I do some tricky long division sum in my head?' I thought that way I could improve my long division while also getting over the guy I liked. I never liked maths and this did not work for me as I just gave up and thought and daydreamed about the guy within seconds Haha. Butttttt, you may enjoy maths so you could always see if that works for you.
- Try to enjoy being single. You are free; you don't have any restrictions and you can do what you want. In saying this, try not to be a slut, but if you want to kiss one guy, then the next day find a new guy to kiss on Tinder, you can.
- Try to have unconditional love for this person. You want them to be happy if it includes you or not. You truly want THEIR happiness over your own.
- Don't confuse love with need... Do you want HIM or do you want someone?

- Let it alllllll out with someone you trust. It could be your mum, dad, close friend (make sure you trust them) or even a counsellor. Don't bottle up your feelings. It will only make them worse and they will explode when you least expect it.
- IT'S THEIR LOSS

Let me say that one again ... IT'S THEIR LOSS...you are amazing!

- Something I've recently started to go by is the motto *'I don't want a boyfriend... I want a boy who makes me realise that I want HIM as my boyfriend'*
- As mean as it is, think about what you didn't like in the person and what you found unattractive.
- Hide memories or anything you can that may remind you of this person.
- Realise that you don't control other people's feelings.
- Learn from something you may try to improve for your next relationship...e.g., if you were too naggy, needy or insecure, realise that and say to yourself that you will try hard to change that not only in your next relationship but in yourself as a person.
- Dissolve the illusion. Stop putting the fantasy figure person on a pedestal.
- If they were the right person they would be with you.

The best way out is always through
– Robert Frost

Freedom

Although a lot of this book has focused on giving you confidence, building you up and helping you believe in yourself, this chapter is a little bit different. I'm not telling you to be unsure of yourself and to lack confidence, but in this case I'm actually going to tell you that overconfidence can kill…yes, literally kill. What am I talking about here? I'll give you a clue: what twists and turns and can throw you upside-down? (I'm not talking about a ride at a carnival.) What can be one of the best things to happen to you and can open up so many opportunities while also increasing your independence? And what type of heavy machinery is most likely to be in your life almost every day? And what is one of the most likely causes of death that could happen to anyone you know or even you at almost any time? Yep, I'm talking about driving a car.

Now along with all the other stresses we have growing up, driving can be yet another stressful activity to add to your 'list of stresses'. When I was first learning to drive at 16 in Melbourne, Australia, I remember my dad trying to teach me. He would always say to me, 'Megan, I know that you are not concentrating and you are focusing on other things.

You NEED to concentrate; you are operating heavy machinery disguised as a shiny car...one wrong move and your life could be gone forever'. As much as I don't like to admit it, my dad was right. I would pretty much focus on anything and everything but driving. School work, bullying, whether I should get my tongue pierced, boys, what hours I was working that week, just to name a few. There is something about a car, I swear, that just makes you zone out and go into deep thought. After a few months of driving I paid for my lack of concentration. One day when I was stuck in traffic I was about to cross a railway crossing. The cars were banked up ahead of me, stopped at a red light. I assumed as I drove over the crossing that they would move forward but they actually seemed to be going nowhere fast. Then the unthinkable happened! The crossing lights started flashing – while Dad and I were still on the train tracks! Now you may be thinking, 'Hey, it's not rocket science... just reverse the car', but I couldn't as everyone was jam packed behind me as well as in front. Dad and I were stuck on the tracks, boom gates closing down on us and the train fast approaching. The boom gates were almost down when the person in the car behind thankfully found space to reverse, so that we had room to reverse back. I could hardly think straight as I was in such a state of panic, but somehow I managed to get my brain into gear just in the nick of time. We literally just missed the boom gates. Then the train passed while we were trying to catch our breath. It was so scary but we made it. This story just shows you that you really, really have to be

on the ball when driving. It could be a split second between life and death.

CONCENTRATE WHEN YOU ARE DRIVING!

Another instance where I made a small mistake when learning to drive was when I actually lost track of where I was going, somehow managed to veer off the road and knocked down a whole primary school crossing fence. Dad just said, 'You need to concentrate more, and you'll be paying for that fence!'

So here you have it: accidents do happen. And they can easily happen to you. Being over-confident and under-experienced is a recipe for disaster.

There was one thing that my final driving instructor told me seriously when I finally got my licence (it took me three go's, third time lucky! Haha), as he dropped my freshly legally licensed driver's ass home. Despite my excitement, he said in a very serious way, 'Now, don't become a statistic. The highest rates of car accidents happen within the first six months of a P-plater getting their licence.' What he meant by this is: don't become another figure to add to the death by road toll.

Even though I was basically jumping out of my skin in excitement I did take what he said very seriously. As a fresh young 19 year old, I knew that I had the world at my feet and my whole life ahead of me that I wanted to live to the full. I decided that I was going to be the safest of safest drivers out there – my friends even started to call me 'granny' because I drove so slowly. Now even if YOU are a safe driver, as much as it sucks, you actually need to be on the lookout, not only for yourself on the road but all the other drivers who may

OOPPS!

be doing silly/wrong things that ultimately could take you down with them.

Now I'm going to share you an intense story, so I'm warning you that it is quite full on and to 'read at your own risk'. This story is about something that was partially my fault. I hope it helps you to realise how easily it can happen to you or someone that you are in the car with. It will also show you to speak out if you are scared, to only get in cars with safe drivers and to realise that the road can be death waiting to happen and that sometimes it's not your fault entirely, but you can be dramatically affected.

So I'll shut up about lessons and get to the story:

At 18, I didn't have my licence. I was lazy and hadn't got it yet so I was left not being able to drive myself around. One night my friend called and said, 'Hey, come over. We are going out in the city (clubbing); would be fun if you could come.' I texted her with, 'I'd love to but I have no way of getting to your house', so she offered to pick me up. At first I refused as I hadn't been feeling very well that day but thought that going out might be a good idea to take my mind off how I was feeling and ultimately make me feel better. (18 year old logic 0 – if you feel sick the best thing to do is to obviously stay home and rest.) But at this point in time, all I wanted to do was party, party, party. So she came to pick me up and yes I did still feel bad as she was never a huge fan of coming out to pick me up, but out of her generosity that night she did. She specifically did say, 'I haven't got much time but I'll come pick you up.' I still remember the night like it was yesterday even though it happened almost four years ago on the

18 yr old logic 0

9/8/2011. I was dolled up ready to party; she was dolled up ready to party, when suddenly, as we were driving to her house I started to feel really sick again. I realised that I was not well enough to go out and I said to her, 'Hey, I'm **so** sorry but is there any way you could take me back home? I'm feeling really unwell.' She was NOT happy about this to say the least (which was completely understandable) and she turned around and slammed on the accelerator. It felt like we were going 200kmph (we weren't really going that fast but it sure felt like it). It was pouring with rain and I remember grasping the side of door handle thing and thinking, 'I hope I make it out of this car alive', when suddenly, as we were turning a corner, the car skidded and did a 180° turn onto the opposite side of the road. Then we fell into a ditch and rolled one 360° turn, two 360° turns, three 360° turns, and then another 180° turn. Yes, we rolled three and a half times. I remember thinking when we were going through those rolls, 'This is the end of me', when it suddenly stopped. We both sat there, hanging upside-down in the car. I moved my arms and legs and to my disbelief, I was intact and in no pain at all. I asked my friend how she was and she goes, 'Oh crap. I have no insurance.' I thought, 'DUDE, WE ARE EFFFING ALIVE!' But I don't blame her. The shock of something like that will cause anyone not to think straight. I remember at this time I even thought, 'Oh, I hope the powder in my new makeup is intact.' Absolutely insane, the both of us. So anyway we tried to escape the car but the doors wouldn't open as they were both (two-door car) jammed from the rolling. We literally sat there for five minutes not knowing what to do. It was really dark

Miracle ⋆♡

and would have been very hard for the cars passing by to see us as we were in a bushy suburb and had rolled all the way to the side of someone's property. In saying that, it's very lucky we didn't roll the other way because the other way was down a hill. After what felt like forever, someone pulled over and from the outside managed to yank the door open so we could escape. I wish I could thank him properly but never even found out his name. We got out of the car and literally walked away with a few grazes on our knees (no idea how they even got there) but it was an absolute miracle. There is no other word to describe the fact that both of us walked away completely unharmed (physically) from a three and a half times roll over at the age of 18 and 19. We were so close to, as my driving instructor had said, 'becoming another statistic'. The ambulance came to double check if we were okay injury-wise, and we were fine. My friend's mum then dropped me home where I explained to my parents what had happened. They had assumed that I had been in a minor crash (I had called them earlier after the crash), up someone else's ass, not a three-and-a-half-times rollover. I was still in a massive state of shock and felt like I was in a dream for about a week. Everyone at uni was asking what was wrong and then I would just burst into tears. I had nightmares of the accident for so long after; then flashbacks, even in the daytime. Everyone suspected I had minor post-traumatic stress... I probably did but it was never diagnosed. It took about three to four months for the nightmares to disappear, and also a long time for me to get into a car and not freak out at every corner that was turned when someone other than me was driving. The scene of the crash used to flash back at almost every corner that was turned and I even refused to get into a car when it was raining for at least four months. I'd even ask every person to slow down, even if they were doing the limit. I felt so rude but it was the only way to prevent the flashbacks. Most of this has gone away now (you'd hope so after four years) but I'm not going to lie, it took me at least a year before I felt even remotely safe in cars again. My friend called me the day after the accident and when I offered her money to pay for the car that had been written off, she politely refused. She also had a completely changed mindset. Out the window was the 'Oh no, my car has no insurance' to 'We are so lucky to even be alive'. She had taken the car to the wreckers and the man there had told her that we were so lucky and to go out and buy a lottery ticket. Considering the state of the car he was so surprised that we had both walked away unharmed. He said most people don't walk away from a three and a half times roll over intact. Most of them don't walk ever again – they don't even survive. Both she and I have now realised how blessed we were/are to even be alive despite the costs of the new car. We had the most important thing...our lives.

please slow down!

If you are curious about the car, it was Peugeot little blue hatchback with a five-star safety rating. Honestly if it had been one of many other cars I don't think I'd be here today living to tell the tale.

It's so crazy to think that we survived and even crazier to think this happened to one of my best friends. She is literally the LAST person you would think would ever get into any trouble, let alone a car crash. She is/was a goody two shoes, smart, good head on her shoulders, actually enjoys science and maths, prissy private school girl, even a self-confessed nerd. Not a speeding, hooning ratbag who disobeys the law regularly and who a lot of people would expect to have a car crash. This is a girl who has the brains to ace any test and/or exam thrown at her. She is responsible, hardworking, and even makes speeches for the Dean of Education regularly. However, she became irritable and let her focus on safe driving lapse. I'm telling you all this not to brag about how awesome one of my besties is but to show you that this sort of thing **can really happen to anyone.** That includes YOU!

Don't go around thinking you are invincible on the road even if you are in fact invincible in every other area of your life. I've said it once and I'll say it before **the road is not the place to be over-confident and under-experienced.**

Try not to go around having the mindset of:

- 'Oh, it won't happen to me.'
- 'I'm wayyyyy too smart to have a car crash.'
- 'I'm not some scummy rebel who speeds.'

- 'I'm seriously just not dumb enough to have a car crash.'
- Or worst of all do what my friend did and express your emotions (in her case, anger) out through her driving.

You need to be so, so careful on the road. Just because you pass the test to get your licence, this doesn't mean that you are some superhero wonder driver on the road.

Also a point to remember is watch who you get into a car with. If you are scared of someone's driving, get out, catch the bus, or even a cab. It may be embarrassing but if you fear for your life with someone else's driving, think back to this chapter and get out while you can

Quit while you're ahead!

- Watch out for other idiots on the road. You need to not just look out for yourself, but also them. As I said a lot of people will drive under the influence of drugs, alcohol, their own emotions, when really tired, the list goes on. You need to be well prepared for this.

So many people also get road rage. Try your best to keep out of the rager's way. A few people I know will actually, purposefully, slow down if someone is tailgating them. What's the point? You only piss them off more and create more rage on the road, which can lead to more accidents. Don't be a little shit. Just simply pull over at the safest place and let their raging ass speed right past you.

A few other simple tips to follow when driving to stay safe are:

Don't rush...it's better to arrive alive than be dead on time.
– My mum

- SOME TIPS:
- If you are doing an especially tricky turn and/or drive, turn down the music, or even better turn it offffff.
- No driving when really tired.
- NO PHONE, IPOD, OR ANY SCREEN. Not even at traffic lights.

- Try not to get carried away singing.
- If unsure whether to put lights on or not put them on, better safe than sorry.
- Try not to let your petrol get below ¼ tank... in case of emergency (I struggle with this. I like to live on the edge :P).
- Remember that driving other people is very distracting. Block them out and focus on the road.
- Make it an official rule that everyone wears their seatbelts in your car. Always.
- I personally have no clock in my car, to ensure that I am not rushing and racing to get

somewhere on time. Nowhere you are driving to is worth you speeding.

- Stress ball in car ready for traffic.

- Have a phone charger in case you are in trouble and out of battery due to too many selfies that day.
- Have snacks just in case you are feeling dizzy and/or lightheaded when hungry. Also always have water on you.
- 'It's safe to speed here.' No it's not. Limits are there for a reason.

I'ts <u>never</u> safe to speed!

- Don't drink/do drugs then drive. *Only a little bit over...you bloody idiot* – TAC
- Drive according to the conditions. As my mum says, 'When it's wet, drive as if you're on ice skates.'
- Plan, time management: have the plan of where you are going ahead of your trip
- *15-minute powernap could save your life.* – TAC
- Allow MORE than enough time to get to places. Aim for ten minutes early.
- Leave car at home if drinking; resist the temptation to drink drive.
- Overall driving is truly one of the best things, but be safe and take your health and safety seriously.
- And last but not least... **Don't become a statistic**.

Ending Chapter

As I close the book I hope that in even just one way it has helped you to look at your life, your trials, your heartbreaks, your setbacks, and any experiences you may have had in the past or may have in the future differently.

I hope it has made you realise that every negative has a positive side to it; whether you see it now or later on in your life, know that it exists.

It's up to YOU to look for the positive in the 'negative' and grow from your struggles, trials and setbacks.

Opportunity often comes disguised in the form of misfortune or temporary defeat
– Napoleon Hill

You may have to look at your experiences and problems upside-down, inside out, back-to-front, from a bird's eye view, from below the ground or even from a diagonal view to see the blessing in the storm, but I PROMISE you, it exists!

I want you guys to realise and understand that despite how hard life can get and how much you may want to give up and maybe even take your life, remember that suicide is a permanent solution to a temporary problem. It will affect so many people in so many unimaginable ways. If you know how hard pain is, surely the last thing you want to do is put someone else through pain.

Reality is that life can fu*king suck sometimes.
Life can fucki*g suck sometimes.
LIFE CAN F*CKING SUCK SOMETIMES.

*{But believe me there **IS** light at the end of the tunnel and*
if you're going through hell...
KEEP GOING.
– Winston Churchill}

I hope that my stories and quotes throughout the book have helped you to realise that **we are all weird and fu*ked up** and that there are other people who have gone through the same and similar shit as you (may be worse, may be better; let's not compare problems) but still pretty bad stuff and they make it out of it alive.

Somebody once said to me, 'Oh yes, I have those days when I think about ending my life and committing suicide... But don't we all?'

YOU ARE NOT ALONE.

YOU CAN AND WILL FIND PEOPLE THAT UNDERSTAND YOU.

Growing up in this day and age can actually suck so much.

BUT growing up can also be **awesome.**

From this day forward you are a different person. You are a changed, more positive person who is thankful for everything you've been through...the good, the bad and the ugly.

The glass is half full.

And if you are struggling **I BEG, BEG, *BEG* YOU TO SEEK HELP, ASAP**. No waiting, don't put it off, DO IT TOMORROW, DO IT NOW! Despite what you may have on, **your health is more important than anything.**

- Call **Kids Help line** (their highest age is 24) 1800 55 1800
- Call **Lifeline** – 13 11 14
- Or contact **Beyondblue** Call: 1300 22 4636
  Chat online: between 3pm-12am every day
  Beyondblue website www.beyondblue.org.au
  Email: response within 24 hours
- See the doctor.
- Go onto antidepressants, I know soo many people they have worked so well for. Don't be ashamed to take them. Literally the most commonly prescribed drugs in America are antidepressants.

- Probably half the people you know have either been on them or are on them now.
- TALK TO SOMEONE.
- See a psychologist or psychiatrist. It's NOT bad and you are NOT crazy.

But whatever you do, don't bottle up all your feelings. Talk to someone…seek help… It gets better than this. I promise you.

Hush little baby don't you cry,
Don't cut your arms, don't say good bye,
Put down that razor, put down that light,
It might be hard
But you'll win this fight.
– Unknown

Now let's try our best to *live life fully while we're here; experience everything; take care of ourselves and our friends.*

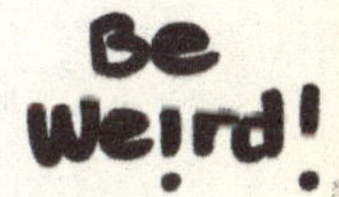

Have fun, be crazy, be weird.
Go out, screw up! You're going to anyway,
so you might as well enjoy the process.
Take the opportunity to learn from your
mistakes, find the causes of your problems
and eliminate them.
DON'T TRY TO BE PERFECT.
Just be an excellent example of a human being.
– Anthony Robbins

And just when the caterpillar thought the world was over...IT BECAME A BUTTERFLY!
– English Proverb

About the Author

Still waters run deep.

The Songs To Which I Owe So Much

- *MR BRIGHTSIDE*– The Killers
- *Shut Up* – Simple Plan
- *The Anthem* – Good Charlotte
- *Believe* – Yellowcard
- *In too Deep* – Sum 41
- *Lullaby* – Nickelback
- *Welcome To My Life* – Simple Plan
- *Addicted* – Simple Plan
- *Teenage Dirtbag* – Wheatus
- *The Middle* – Jimmy Eat World
- *The Reason* – Hoobastank
- *The Black Parade* – My Chemical Romance (Gerard Way, you're amazing!)
- *The Little Things* – Good Charlotte
- *Numb* – Linkin Park
- *Promises* – Sanctus Real
- *Only One* – Yellowcard
- *Heroheroine* – Boys Like Girls
- *Affirmation* – Savage Garden

References

About popularity. Kevin H. Rubin, PH.D with Andrea Thompson (2002). *The Friendship Factor.* England: Penguin Group. 181-206.

Rejected by 140 publishers, Jack Canfield and Mark Victor Hansen.
http://www.booksandsuch.com/blog/why-are-great-projects-rejected/

Miranda Kerr. http://www.dailymail.co.uk/tvshowbiz/article-2983642/You-skin-Miranda-Kerr-says-learned-not-things-personally-experiencing-rejection-losing-modelling-jobs.html

Henry Ford. http://m.insurancebusinessonline.com.au/au/featured-content/how-to-overcome-excuses-212536.aspx

http://www.goodreads.com/quotes/306227-associate-yourself-with-men-of-good-quality-if-you-esteem

Kids Help Line. 1800551800
http://www.kidshelp.com.au

Beyondblue. 1300224636
https://www.beyondblue.org.au/get-support/get-immediate-support

Lifeline 131114 https://m.lifeline.org.au

Walt Disney was fired because he lacked imagination
http://www.businessinsider.com.au/17-people-who-were-fired-before-they-became-rich-and-famous-2012-3#walt-disneys-newspaper-editor-told-the-aspiring-cartoonist-he-wasnt-creative-enough-1

EGO TRAPS: If you think... Unknown.
https://www.google.com.au/#q=ego+traps+&imgrc=_8B--jz2gIU8SM%3A

Research carried out by the Carnegie Institute of Technology shows that *85 percent of your financial success is due to skills in 'human engineering'*...at a higher price. Jensen, 2012.
http://www.forbes.com/sites/keldjensen/2012/04/12/intelligence-is-overated-what-you-really-need-to-succeed/

Making people feel special: Dale Carnegie (1936). *How to Win Friends and Influence People.* United States: Simon and Schuster.

S.M.A.R.T Goals by George T Doran.

Laura Henshaw and Stephanie Smith blog 'Keep it Cleaner' Social Media and Body Image article. http://keepitcleaner.com.au/blog/view/23/.

Howard Gardner's Multiple Intelligences Theory http://www.tecweb.org/styles/gardner.html

Test: http://www.edutopia.org/multiple-intelligences-assessment

Cardiovascular diseases leading case of death in 2010. http://www.who.int/mediacentre/factsheets/fs317/en/

YouTube video that was counting down the top 10 most addictive drugs... https://www.youtube.com/watch?v=Edi3ta0lkAA

What I learned in health class at school was that in Australia coronary heart disease was the leading cause of death which can be caused by smoking. http://www.aihw.gov.au/WorkArea/DownloadAsset.aspx?id=60129547723

Schizophrenia: 'A serious brain disorder that distorts the way a person thinks' and 'Schizophrenia is a lifelong disease that cannot be cured'

http://www.webmd.com/schizophrenia/guide/mental-health-schizophrenia.

'Drug misuse increases the risk of developing schizophrenia'
http://nhs.uk/Conditions/Schizophrenia/Pages/Causes.aspx

'Frustration attraction', which means 'wanting the person more when barriers are increased'. Helen Fisher states in Cupid's Comeuppance article Psychology Today. https://www.psychologytoday.com/articles/200409/cupids-comeuppance

This is not entirely the guy's fault...
http://www.dailymail.co.uk/health/article-2031498/Sex-Why-makes-women-fall-love--just-makes-men-want-MORE.html

Chicks before dicks. Urban Dictionary.
http://www.urbandictionary.com/define.php?term=chicks+before+dicks

Stendhal's Crystallization'theory.
https://en.m.wikipedia.org/wiki/Crystallization_(love)

Emotional connection, What It Is and Why It Matters. Article found on:
http://inspiredcommitment.com/making-it-count/emotional-connection-what-it-is-and-why-it-matters/
Info on page 166 about emotional attraction :
http://classroom.synonym.com/mean-emotionally-attracted-someone-8325.html

Only a little bit over? You bloody idiot. TAC campaign.
http://www.tac.vic.gov.au/road-safety/tac-campaigns/drink-driving/another-bloody-idiot-tv-ad

A 15-minute power nap could save your life. TAC.
https://m.youtube.com/watch?v=WOAMYQoLpg0

Guys don't necessarily associate sex with attachment:
http://www.dailymail.co.uk/health/article-2031498/Sex-Why-makes-women-fall-love--just-makes-men-want-MORE.html

Respect: A feeling of deep admiration for someone or something elicited by their abilities, qualities or achievements. English Oxford Dictionary.
http://www.oxforddictionaries.com/definition/english/respect

Showing respect for someone means you act in a way that shows you care about their feelings and well-being.
http://talkingtreebooks.com/what_is_respect.html

Respect: A quality seriously lacking in today's society.
Respect? What the hell does that mean?
www.urbandictionary.com/define.php?term=respect

Respect: Something that no one has for each other nowadays.
https://www.urbandictionary.com/define.php?term=respect&defid=1881184&page=3

Research carried out by the Carnegie Institute of Technology shows that 85 percent of your financial success is due to skills in "human engineering," your personality and ability to communicate, negotiate, and lead... (Jensen, 2012).
Jensen,K. (2012). Intelligence is overated: What you really need to succeed. Forbes. Retrieved from http://www.forbes.com/sites/keldjensen/2012/04/12/intelligence-is-overated-what-you-really-need-to-succeed/

Health is a state of complete physical, mental and social well-being and not merely the absence of disease or infirmity. World Health Organisation.

Even scientists have proven that when you are in love with someone they give you a similar rush as what you get when you do cocaine. It's addictive.
http://www.therooster.com/blog/high-love-why-falling-love-doing-cocaine
https://www.youtube.com/watch?v=OYfoGTIG7pY#t=89

There are two things people will do when they are jealous: *1. Be mean to the person that they are jealous of. 2. Use the jealousy they feel to push THEMSELVES to be a better person.* Upside of Negative Emotions Issue of Psychology Today Magazine.

the most commonly prescribed drugs in America are antidepressants http://edition.cnn.com/2007/HEALTH/07/09/anti-depressants/index.html?eref=RSI

Yoga is great not only for flexibility but to help you stop worrying and stressing out! Also makes your pelvic floor muscles stronger. You'll thank me in the future. http://www.menopause.org/for-women/menopause-flashes/sexual-health/for-better-sex-3-ways-to-strengthen-your-pelvic-floor.

YouTube video that was counting down the top 10 most addictive drugs and it kept counting down from cocaine to heroin; then it finally got to the number one most addictive drug, which was actually nicotine! https://www.youtube.com/watch?v=Edi3ta0lkAA

What I learnt in health class at school was that in Australia coronary heart disease was the leading cause of death which can be caused by smoking. – http://www.aihw.gov.au/WorkArea/DownloadAsset.aspx?id=60129547723

Guys don't necessarily associate sex with attachment, but girls do. Guys can easily have a 'f*ck buddy' but as for girls this is a little bit harder. This is actually due to science as when we have sex, 'oxytocin' is released, which is the 'cuddle hormone' which will bind you to him emotionally…that is why when women sleep with men they usually get attached. Whereas men manage to more easily remain neutral and emotionally detached because the main hormone released for them during sex is the 'pleasure hormone' Dopamine.

http://www.dailymail.co.uk/health/article-2031498/Sex-Why-makes-women-fall-love--just-makes-men-want-MORE.html

According to *Psychology Today* it's called 'frustration attraction' 'wanting someone more when barriers are increased'. https://www.psychologytoday.com/articles/200409/cupids-comeuppance

Rhonda Byrne (2006). The Secret. Australia, USA: Atria Books, Beyond Words Publishing.

The Secret. Movie.

You Can Do It. Emotional Resilience Program. https://www.kidsmatter.edu.au/primary/programs/you-can-do-it-education-program-achieve

Gary Chapman *Five Love Languages* http://www.5lovelanguages.com/profile/singles/

Miranda Kerr. *Treasure Yourself: Power Thoughts For My Generation* October, 2010. Hay House. UK.

Tony Wrighton (2011). *How To Persuade In a Minute.* United Kingdom : Virgin Books and Random House. 77-90.

Jessica Grogan, PH.D (2014). *'The Myth of Cool'*

Life is More Complicated Than Your High School Popularity Contest.' Let It Go issue of Psychology Today Magazine (December) 23.

Matthew Hutson, (2015). 'BEYOND HAPPINESS: THE UPSIDE OF FEELING DOWN'. The Upside Of Negative Emotions issue of Psychology Today Magazine (February) 2015.

Susan Krauss Whitbourne Ph.D. (2015) *'Why We Feel Insecure, and How We Can Stop Can you make yourself feel bigger without making others feel smaller?'* https://www.psychologytoday.com/blog/fulfillment-any-age/201507/why-we-feel-insecure-and-how-we-can-stop

Cindy Lu (2007) *'The Four man plan: a romantic science'*. London, United Kingdom. CreateSpace Independent Publishing Platform (September 7, 2007) Random House.

Sherry Argov (2000) *'Why Men Love Bitches: from doormat to dream girl – a woman's guide to holding her own in a relationship*. The United States. Adams media, An F+W publications company.

NOTE:

Some names and identifying details have been changed to protect the privacy of individuals.

I have tried to recreate events, locales and conversations from my memories of them. In order to maintain their anonymity in some instances I have changed the names of individuals and places, I may have changed some identifying characteristics and details such as physical properties, occupations and places of residence.

Although the author and publisher have made every effort to ensure that the information in this book was correct at press time, the author and publisher do not assume and hereby disclaim any liability to any party for any loss, damage, or disruption caused by errors or omissions, whether such errors or omissions result from negligence, accident, or any other cause.

New Releases... also from Sid Harta Publishers

OTHER BEST SELLING SID HARTA TITLES CAN BE FOUND AT

http://sidharta.com.au   http://Anzac.sidharta.com

***

HAVE YOU WRITTEN A STORY?

http://publisher-guidelines.com